The Overloaded Liberal

The Overloaded Liberal

Shopping, Investing, Parenting, and Other Daily Dilemmas in an Age of Political Activism

FRAN HAWTHORNE

BEACON PRESS

BOSTON

Beacon Press
25 Beacon Street
Boston, Massachusetts 02108-2892
www.beacon.org

Beacon Press books
are published under the auspices of
the Unitarian Universalist Association of Congregations.

13 12 11 10   8 7 6 5 4 3 2 1

This book is printed on acid-free paper that meets the uncoated paper ANSI/
NISO specifications for permanence as revised in 1992.

Text composition by Wilsted & Taylor Publishing Services

Library of Congress Cataloging-in-Publication Data
Hawthorne, Fran.
The overloaded liberal: shopping, investing, parenting, and other daily
dilemmas in an age of political activism / Fran Hawthorne.
p. cm.
Includes bibliographical references.
ISBN 978-0-8070-3263-3 (hardcover: alk. paper) 1. Green marketing—
United States. 2. Green products—United States. I. Title.
HF5413.H39 2009
640—dc22   2009027663

To my son, Joseph
(because that's who the future is for)

Contents

Introduction

I have to confess that I was kind of smug about my lifestyle before I started this book. I knew that I took a lot of steps to save energy, to support unions and small stores, and to put my money in mutual funds that invested in causes I believe in, and I was quite pleased with myself for all of that. I used cloth napkins instead of paper. I never crossed a picket line. I brought my own shopping bags to stores. I recycled nearly every scrap of paper, metal, glass, and plastic possible, and then I bought recycled paper, and ... Well, I won't go through my whole self-satisfied list right here. (If you're interested, it's at the end of this Introduction.) Let's just say that every time I opted for the more expensive, no-antibiotics, no-added-hormones ground beef, I thought I was managing to live pretty much according to my liberal values.

Except that guilty reminders were always tapping at the edge of my brain. If I really were an ethical consumer, wouldn't I buy the beef at the farmers market and the food co-op, not the chain grocery store? In fact, wouldn't I avoid eating beef altogether? But if the ethical goal is to avoid eating beef, why was anyone bothering to make antibiotic-free beef, if not for people like me who care about animal welfare and the environment? Wasn't this better for the environment, or at least the cow? And if the grocery store I sometimes went to was, as it claimed, an "individually owned and operated," unionized member of a purchasing and distribution cooperative, was it really an evil Big Chain?

So I started this book with a list of questions and contradictions, along with the hope, of course, that I could find some answers that would relieve my guilt. What I really wanted was an expert who could magically prove that the convenient super-market was just as ethical as the once-a-week farmers market and the pricier natural-foods store. Instead, I produced more questions. And more. And my smugness deflated abruptly.

There was so much I wasn't doing, or was doing wrong. How dare I use an energy-gobbling clothes dryer, or buy plastic food wrap? Did I realize I'd helped put five local bookstores out of business by shopping at Barnes & Noble? Why wasn't *all* my money, not just some of it, in a socially responsible mutual fund? Maybe I was checking my carbon footprint, but what about my water footprint? Still, many things weren't clear. Should I support the labor movement by buying clothing from a union factory in North Carolina, or would it be more ethical to help women climb out of poverty in Bangladesh by buying the skirts and blouses they made in their sweatshops? Is a flat-screen computer monitor good because it wastes less energy than the bulky, older monitors or bad because of the dangerous chemical coating?

No kind of food seemed ethical or safe. Fish have the Omega-3 fatty acids that are good for your heart, but we've gobbled up so much that some of the most popular types—like Atlantic cod, halibut, grouper, and bluefin tuna—are dangerously depleted. Plus, other sea creatures get caught and killed in the fishing nets. And how about all the energy that's expended to fly these fresh-caught fish from way out in the ocean to our stores? As an alternative, about one-third of fish intended for human consumption are raised on industrial farms these days, but it's debatable whether that's much of an improvement. The captive fish often are shot up with dyes and antibiotics, while they pollute the nearby water with tons and tons of fish-poo. And what do they eat? Smaller, wild fish, churned into fish meal by the barrelful, a practice that now threatens to deplete species like herring, mackerel, anchovies, and sardines.

Nor could I trust any company. Nice, all-natural Tom's of

Maine was bought out by Colgate-Palmolive Co., which uses animals to test the weird chemicals in its other toothpastes and soaps. Equally natural Burt's Bees also sold out to a conglomerate, Clorox Co. Even worse, Burt's Bees must produce tons of climate-altering carbon emissions by importing its honey from Ethiopia instead of relying on local bees. Some animal-rights groups have even criticized Ecover, the Belgian manufacturer of ultra-green household cleaners, soaps, and detergent, because it doesn't completely reject animal testing, according to *The Rough Guide to Shopping with a Conscience.*

I was swamped with self-doubt. Depressed. Panicked. I walked into bookstores and felt hopeless in front of shelves upon shelves groaning with books about ethical shopping and green lifestyles, all of them referring me to Web sites and more lists.

I interviewed dozens of environmental, financial, labor, and consumer activists, and they all had different angles and priorities. Each activist was so sure of the prime importance of his or her niche. I couldn't possibly live right, not without a lot more hours in the day for research, plenty of assistance to help with that research and shopping, a small fortune to pay the higher costs of things like wild Alaska salmon, and a mental breakdown.

According to the analysis of Jonathan Haidt, associate professor of social psychology at the University of Virginia, liberals ought to find it easier than conservatives to live according to their values. Haidt has defined what he sees as five psychological systems, each of which results in a set of related values: harm/care, fairness/reciprocity, in-group/loyalty, authority/respect, and purity/sanctity. Grouping them politically, he says all five are equally important to conservatives, while liberals care most about the first two sets, harm and fairness. Because conservatives have more values to juggle, "they have the potential for more conflict in daily life," Haidt told me. But liberals face other problems, because "liberals hyperdevelop their sensitivity to harm and fairness." When observant Mormons, who tend to be politically conservative, shun coffee and alcohol, they are living out the value of purity. When animal-rights activists broke into a mass-production egg farm in Maryland in 2001 and took away eight hens, they were, like good liberals, acting out the value of preventing harm (rescuing the hens from horrible conditions) while spurning the conservative value of authority (trespassing and stealing from the farm owner).

However, I don't think liberals are limited to two, easy-to-juggle value sets. We liberals certainly can have a sense of loyalty and belonging to an in-group, as manifested when we join food co-ops and community-supported agriculture programs (or when we sneer at those who aren't in our group, like Bible Belt "rubes" and National Rifle Association members). And isn't buying organic a form of seeking purity?

Many liberals sure don't seem to have an easy time. Dilemmas bombarded me whenever I chatted with people about shopping, or food, or kids, or the weather, or almost any aspect of daily life. One friend careens constantly between buying super-expensive organic berries that are imported from Chile (the price! the carbon emissions!) or less-expensive local berries that aren't organic (the pesticides!). Another, with several children, fretted about whether a standard minivan or a hybrid SUV would use less gas and emit less carbon dioxide. At one point, members of my New York City synagogue were shooting e-mails back and forth as to how to find meat that was kosher, organic, and halfway affordable. The more research I dug into and the more experts I talked with, the more I realized that I simply couldn't resolve all the contradictions.

What I finally understood was that the questions I added to my list, as a result of writing this book, were more important than the answers.

I would not end this journey the same person I was when I began it. No, I couldn't possibly carry out every piece of advice I picked up. But after what I was learning, I couldn't continue doing all the same things I'd done before. My challenge would be to figure out which balls I would be able to keep in the air while I juggled, and which I could afford to drop.

Introduction Part 2: The "Before" List

Here's some of what I already was doing, before I started writing this book, in trying to live according to my values:

Environment

- using rags and sponges instead of paper towels (usually)
- using cloth handkerchiefs instead of tissues (usually)
- refilling water bottles
- returning metal hangers to the dry cleaner
- recycling printer cartridges and cell phone batteries
- reusing tin foil and plastic storage bags (if they're not too icky)
- composting fruit and vegetable scraps
- taking the subway or walking almost everywhere (I get no Brownie points for doing this, since I live in New York City, where driving is impossible anyway.)
- installing compact fluorescent (CFL) light bulbs
- paying extra for power from wind and hydroelectric sources
- turning off lights constantly (and nagging my family to do the same)
- not running the water while brushing my teeth (This is such a no-brainer that I shouldn't get Brownie points here, either, but the green advice books feel compelled to include this.)

- sweeping rather than vacuuming (often)
- running the washing machine on warm, not hot
- running the dishwasher—only when full, of course—on "water miser"
- requesting that the sheets and towels not be washed every day when staying at a hotel

Workers' Rights, Which Includes Supporting Local Stores

- not buying from manufacturers or stores that are being boycotted by groups I agree with (This applies if I hear about the boycott; I don't deliberately look for lists of boycotts.)
- refusing to use the self-checkout line at the supermarket, no matter how long the other lines are, because these ultimately will eliminate cashiers' jobs
- filling one-time prescriptions at the local, independent pharmacy (but not ongoing prescriptions)
- avoiding Wal-Mart and Whole Foods

Food

- choosing organic carrots (always), milk without added hormones (usually), and meat without antibiotics (sometimes)

Socially Responsible Investing

- keeping a small savings account at a community bank known for social activism (and therefore probably earn lower interest than if I put the money into a CD in a big savings bank)
- maintaining Individual Retirement Accounts in two socially responsible mutual fund companies

Direct Social Action

- organizing an annual clean-up in our local park
- walking the 39-mile Avon Walk to raise money to fight breast cancer (I've done this three times so far, but there are no guarantees for the future.)
- voting at every election, for every office (not counting really obscure positions, like local-level judge, because there's just a limit to what I can be fully informed about)
- bringing my kids with me as often as possible, to instill in them a sense that community activism is a normal part of life, like breathing

CHAPTER ONE

JUGGLING LESSONS

One evening in 2008, I happened to be in a restaurant near Boston, trying to order dinner. As long as I was in New England, I figured that I ought to sample a local specialty. That also would be good for the environment, because big trucks wouldn't have guzzled tons of gas transporting the raw ingredients here from their original locations. But the menu didn't specify which foods were local. The only items I was pretty sure were from Boston were lobster and clams, which I can't eat because I keep semi-kosher, and haddock, which usually is caught by trawling methods that damage the seabed and other species.

Okay, how about a nonlocal but safe type of fish instead? I knew that tilapia, a flakey, white fish, wasn't endangered. It wasn't on the menu, however. Moreover, all the fish dishes were either baked in bread crumbs or fried, which would be fattening.

So forget about fish. Anyway, I really craved a salad. That would be nice and healthful and low-calorie. Another point in salad's favor: it cost about two-thirds the price of the haddock. However, I wanted some protein in my salad. I'm not vegetarian or strictly kosher, so I could have the tossed salad with grilled chicken. But since the menu didn't indicate any particular farming methods—nothing about being organic or free-range—the chicken probably came from some industrial farm in Maryland, where it would have been pumped full of antibiotics and salt, jammed with thirty thousand others into a dark, dusty shed reeking of their own waste, crippled by in-breeding to produce breasts so unnaturally large that it could barely walk, and finally ferried several hundred miles to Boston. While the salad greens might be healthy for me, the chicken wouldn't be, not for me, the earth, or the chicken itself.

At that point, the wisest thing to eat seemed like the chocolate cake.

All this agonizing, which probably took me a good five minutes, was for just one item in one meal on one night for one person with a fairly consistent set of values. For many people, something like this happens several times a day, a dozen times in a week. Americans, along with middle-class people in other developed countries, today live in a society that is at once the most politically aware and the most consumer-oriented in human history, and increasing numbers of us want to combine those two trends in our daily life. And in theory, that sounds great. Why not use all legitimate means at our disposal to further our values? We are told constantly that we should be educated, empowered consumers, that our purchasing and investing dollars are a form of influence to be wielded. Shopping for groceries, buying clothes, doing laundry, selecting a brand of toothpaste, cleaning the house, choosing a bank, deciding where to live, investing in stocks, raising our kids, and getting from place to place aren't just functions. They can be political declarations, even tactics to improve the world. In fact, it would be hypocritical to live in ways that didn't support our beliefs.

In theory, sure. But a life where you have to think about every single step you take is a life of impossible stress and constant debate.

To make matters worse, most of us probably care passionately about more than one issue. Although the issues might all seem to fall at the same end of the political spectrum, within a rational and related value system, they can turn out to be as contradictory in practice as my dinner in Boston.

Or dinner with Carroll Muffett. As deputy director of campaigns for the environmental group Greenpeace—and before that, an official at Defenders of Wildlife, which advocates on behalf of endangered species—Muffett is probably as green as you can get. One day, he and his family wanted to eat dinner with the family of his daughter's best friend, whose father works for a labor union. "It was nearly impossible for us to have dinner together, outside of spaghetti or rice and beans," Muffett recalled. "As an environmentalist, I can't eat most kinds of fish, or beef unless it's local. They couldn't eat grapes because of labor issues, or even some mushrooms. I'm pretty aware, but those are things I had no idea about."

Even a decision to shun McDonald's isn't as ethically clear-cut as it might seem. Certainly no conscientious parents would ever take their offspring there, right? After all, its high-fat, assembly-line food is a big reason why childhood obesity is epidemic in the United States.

Yet McDonald's scores fairly well on many consumer-advocacy lists. Amy Domini, chief executive of Domini Social Investments, who helped pioneer the philosophy of investing according to ethical criteria, includes the chain in her socially responsible mutual funds, with some perennial moral struggles. "On every issue people have brought to them for twenty years, they always say, 'Oops, you're right, we'll change it,'" she pointed out. McDonald's worked with the Environmental Defense Fund early on to replace its Styrofoam clamshell burger containers, which were made with ozone-destroying chlorofluorocarbons, and it has pressured suppliers to improve conditions for the hens that supply its eggs and the pigs that become its bacon. Furthermore, its customers probably won't get salmonella or *E. coli* poisoning from undercooked food. "If you want to make sure you're eating a hamburger as sterile as possible, go eat at McDonald's," advised Carol Tucker Foreman, one of the deans of the consumer movement as a former U.S. assistant secretary of agriculture and now a distinguished fellow of the Food Policy Institute at the Consumer Federation of America. "They have the highest standards. They can't afford not to. You may get a lot of fat, and it may be tasteless, but they'll cook that son of a bitch to death."

And eating at restaurants is just one tiny example of the dilemmas, contradictions, and difficult choices we face when we try to juggle all of our values in daily life.

I believe people should have decent working conditions, fair pay, and respect on the job. So I support the union movement, and I'd like to buy union-made clothes. I don't want my dollars propping up sweatshops overseas. But I also care about helping people in developing nations, and for the women who are employed there, those sweatshops actually can be highly desirable workplaces, far preferable to toiling in the rice paddies of their native village. But—one more but—I care about the environment. And it takes huge amounts of fossil fuel to ship clothing from Bangladesh, Cambodia, and other faraway countries, thus depleting scarce resources, increasing our dependence on oil-producing dictatorships, and emitting tons of the greenhouse gases that are whipsawing Earth's climate. (Of course, none of my preferences may matter in real life. Just try to find reasonably priced clothing at a typical store that *isn't* made overseas— and if you do locate the rare item made in the USA, try to find a union label.)

I believe in helping neighborhood stores and farmers stay in business, so that multinational conglomerates don't take over the world. Also, think of the gas I'd save if I shopped within a few blocks of my home, rather than driving miles to a big chain store. Or would I save? Instead of trudging from the farmers market to the natural-food store to the local drug store to the food co-op, would it be more efficient to get everything all at once, at one big store?

I believe in recycling, to save resources and energy. However, neither of my small, nearby stationery stores carries recycled-paper writing pads. But Staples, the big stationery chain, does. And, oh, the prices at Staples are generally so much cheaper.

Another way to recycle is to donate my old cell phone to a company that will send it to a poorer country in Africa, Latin America, or Asia, where it could be used for a few more years by a happy customer. That sounds good. But what happens after the phone finally, irrevocably, gives out? Most likely, local children will rip it apart for valuable components they can sell, clambering through dangerous mounds of trash, breathing in poisonous chemical fumes, and getting splashed with acid in the process. Would it be better just to discard the thing immediately, so it can be safely recycled or otherwise disposed of in an American facility?

I believe in eating food that's grown or raised without pesticides, chemical fertilizer, antibiotics, and added hormones, because it's better for the planet, for whatever animals are involved, and for my body. Most likely, the farmers at my local farmers market raise their crops and animals according to many of these principles, but they may not be quite pure enough to qualify for an official organic certification. Meanwhile, Whole Foods Market, Inc. always offers a huge, beautiful display of produce that's certified organic. In the New York City outlets closest to where I live, however, most of those lovely fruits and vegetables come from California. Is burning gasoline to transport this organic food three thousand miles worse for the environment than the synthetic fertilizer my local farmer may have used? To further complicate the equation, Whole Foods is notorious for fighting any attempt to unionize its work force, and as I said, I believe in supporting unions.

True, I can buy some organic food at many supermarkets

these days, and probably for a lower price than at Whole Foods. So who needs Whole Foods? Still, if Whole Foods hadn't pioneered mass-market organics, would other stores ever have begun selling those products? And if Whole Foods disappeared, would the others stop? Maybe I should shop at Whole Foods as a sign of appreciation.

I believe in supporting businesses that respect their workers, the environment, and the broader community. One way to express this support is to invest in socially responsible mutual funds like those Amy Domini oversees. There are funds that invest in companies that develop alternative energy, and funds that shun producers of tobacco and weapons. One fund looks for companies that mentor and promote women. So which fund should get my dollars? Do I care more about the environment, or tobacco, or women's rights?

"Even for the best-intentioned person," Carroll Muffett of Greenpeace said, "it is really impossible to make ethical choices about everything. People are busy in their daily lives. They have jobs, families, houses. You can try—you should try—but you shouldn't beat yourself up because the tissue paper you're using has no recycled content."

With all these contradictions and so much to investigate, plus limited budgets, how can anyone possibly live according to his or her values?

Yet, with so much at stake—climate change, sweatshops and child labor, personal health, oil wars, poverty, pollution, animal cruelty—how can we not?

Most people have never faced these sorts of dilemmas on such a wide scale before. For one thing, until the mid-twentieth century, a mass consumer society did not exist. The general populace had neither the excess cash nor the leisure time to worry about how to spend their money in any but the most practical ways. And until the last couple of centuries, ordinary citizens also lacked the political freedom to proclaim their beliefs publicly. These two strands of consumer and political awareness emerged just in time to confront a slew of problems worthy of their passion, as the detritus of centuries of human fishing, farming, hunting, building, damming, excavation, pollution, industrialization, colonization, and wars was finally reaching the limits of the planet's endurance.

Sure, individuals always are resolving ethical dilemmas in daily life. But we often grab our choices almost automatically, without thinking too much about how to reconcile competing values. Bruce G. Friedrich, vice president of the international grassroots campaign of the animal rights group People for the Ethical Treatment of Animals (PETA), likens the unconscious juggling to speeding: "We make decisions about things like speed limits every day, knowing that every 10 mph increase in the speed limit could cause a fatal accident," he said. We also know, somewhere in the back of our minds, that speeding uses more gas. However, even if we believe in saving lives and saving gas, what pushes our feet to press harder on the gas pedal is the more immediate knowledge that we're going to be late to wherever it is we're going.

"Life is governed ethically by an enormous amount of custom and routine," said Arthur Caplan, chair of the Department of Medical Ethics at the University of Pennsylvania. Very few people, he said, are what are known in ethical theory as "act utilitarians"—that is, "for every decision, you compute the pros and cons and the benefits and downsides."

On the opposite end of the scale from the automatic, everyday ethical decisions, society has also always had crusaders, ordinary people fired up for a grand moral cause, from the nineteenth-century abolitionists and suffragettes, to the twentieth-century abortion-clinic protestors and Mississippi Summer voter-registration volunteers. They may be trying to influence something that happens in daily life, like getting an abortion or voting. However, the specific methods that the crusaders apply in order to achieve this influence—marching, picketing, helping runaway slaves escape—are not activities in most people's usual experience. To put it another way, traditional activists use extraordinary measures to change some aspect of everyday life, rather than harnessing everyday life to change something bigger in the world.

Whenever people might be bothered momentarily by the wider implication of some daily action and tempted to apply ethical considerations to that action, practicality always seems to push aside those "softer" values, particularly when money is tight. In his 2007 book *Supercapitalism*, former U.S. secretary of labor Robert B. Reich argues that even if consumers want to be ethical, they've allowed society to put their financial interests ahead of their ethical concerns:

> These issues of economic security, social equity, community, our shared environment, and common decency…were—and still are—concerns to us in our capacity as *citizens*. [emphasis in the original] But as power has shifted to us as consumers and investors, these issues have been eclipsed. We've entered into a Faustian bargain. Today's economy can give us great deals largely because it punishes us in other ways.

Over the past half-century, however, the concept of consumer-political-ethical activism has been building slowly. In the 1950s and 1960s, the bus boycotts and lunch-counter sit-ins of the civil rights movement proved that consumer power could be leveraged to tear down unfair laws. As the 1960s segued into the Me Generation of the 1970s and 1980s, activism took a turn toward materialism, but it employed the same principle of consumer empowerment. Affinity cards and frequent-flyer clubs taught shoppers to turn even the most mundane purchases into a twofer, first to buy the item at hand, then to rack up points toward another goal. Consumer power exploded with the Internet a decade later. Information about corporate behavior, product ingredients, product availability, scientific warnings, investment returns, and international conflicts now was widely available, shared across the globe within seconds, making mass actions easier to organize. "Helicopter moms" zoomed into their kids' lives, obsessing about the potential toxins in their lunch boxes, their water bottles, their school cafeterias, and the junk food at their friends' homes.

Probably the strongest, most broad-based consumer-political movement to emerge was environmentalism. By the late 1990s, everyone from kindergartners to CEOs was talking green. If hard-core environmentalists scoffed that a lot of the talk was merely marketing hype, it at least proved that public awareness was strong enough to make greenness an advantage in the marketplace. Grocery stores gave rebates for reusing plastic bags, cities carved out bike lanes, and highway rest stops put out recycling bins (yes, at the same rest stops where gas-guzzlers fill up with more gas). Colleges competed to attract applicants by touting environmental touches like the biodegradable forks in their dining halls, and the *Princeton Review* in 2008 began including a "green rating" in its annual college guide. Even Wal-Mart Stores, Inc., the chain that liberals love to hate, launched a major eco-program to recycle excess plastic, run its trucks more efficiently, and, eventually, operate solely on renewable energy.

And more: Hotels bragged that they actually wouldn't clean your room; in other words, they wouldn't change the bed sheets and towels unless a guest specifically requested it, in order to save water. A group of direct mailers called the Green Marketing Coalition in 2008 announced a set of environmental guidelines, such as using recycled paper made without chlorine. (Wouldn't they save even more trees if they just stopped sending us all that junk mail?) Firemen's Fund Insurance Companies that same year created a special "green" policy for "homeowners who currently own green homes or who want to upgrade their residence with green features after a loss using environmental safety and efficiency standards." What sorts of standards? Probably the most well-known is the Leadership in Environmental and Energy Design (LEED) Green Building Rating System, which defines four levels of "greenness" for such factors as water efficiency, energy efficiency, and materials. But if a building owner doesn't like that, the book *The Sustainability Revolution* by environmental consultant Andres R. Edwards, published in 2005, has a three-page chart with thirty-eight more sets of environmental principles and standards.

Truly, I'm glad we have these consumer options, hype or not. But one risk, when something becomes so popularized, is that there's too much information and too much to do. All those green building standards. A half-dozen brands of organic corn chips. How do you choose?

No one expects the average consumer to know every political, sociological, health, and environmental implication of every possible encounter in daily life, of course. Not even an activist like Kimberly Danek Pinkson can do that. In 2006, Pinkson founded an organization in Northern California called the EcoMom Alliance, which is basically what the name implies: a group of mothers who lobby their local schools, governments, merchants, and neighbors to be more environmentally sensitive. "When I read labels at the store, ninety percent of the time the things don't mean anything to me," Pinkson said. "I haven't memorized every toxin I should avoid." Added Carroll Muffett, "It is fundamentally unfair to ask consumers to bear all this" research effort.

So we have books to analyze the labels and do the research for us. *True Green: 100 Everyday Ways You Can Contribute to a Healthier Planet. The Little Green Book of Shopping: 250 Tips for an Eco Lifestyle. 1001 Ways to Save the Earth.*

Wait a second. Am I supposed to do ONE HUNDRED or TWO HUNDRED AND FIFTY or ONE THOUSAND AND ONE things just for the environment? And that's not counting all the other causes I care about.

Living an ethical life is so much work, in fact, that it *is* some people's full-time work. They earn a living by advocating ethical living. One of them is Chip Giller, who runs a Web site called Grist, which offers news, analysis, advice, and even humor about environmental issues. The site's advice column, "Ask Umbra," answers the most ultra-green questions imaginable, including whether to use cloth or disposable diapers (no preference) and how to recycle food waste (depending on where you live, you may be able to leave it at the curb or take it to a central collection bin). Grist and its networking tools get more than eight hundred thousand unique visitors a month, an indication of how popular the whole green movement has become.

Alex Steffen, a former journalist, also labors full-time running an ethical-lifestyle Web site, Worldchanging. It tends to have more sober articles and lectures. No puns or trivial advice here. "I've readjusted my entire career to work on this issue," Steffen said.

Wood Turner left his public relations job in 2006 to create a ranking of the carbon emissions of the biggest companies in the nine largest consumer sectors: apparel, beer, electronics, food products, food services, household products, Internet/software, media, and shipping. With the help of several freelance and volunteer assistants, Turner analyzes companies based on twenty-two criteria. Has the company measured its greenhouse-gas emissions? If so, does that measurement include indirect emissions from its supply chain, employee travel, and even the other companies it invests in? Does the company also try to educate its employees, industry colleagues, and customers on ways they can reduce their own carbon impact? Each answer is worth two to ten points, for a total of one hundred, and the rankings are posted on Turner's Web site, ClimateCounts. The information comes from publicly available data and the companies' responses to letters Turner sends them.

"We built the organization as a proxy for the average consumer," said Turner, whose official title is project director. And apparently there are a lot of these consumers. Turner said that in its first eighteen months, ClimateCounts distributed a half-million copies of its pocket consumer guide. The idea is to help us shop ethically. If I'm going to continue my addiction to diet soda, Coke scores better, with sixty-one points, than Pepsi, with thirty-seven points.

But look what happened: among the six media companies, Rupert Murdoch's News Corp. got the second-highest ranking, a nice, green sixty-three.

Yikes! Arch right-winger Murdoch, owner of the liberal-bashing Fox News and *New York Post?* What liberal could possibly give a top rating to this company, no matter how much newsprint it recycles? Greenhouse gas "is not really a political issue," was Turner's total explanation. So does that mean I can't be true to my partisan politics and my environmental politics at the same time? (Note to self: there goes any hope of getting a job at the Murdoch-owned *Wall Street Journal.*)

To read all those cheerful advice books and to listen to a lot of experts, you'd never guess there was a conflict in the world, no clashes between competing values, or between ethics and reality. *True Green* tells readers to use cloth diapers, then save water and electricity "by washing in bulk and line drying." Well, as a mother of two, I have tried cloth diapers and line drying. Line-dried diapers are rougher than machine-dried, which will make your baby miserable and probably cause rashes. And what new parent has time to wring out all those wet diapers, pin them up one by one on the clothes line, and run around checking to see if they're dry? (Anyway, didn't Umbra, the Grist columnist, say that disposable diapers are just as green as cloth?)

For parents with slightly older children, *Llewellyn's 2009 Green Living Guide* suggests growing your own organic vegetables. As the book says, "Gardening is a great way to teach your toddler about nutrition and get them to eat healthy food." Also to eat dirt, rocks, bugs, and inedible plants as the toddlers wander around that lovely garden while you water and pull weeds. (Give the book credit, at least, for trying to save harried parents the cost of buying the veggies.)

The useless, chirpy advice extends beyond child-rearing. While urging people to buy only items that are certified as fair-trade—made by workers overseas who are treated decently and paid a living wage—another *Llewellyn* writer concedes that it's hard to discern whether a certification is legit. "The certification industry is fairly young in the garment sector and sadly full of 'freeloaders' who have seen the opportunity and deliberately try to deceive the consumer," the book warns. Therefore, the author continues, "When buying a garment, take a look at the certification mark, which should have a web address. Make a note of it and then go home and do some research. If you are satisfied, then go back and buy it." Right. If no one else has grabbed the only one in your size in the interim, and if you have the time to make two trips to the store, and by the way, how much gas are you wasting by repeating your trip?

It's always easier to take on more responsibilities if you don't have many to begin with. From my reporting, I'd guess that a lot of liberal activists are in their twenties and thirties, in good health, with decent-paying, white-collar jobs and no kids or aging parents to care for. No doubt they have the time to sort through their recycling and the money to buy organic food. How about those of us with more complex lives?

Lisa Wise, for example, is the executive director of the Center for a New American Dream, a think tank in Washington, D.C., that aims to teach people how to be socially responsible consumers. Admirably practicing what she preaches, Wise lives with three roommates in a house with energy-efficient appliances, compact fluorescent (CFL) light bulbs, motion sensors, low-flow toilets and shower heads, and an irrigation drip system in the garden instead of a hose, all of which save energy or water. Wise and her roommates shop as much as possible by bicycle, and when a car is absolutely necessary, they combine trips. So if she can live virtuously, why can't everyone? As Wise sees it, people who talk about juggling conflicts are just looking for excuses. "There are a million ways for people to explain why they can't do things efficiently," Wise told me. "There are always efficiencies people can create in their lives."

Still, I asked her, aren't "green" products often more expensive than standard ones? And aren't liberals supposed to be concerned about lower-income and working-class people? Her answer: "By and large, if they cut their frivolous consumer-based spending and then focus on buying green, it would pencil out in the consumer's favor. One less iPod helps you buy organic."

One less iPod? Frivolous spending?

Is that really the only financial dilemma that some activists can imagine? How about the dilemma faced by a single mom without dental insurance whose teenage son needs braces? Or a part-time department store clerk whose husband just lost his job at General Motors? Now ask them to pay extra for organic veggies in order to save the earth.

When confronted with these sorts of conflicts, self-righteous advocates usually don't have an answer that will help in real life. So they launch into a description of the ethically pure planet they expect to inhabit in the future, a world in which we all take mass transit, run our energy-efficient homes solely with solar and wind power, and walk to the bustling nearby farmers market. Or else they start explaining the theory of long-term social impact and why mass-produced hamburger isn't really as cheap as it seems because of the hidden costs of pesticides and chemical run-offs that society ultimately will have to pay for.

For example, I asked Bruce Friedrich of PETA what he considered the most ethical source of energy. Is it okay to buy my electricity from a utility that uses nuclear power, because it emits no carbon gases? Or do the risk of a nuclear accident and the lack of permanent storage for radioactive waste outweigh the carbon benefits? (More on this in chapter 4.) "The real solution is not to figure out how we can continue to consume so gluttonously," he replied. "The real solution is to come up with wind power, solar power, other means of energy sources that don't have catastrophic effects." Well, yes, but right now, I need power to run my computer, lights, refrigerator, washing machine, and other basic needs. (At least no one is telling me to scrub my clothes on a tin washboard.)

Even some activists are annoyed by their colleagues' smugness and extremism. (Interestingly, they are usually the ones with children, and thus more grounded in reality.) Chip Giller—who has two young kids—said he started Grist in 1999 "deliberately to help lighten up a movement that was known for a good while as being self-righteous and preachy and taking itself a little too seriously. There has been an impression created that environmentalists are purists. I think it's been a turn-off." Kimberly Danek Pinkson, the founder of the EcoMom Alliance, and a single mother, agreed. "That's why the environmental movement didn't take off for thirty years," she said. "It was too holier-than-thou. Too either-or." The original public image of the movement, she said, was "live on the commune, don't wear make-up, don't drive anywhere, you're a bad human being and there's no in-between if you're not willing to go the whole distance and be perfect like me."

Pinkson got the idea for her alliance after helping to organize a local event for the United Nations' World Environment Day in June 2006. About a month later, she overheard a conversation among a group of friends. "One of them was talking about how she attended that event, then she went home and switched all the bulbs to CFL. I watched as the conversation took off like wildfire, from 'What's a CFL?' to 'I want those. Where can I get one?' to what kinds of cleansers these moms were using, what kinds of cosmetics, were they using recycled toilet paper?" Pinkson recalled. "I was watching that and thinking about the power of women as role models and as a market force."

Living in upscale, liberal Marin County, just across the Golden Gate Bridge from San Francisco, Pinkson is all too familiar with today's version of the purer-than-thou environmentalists. A 2008 cover story in *San Francisco* magazine described a society of ultra-green local mothers who reuse their children's bathwater, dig out recyclables from their neighbors' trash, and confess their sins to "eco-therapists." One woman listed all the ingredients she checks for in every container of food: genetically modified organisms, soy, corn syrup, trans fats, lecithin, high sugar content, overly processed wheat, whether the chickens were free-range or the eggs are from free-range chickens, and added corn, soy or canola oil. The *New York Times* soon followed with an article focusing on one EcoMom Alliance gathering during which neighbors jumped on the hostess "for her wall-to-wall carpeting (potential off-gassing), her painted walls (unhealthful volatile organic compounds) and the freshly cut flowers that she had set out for the occasion (not organic). Their problems with the SUV in the driveway were self-explanatory."

Pinkson seemed to take it in stride when I reminded her of the article. "Yes, she's got that carpeting and that kind of car. But she's trying to do something [just by being part of EcoMom], and that's fantastic," Pinkson said. "The people who are criticizing these women are missing the boat. You can't wake up one morning and decide to be perfect."

In fairness, the super-self-satisfied advocates have a valid point. Sometimes there is no conflict between values, or between values and real life. Turning off lights saves money and also reduces emissions. If we bought more fair-trade goods from small-scale farmers and craftspeople overseas, maybe they could earn enough that they wouldn't chop down priceless rain forests for fuel or kill endangered animals for food. "Ecology and economy are becoming ever more interwoven...A world in which poverty is endemic will always be prone to ecological and other catastrophes," says the 1987 report "Our Common Future" from the United Nations' World Commission on Environment and Development, known as the Brundtland report.

Nevertheless, plenty of choices, like my dinner in Boston, just aren't clear-cut. As consumers and citizens, we often have to draw lines.

When Wood Turner created ClimateCounts, he had to decide what criteria to use for ranking the consumer-goods companies. The possibilities are "sort of overwhelming," he admitted. "You want to slice every company in every way you possibly can: labor, human rights, childhood obesity, animal welfare." But to analyze all those slices, he would need a cast of thousands to do the research, and the spreadsheet that emerged probably would be unreadable.

So Turner narrowed the ranking to a single core issue. He chose global warming, he said, because the impact is so enormous that it supersedes everything else. "If we're not thinking in a very comprehensive way about how we're facing climate change, the many other issues that we're facing as a society don't amount to much," he explained. If the Russian permafrost melts and coastlines are washed away, if fertile plains become deserts and ice patches become fertile plains, if habitats change so drastically that the animals that live there can't survive, people won't really care whether their strawberries are organic or hens are squeezed into filthy cages. In Turner's view, "Climate change has implications for every issue that we're facing."

Like Turner, the most active of the activists zoom in on just one area, among all the causes they may care about, to be their central concern. Even for professionals, it's impossible to become an expert in everything.

The crucial question, then, is how do these activists select their focus area?

Why does Bruce Friedrich of PETA work so hard to protect animals, instead of trying to reduce the risk of global warming? Part of the answer is precisely that the environment already has plenty of defenders. "Animal protection gets vastly fewer resources and attention than human and environmental causes," Friedrich explained. "Human and environmental causes are based in a real way on self-interest, whereas animal preservation means fighting for a very real paradigm change." Emphasizing the traits that animals and humans share, especially the ability to feel pain, Friedrich and others equate animal rights with civil rights and women's rights—that is, to treat animals differently from people is "speciesism." In the 2006 animal-rights manifesto *In Defense of Animals*—a collection of eighteen essays, edited by the veteran activist Peter Singer—Richard D. Ryder, a former chair of the Royal Society for the Prevention of Cruelty to Animals Council in Britain, traced the history of this movement to the 1970s. Ryder writes: "Once colonialism, racism, and sexism had been intellectually challenged, then the next logical stage in the expansion of the boundaries of the moral in-group was an attack upon speciesism."

If you're an incorrigible speciesist, on the other hand, and your priority is fighting poverty, Christian E. Weller says the most effective strategy is to support the labor movement. Weller is an associate professor of public policy at the McCormack Graduate School of Policy Studies at the University of Massachusetts at Boston, as well as a senior fellow at the Center for American Progress, a liberal think tank in Washington, D.C., closely tied to former president Bill Clinton and Secretary of State Hillary Rodham Clinton. He also has indirect union credentials as the husband of Beth Almeida, a onetime official of the International Association of Machinists and Aerospace Workers. "Buying union is the only thing that I consistently consider when buying large consumer items," Weller said. "I study the economic troubles in the U.S. very closely, and one of the fundamental problems of the past three decades has been the lack of strong wage growth across the lower- and middle-income ranges. While a higher minimum wage is helpful in raising incomes at the bottom, only unionization can really help to put wage growth in line with productivity growth for middle-income workers."

Chip Giller shares Wood Turner's idea of harnessing consumer power for environmental causes, but he doesn't single out climate change. "We look at food, climate, transportation, making more livable communities—to make green normal, to make it a pervasive and expected part of people's personal and professional lives," he explained. That's why Grist posts so much practical advice about shopping and housekeeping. Rather than denouncing the horrible conditions on poultry farms, as PETA might, Grist at Thanksgiving had a column on how to find a "heritage" turkey, raised on a local farm with open space and organic food. "Really, what we want is societal change, and to do that you need to get to people where they're at," Giller said.

Alex Steffen disagrees. While he also dedicates himself to environmental causes, he thinks consumer advice is frivolous. "The scale of the changes we're called to make is such that they can't be accomplished in small steps," he scoffed. "I don't think that the lifestyle changes really work." In fact, analyzing whether to buy Coke or Pepsi can be dangerous, in his view. "To the extent that it [ethical shopping] makes people feel that the problem has been solved, it's not a good thing. If everyone who's spending their time worrying about whether it's better to buy something local or something organic spent more time trying to influence the farm bill, we would have a whole food system that's more sustainable." So his Web site, Worldchanging, urges readers to think broadly: to volunteer on campaigns, lobby, blog, and write to politicians.

Saving the earth from global warming. Saving the oceans and forests. Saving endangered species. Making sure people earn decent wages. Making sure farm animals have decent living conditions. All of these are good and important causes. And there are even more that I haven't mentioned yet, issues like horrendous global poverty, terrorism, and women's rights in developing countries and under Islamic *shari'ah* law. All of the advocates make convincing arguments. After talking to them, I was more torn than ever.

But not hopeless. Quite the opposite. This may sound goody-goody, but I truly was inspired by all the ways I could work to make the world a better place. The next step was to find out more information so I could decide which way to go.

Oh, and about the dinner in Boston? In the end, I ordered the haddock, with a vegetable side dish. But I really wanted that salad.

CHAPTER TWO

MORALS AT THE MALL

Shopping, as we are constantly reminded, drives American society. Consumers are responsible for two-thirds of the nation's economic activity, or about $8 trillion worth of transactions annually in recent years. After the terrorist attacks of September 11, 2001, and again during the financial meltdown of 2008–2009, the federal government pushed Americans to spend, spend, spend in order to show Al Qaeda that we were undaunted and to pull the country out of recession, respectively.

With those kinds of dollars bumping around, the U.S. consumer has a tremendous impact on climate change, pollution, global working conditions, the price of oil and other commodities, the survival of endangered species, the union movement, poverty, international financial stability, and the wars that often erupt from these pressures, even if the consumer isn't actually trying to target spending for ethical or political reasons. A decision to buy a new cell phone, a shirt, a car, a box of laundry detergent, or even this book has consequences. The decision helps determine whether land is dug up in Central African gorilla habitats and war zones to mine for the metallic ore coltan that is used in manufacturing cell phones; whether girls leave their villages in Vietnam and Honduras for jobs in shirt-making factories; whether water is drained from the Aral Sea in Uzbekistan to irrigate fields to grow cotton for the shirt; whether auto companies devote more effort to researching electric cars; whether

OPEC jacks up the price of oil; whether lab mice are injected with chemicals that might be used in the detergent; whether chemical additives from the detergent, mixed in with waste water from sewer pipes, accumulate to dangerous levels in fish and plankton; and whether trees are cut down to produce the paper for this book. In addition to these direct effects of the manufacturing process, there are also the costs and effects of shipping, stocking, advertising, and paying for these goods.

Most of us, given our druthers, probably would prefer not to spark a civil war over coltan mining, prop up oil dictatorships, or poison fish. We'd much rather buy stuff made in ways that treat animals, humans, and the earth with respect. And we are lucky that, in Western society, we have many, many ethical alternatives nowadays. A host of toothpastes, shampoos, soaps, and hand lotions contain all-natural—and delightful-sounding—ingredients like ginger-peppermint oil, sweet almond oil, sugar beets, myrrh, lavender, and green apples. There are recycled paper goods of various kinds, and organic-cotton clothing and bed sheets. You can buy beautiful secondhand clothes, barely worn, at the most fashionable thrift shops. In my wardrobe I've got a hemp hat, and the *New York Times* in 2007 found underwear made of soy.

But we live in a busy world. We don't have the time to check the "made in" label, the working and environmental conditions, the carbon footprint, or the roster of ingredients for every item we contemplate, every time we go shopping—let alone mix olive oil and vinegar to make our own, natural, wood-furniture cleaner. (That's a recipe from *Consumer Reports:* six teaspoons of light olive oil plus three cups of distilled white vinegar, if you want to know.)

Yes, plenty of books and Web sites are happy to step in. Too many. PETA's CaringConsumer provides lists of companies that do and don't use animals to test consumer products. Another Web site, GoodGuide, claims to rate thousands of hair-care, baby-care, laundry, make-up, sports, and household products according to six hundred factors such as philanthropy, working conditions, energy use, and environmental emissions. Wood Turner's ClimateCounts analyzes several of these same companies by similar environmental criteria—yet, confusingly, sometimes with different results. For example, Procter & Gamble is the top company in ClimateCounts's "household products" category; however, one of its Crest toothpaste brands comes in among the worst at GoodGuide.

That's not all the rosters, not by far. Greenpeace has ranked toy companies based on whether their toys contain polyvinyl chloride, the United Auto Workers (UAW) has a list of "Union Made in America" cars, and the AFL-CIO surveys nearly two dozen product categories on the Web site Unionlabel. *The Rough Guide to Shopping with a Conscience* offers two full pages of what the book calls "high-profile boycotts under way at the time of writing." In 2007, the list included boycotts against individual companies such as Nestlé (for pushing infant formula in the developing world) and Adidas (for making soccer shoes out of kangaroo skin); actions against big groupings, like donors to then-President George W. Bush; and boycotts of companies doing business in Myanmar, China, and the United States. (It's a bit tough to follow that last boycott if you actually live in the United States.)

However, these competing guidelines don't magically solve our shopping problems. Which list should we use? What criteria? Environmental record? Political contributions? Use of animal products? Labor record? Shoppers have to remember to consult the right authority before running off to the mall. Or lug a couple of books and long computer printouts. Or hold up the checkout line while frantically scrolling through a dozen Web sites on their BlackBerries. Most important, while consumers are worrying about the lab mice and the dried-out Aral Sea and the carbon emissions, they risk forgetting the reason they went shopping to begin with. You probably didn't set out to buy an organic, union-made piece of cloth. You set out to buy a skirt that you could wear to an important job interview, that would match your navy blazer, that was within a certain price range, and that wouldn't make your butt look too big. Don't those qualities matter anymore? If, after hours of searching, you finally, finally find the perfect skirt that meets all those criteria, are you really going to reject it because the material isn't organic or it was sewn in a sweatshop in El Salvador? Let's be honest.

Kimberly Danek Pinkson, the founder of the EcoMom Alliance in California, admits that her young son Corbin owns plastic (nonrecyclable) action figures made in China (not local). You just try to take Rescue Heroes away from an eight-year-old. "If I completely turn him away from the culture we live in, he's going to revolt and turn the other way," Pinkson figured.

There's got to be a manageable system for organizing the cacophony of too much consumer information and too many competing demands. For starters, maybe it's possible to single out some stores and manufacturers that a liberal shopper can generally trust, without having to research every item they sell. These would be places that use ethical processes and ingredients, that treat their employees fairly, that contribute to the community—in short, that a consumer can feel good about going to.

Sitting in her light-filled living room in New York City, Cathy Monblatt explained her shopping hierarchy: "There's the farmers market, the food co-op, the local organic store, the local nonorganic market, the supermarket, Costco, Wal-Mart. Then there's local and organic. For each item, think of it as a grid. We move up and down the grid."

She analyzes seven possible stores and two possible versions for each item she buys?

"It isn't that we're consciously going through this every time we make a purchase," Monblatt quickly amended. She and her husband, Stewart Pravda (both technology program managers who specialize in finance), simply try to shop in more or less the order she outlined. Local merchants are a priority, and Wal-Mart is beyond the pale.

Monblatt's ranking is in many ways not just a liberal ideal, but also an all-American shopping list. Consider how she starts with small, local markets. The American Revolution was a classic David-versus-Goliath story, and ever since then we've been taught to root for the little guy. Never mind that nearly 80 percent of Americans live in urban areas; in popular mythology, we all belong in Mayberry—we drink coffee at the local diner, buy a birthday card at the neighborhood drug store, and wave hi to our friendly letter-carrier. During every presidential campaign, the candidates trip over each other trying to evoke more of these mythical small-town values than the other guy.

In addition, Americans have been raised to believe in free-market competition. Thus, we should want lots of independent outlets to choose from, rather than only a couple of huge chains.

The Park Slope Food Coop that Cathy Monblatt mentioned—which sells cookbooks, wrapping paper, and face cream, as well as food—fits another national archetype, one almost as old as the Revolution. That's the America of Alexis de Tocqueville in the 1830s, America as a collection of close-knit communities where neighbors aid one another. Think of pot-luck church suppers and Welcome Wagons, pioneers helping to raise each other's barns and the people of Bedford Falls collecting the $8,000 George Bailey needs to save his family's building and loan association in *It's a Wonderful Life*. Similarly, in a food co-op, the members officially own the enterprise and vote on major decisions, and many co-ops, including Monblatt's, require everyone to share the nuts-and-bolts work. (This contradicts a different national image, that of rugged individualism—Daniel Boone striding into the wilderness, Horatio Alger telling poor boys to pull themselves up by their own bootstraps, John Wayne doing almost anything—but who said cultural archetypes have to be consistent?)

Beyond mythology, there are strong ethical reasons for liberals to seek out local merchants. It seems logical that you'd save gas by shopping close to home. A big chain drugstore isn't going to screen out shampoo that was tested on animals, but the little health-food store will. And you create a nice, virtuous circle that keeps money circulating in your neighborhood: the cash you spend at the local hardware store goes to the store owner, who pays taxes to your state and city, which comes back to you in the form of municipal services and lower taxes. Furthermore, local owners often feel a certain degree of loyalty; they'll contribute to a downtown beautification campaign or the city art museum.

While the small-town mythology may be overdone, it's not completely without foundation. In a crowded, busy, impersonal world—a world in which many people spend all day at a computer screen, hardly seeing any live human beings—it's a rare and wonderful treat to walk into a store that's not a carbon copy of one you can find in any strip mall. At the food co-op, the people who take your money at the cash register today may be the same people whose money you took yesterday when you worked the registers. At the farmers market, Cathy Monblatt said, "You can actually get into a conversation with the actual producer. 'What are these mushrooms? What do you use this cheese for?'" (I don't want to get carried away with this point, however. Sometimes it's so crowded and busy at my local farmers market that I think the other customers would shove me if I tried to chat up the farmer.)

The antithesis of the little neighborhood shop are department stores, supermarkets, national and international chains, shopping Web sites, and—epitomized by Wal-Mart—big-box discount giants. Four arguments, sometimes with ethical angles, are offered most frequently to defend these Goliaths: their prices are lower than those of stand-alone stores; they offer a wider variety of goods, including a lot of the organic and natural brands that you used to find only at small, alternative markets; they're more likely to stay in business; and doing all your shopping online or in one big superstore, even if it's far from your home, actually saves gas compared with driving from one tiny shop to another.

Are these arguments valid? Let's start with the easiest to prove. In theory, the behemoths' size should give them the clout to negotiate bulk discounts from suppliers and the space to display and stock far more than a tiny store—enough clout, in fact, to force rivals to match their cheap prices, thus multiplying their beneficial impact on society. Two economics professors, Emek Basker of the University of Missouri and Michael Noel of the University of California at San Diego, analyzed this so-called Wal-Mart effect by looking at the prices of two dozen items at Wal-Mart and other stores in 175 U.S. cities from July 2001 to July 2004, then correlating those statistics with the dates that a Wal-Mart branch opened in the area. The professors' conclusion, in a July 2007 paper entitled "The Evolving Food Chain: Competitive Effects of Wal-Mart's Entry into the Supermarket Industry," supports Goliath's side. They say that Wal-Mart on average charges 10 percent less for most items than competitors do, and its arrival on the scene spurs other stores to lower their own prices by 1 to 1.2 percent. "We find that both the direct and indirect price effects of Wal-Mart's expansion are significant," the paper states. (There's more about price in chapter 7.)

Any consumer can try to confirm the cost and variety claims by comparison-shopping. When I checked a half-dozen items at my neighborhood Staples and two independent stationery stores, Staples' prices were arguably lower for four or five of them. Sometimes it wasn't clear what to compare, however, because Staples had so many more choices for the same category. Should I match one local store's $4.95 one-inch binder against Staples' $2.49 binder, the $3.29 version, the $4.49, or the $6.99? Staples, in fact, had eight different one-inch binders, along with several half-inch, 1½-inch, 2-inch, and 3-inch varieties. Meanwhile, one of the small stores had no binders at all.

However, Stacy Mitchell, a community development advisor, disputes these contentions in her 2006 book *Big-Box Swindle,* which investigates the rise and power of Wal-Mart and its ilk, and she also discussed the issue in a separate interview with me. For instance, the supposed discounts are only for a few "loss leaders" and temporary bargains to lure people in the door, she asserted. The rest of the merchandise typically costs the same or even more than at rival stores. Similarly, author Ellen Ruppel Shell, in her 2009 book *Cheap,* asserts that fully one-third of Wal-Mart's prices are higher than the average elsewhere. And the great savings on the other two-thirds? Thirty-seven cents, on average. As Mitchell writes, "Recognizing the power of first impressions, many offer especially low prices when they first enter an area, only to raise them as competitors disappear and consumers become accustomed to shopping at the big box."

In our interview, Mitchell brought up a variation on the but-in-the-long-run argument: "Whatever these companies have saved us in terms of what we spend, they've taken far more away from us in terms of lost income and job opportunities and sales tax." Obviously some municipality *will* gain income, jobs, and tax revenue when a Big Box plants itself there, but a slew of other towns will lose if the Big Box puts their stores out of business—and the net result, Mitchell argued, is not a one-for-one replacement. Referring to an analysis of Wal-Mart openings and employment published in 2006 by the Public Policy Institute of California, she writes:

They found that the opening of a Wal-Mart store reduced a county's retail employment by an average of 180 jobs, or 3.2 percent. That is, Wal-Mart employed fewer people than the stores that closed or downsized following its arrival. This makes sense, given the efficiencies of big-box retailers and their tendency to understaff stores.

Another blow to the local economy is that a big chain is likely to order its everyday supplies through the national headquarters, rather than picking up pens and paper towels from stores in town. And the consulting firm Civic Economics, in a study of western Michigan in 2009, backed up the "virtuous circle" theory of shopping local. According to the firm, if independent neighborhood stores could grab 10 percent of market share from big chains, the local economy would gain more than 1,600 new jobs, nearly $140 million in new economic activity, and more than $50 million in new wages.

Next is the question of product variety. In our interview, Mitchell contended that true variety comes from a universe of unique stores, each selling its own personalized, albeit limited, selection. "One of the most important things for consumers is the diversity of the marketplace," she said. "All of the stores in a chain carry basically the same thing. The independent stores are smaller on average, but collectively on average they stock a greater diversity."

How about the third Goliath defense, the question of staying power? While it's true that about half of all small businesses fail within the first five years, according to the U.S. Small Business Administration, there's no guarantee the big guys will survive, especially in a tough economy. Chains like Waldenbooks and Starbucks closed scores of stores during and even before the 2008-2009 financial meltdown. And where are Circuit City,

Montgomery Ward, and Gimbel's today? Completely out of business. Anyway, so what if your local store goes kaput four years from now? Sentimentally, you may regret the death of another brave little enterprise, but you can enjoy it while it lasts. (Just don't build up a lot of store credit.)

The hardest issue for a consumer to investigate is the driving-efficiency claim. You'd have to tally your mileage driving around to a few small, nearby stores, then clock the distance to a single warehouse or discount outlet that carried all the things you got at the locals. The big store is probably a long drive away, located on relatively cheap real estate several exits out on the highway. But that could end up being fewer miles in total than a series of trips to several closer stores.

Gauging the efficiency of online shopping is particularly tough, because there are too many variables: If you hadn't ordered your widget from the Web, would you have purchased it at a local store or a big chain? How many people in your neighborhood are getting deliveries on the same day from the same delivery service that's bringing your widget? Even better, does your store deliver by bike, as the Harvard Book Store began doing locally in 2009? Apparently, a lot of liberals already have decided that ordering in saves gas over picking up. When Domino's Pizza polled nearly three hundred thousand customers on October 29, 2008, on a variety of political and pizza-related issues, it found that Democrats were more likely than Republicans to have their pizzas delivered. (The real question is this: why are Democrats ordering pizza from a chain whose founder, Thomas Monaghan, is well-known for contributing to right-wing politicians and causes?)

These theoretical arguments may be compelling, but even socially conscious shoppers don't decide where to get their socks based solely on values like preventing climate change. If you need only a gallon of paint—and you need it fast—you'll pay an extra buck at the local hardware store rather than spend an hour driving out to Home Depot. However, if you really want a 1 ½-inch binder, and Staples has exactly what you're looking for, while the local independent doesn't, why should you get the wrong thing just to support the little guy? When the economy is flailing, you might feel you can't afford to give up that 10 percent Wal-Mart cost advantage; later, when things improve, you can worry about the long-term implications.

For years, I filled my family's prescriptions at the independent pharmacy a block away from my son's elementary school, in part because the mother of a classmate worked there. (Talk about Mayberry!) I loyally stayed with that pharmacy, even after my son graduated from the school, even after the mother left, and even though there are three chain drug stores in my neighborhood that are open longer hours. Financially, it was no problem, since my insurance co-payment was the same no matter where I shopped. Then one day, when I went to reorder a medication I need to take daily, that nice local pharmacist told me my co-payment had doubled. I called my insurance company to find out why. The company explained that I could reduce the price even lower than before the doubling by purchasing through its mail-order arm.

Sorry, Stacy Mitchell, but that was too huge a cash difference to resist, for something that I will be buying every month for years to come.

As my nod to supporting David, I still go to the local pharmacy for one-time prescriptions.

Mitchell herself confessed, in our interview, to sometimes darkening the doors of the big bad chains in order to get recycled paper. The office-supply store in her hometown of Portland, Maine, doesn't sell the paper, because, Mitchell said, the owner remembers the early days of recycling, back in the 1980s, when the paper quality was so poor that it jammed customers' printers. (Personally, I think this may be a hang-up of all independent owners; neither of my two local stationery stores carries recycled paper.) "I juggle back and forth," buying recycled paper from a chain outlet and other supplies from the little store, Mitchell said. Her long-term solution is to try to persuade the local owner to stock the paper. The results so far: "They're thinking about it. One of the great things about local business is that you can talk to the owner."

In any case, most consumers may not have a choice. If, as Mitchell's book says, the top ten retail chains grabbed nearly 25 percent of the dollars Americans spent in stores in 2005, many Americans probably couldn't find an independently owned, nonchain drug store, shoe store, bookstore, or hardware store close enough to be called "local."

Among the huge chains, two names are special: Costco Wholesale Corp. and Whole Foods.

By all classic definitions, Costco is a big-box behemoth. It has more than 540 stores sprawled across forty states, Canada, Puerto Rico, Mexico, Japan, Taiwan, South Korea, and the United Kingdom. It places the stores far away from the center of town. It undercuts mom-and-pop competitors with supposed discounts. It sells thousands of items ranging from toilet paper to TV sets in such gigantic packages that customers must use cars to tote them away. Yet Mitchell told me that "Costco is in a league of its own."

Why? Largely because of good labor relations. Costco inherited that culture from Price Club, one of two predecessors that merged to form the modern company in 1993. Price Club was founded by Sol Price, "whose father was a coal miner and who, in his entrepreneurial youth, read the *Daily Worker* more than the *Wall Street Journal*," Mitchell writes. About one-sixth of Costco's U.S. work force today is represented by the International Brotherhood of Teamsters. Even most of those who aren't in a union—including a lot of part-timers—get health insurance with low premiums, a 401(k) retirement plan, twice-a-year bonuses, and salaries far above the average for the retail world. Not surprisingly, there's relatively little turnover. Compare that with the constant lawsuits and headlines over Wal-Mart's pay and working conditions.

Another good quality is that Costco is one of the few food companies that conducts its own safety inspections, rather than relying on the usual system of unregulated auditors who may have conflicts of interest, according to the *New York Times*. And the prices truly are cheap. Press reports have described how Costco works with suppliers to redesign products and packaging to save money, and how it considered growing its own pumpkins so that its store-baked pumpkin pies could stay at $5.99. In her book, Mitchell discusses a study of prescription drug prices in Utah, done in 2004 by the Sutherland Institute. Her aim was to show that locals charge less than the big chains. However, she found that the independent pharmacies actually were "somewhat more expensive than Costco."

Costco has its flaws, of course. It came in only tenth out of twenty in a Greenpeace ranking of stores that sell sustainable seafood, and Mitchell's book cites examples in which Costco was sued for sex discrimination, destroyed a historic hotel in Mexico, and gobbled up special business-incentive tax breaks just like all the other big, bad guys. So on balance, does that record make Costco worse than the smaller, regional supermarket chains that lack the clout to get juicy tax deals and are 100 percent unionized to boot? Or does Costco get credit for breaking the stingy labor mold of its Goliath cohort? I'd go for the second approach, on the theory that companies should be rewarded when they are brave enough to challenge unfair industry practices, and no one's perfect anyway.

Whole Foods is almost a mirror-image of Costco, a store that—literally—looks better than its peers at first glance, but starts showing cracks on closer inspection. Beautiful organic carrots and kale, apples and avocados, bananas and broccoli, and dozens of other fruits and vegetables are piled high and clearly labeled with the state or country they come from. There are shelves of goat milk, soy milk, rice milk, lactose-free milk, organic milk, and ordinary milk, along with organic and standard varieties of butter, cheese, fruit juice, crackers, jellies, and breakfast cereal, plus a vegan section. Shoppers can be confident that even the nonorganic meat comes from cows and chickens that were fed a vegetarian diet with no antibiotics or added hormones.

With about two hundred branches, Whole Foods is the largest natural-foods company in the United States, if not the world. Its CEO, John Mackey, is a vegan, shunning all meat and dairy, for heaven's sake! Can any other major chain say that?

When Mackey cofounded Whole Foods in 1980, organic goods were the province of a few hippie co-ops and health-foods stores in college towns, and organic farmers firmly kept their distance from the plastic-capitalist world of supermarkets. If today just about every decent-size grocery store has at least a few organic vegetables and dairy products, most consumer experts say that's because Whole Foods created a market for it. "I'm not sure the organic farms would have survived had it not been for the success of Whole Foods," said Amy Domini, the socially responsible investing pioneer. Added Chip Giller, founder of Grist, "Whole Foods has really introduced the concept of eating that's more healthful for the person and more healthy for the planet to a whole new audience, and as a consequence you now see lots more grocery stores introducing organic lines."

Many eco-activists even are willing to give Whole Foods a pass on a couple of blatantly unenvironmental policies: that those mounds of organic fruits and veggies often are transported from thousands of miles away, and that the outlets sell meat and dairy. Both of those practices add a huge dollop of carbon emissions to global warming because of the oil used to ship the produce and the methane emissions from cows. (More on the cows later.) The animal-rights book *In Defense of Animals* includes a partial transcript of a 2004 roundtable discussion on radio station KPFK-FM in Los Angeles with Mackey and two animal-rights advocates. While the advocates push him a little about selling meat at Whole Foods, mostly they ooh and aah over his social consciousness. "It's incredible to sit in one of these meetings," says Lauren Ornelas, campaigns director of the vegan advocacy organization Viva! USA, "and hear John talk about these animal welfare issues, and about making sure that the ducks are not mutilated and that they have access to the outdoors." ("John." Not "Mr. Mackey.")

"If they wanted to be as pure as they can be, they would say, 'We're so concerned about health and the environment that we won't sell meat or food grown more than one hundred miles away. We won't sell coffee because that's grown far away,'" said Michael F. Jacobson, executive director of the Center for Science in the Public Interest (CSPI), a Washington, D.C., consumer group founded by former associates of Ralph Nader. But if a store followed that policy, Jacobson added, "They wouldn't be in business. Their customers want meat and cheese."

So Jacobson and other consumer and environmental advocates understand that Whole Foods can't be as pure as PETA. Nevertheless, Jacobson has other reasons for not shopping there. "Their prices are a big factor. And to some extent, their sanctimoniousness."

Organic goods, plentiful staffing, beautiful décor, and free samples don't come cheap, and it's widely acknowledged that Whole Foods' prices are higher than those at standard supermarkets—typically one-sixth to one-half more, judging by comparisons that the *New York Times* and I did. After the global economy tanked in the summer of 2008 and consumers began to shun organics, Whole Foods announced that it would slash prices and sell lower-cost items.

Price is not the only rap against the chain. "They're viciously anti-union," said Stewart Acuff, the assistant to John J. Sweeney, who was president of the AFL-CIO when I interviewed Acuff. (This is in an industry that's otherwise highly unionized.) When employees in Whole Foods' Madison, Wisconsin, branch voted to join the United Food and Commercial Workers International Union in 2002, the company fired two leaders of the organizing drive, then dragged its feet on negotiating for so long that the labor effort collapsed, according to news reports. The following year in Virginia, the National Labor Relations Board launched an investigation into charges that Whole Foods tried to coerce workers and manipulate a union vote; that union, too, never materialized. At various times, labor leaders have picketed and called for boycotts of the chain. In response, Mackey argues that his workers don't need a union because he pays better than the industry average, provides good benefits, and offers a lot of flexibility and opportunity.

For all the labor animosity, Acuff hesitated when I asked him whether it would be ethical to shop at Whole Foods. His eventual answer surprised me: "If the workers there were engaged in an active struggle, it would not be. But unless and until they are, I'm not in a position to make that kind of a judgment. Ultimately, we can't deliver respect, rights or dignity externally; people have to have a fight about it." Maybe, but I still would feel like a scab by shopping there. If the employees have become so discouraged that they're no longer trying to organize, does that wipe out all history and turn the company into a nice place to work?

Anyway, there are still more reasons to avoid Whole Foods. Despite a slew of posters in its stores extolling the local family farmer, company practices are pushing small farmers and neighborhood health-food stores out of business. Books and news articles have reported for years that the chain gets most of its goods from big "industrial organic" farms, and those signs about the countries and states where the produce comes from are solid proof of how much isn't local. To be fair, a chain of two hundred outlets needs to buy in bigger bulk than a few small farms can provide. Of course it can be difficult to find local produce on the East Coast in winter. Still, if there's one thing New York State harvests plenty of in the fall, it's apples, so why would a Manhattan Whole Foods carry six kinds of apples from Washington State in early November, and none from New York?

If Whole Foods does use small, local suppliers, Stacy Mitchell found, it often levies onerous requirements, such as demanding $5 million in liability insurance. Then it undermines those suppliers by selling its industrial-organic brands for less than it charges for the local versions. And when a Whole Foods arrived in her Maine neighborhood in 2007, Mitchell said, "it forced the closures of a number of independent food retailers, including a small natural-food store that had been around for a long time."

Whole Foods management seemed to admit that there's a problem, at least indirectly. The *New York Times* in 2007 reported that "foragers have been hired to seek out local farmers; the company has offered $10 million a year in low-interest loans to help small farmers produce more and stand-alone stores will open their parking lots to farmers' markets on Sundays." (The concept of local food will be discussed in more detail in chapter 3.)

Behind the granola-and-vegan image, Whole Foods and its CEO can play nasty. In 2007 the Federal Trade Commission charged that the company's attempt to buy its largest rival, Wild Oats Market, would stifle competition and lead to even higher prices. As the legal maneuvers wound on, the FTC discovered that Mackey had been posting messages anonymously on an Internet chat room for years, posing as an ordinary investor named "Rahodeb," to praise his own firm and trash opponents. He wrote such unsubtle comments as: "I like Mackey's haircut. I think he looks cute!" and "OATS [Wild Oats] has lost their way and no longer has a sense of mission or even a well-thought-out theory of the business."

Whole Food ultimately did acquire Wild Oats, after agreeing to shed nearly three dozen of its stores and leases. With or without a merger, though, the overall picture for consumers doesn't change. We don't need Whole Foods. Through its very success in spreading the organic message, the chain has outlived its usefulness. If you want the basics, such as organic precut carrots or milk, you probably can get them for a lot less money at a unionized market that even may be locally owned. For more variety, there's the range of specialty stores like the ones on Cathy Monblatt's list.

Greens and liberals probably won't abandon the chain, however. By shopping at Whole Foods, "you can feel good about yourself. You're doing something for the environment," Jacobson of CSPI summed up. "Their prices are generally outrageous, but there are enough people around that are willing to make that trade-off. And the loss of small natural-food stores," he added, "is kind of collateral damage."

Still, consumers probably can't get everything they need at a food co-op, farmers market, Costco, or even a bevy of wonderful little shops on Main Street. Eventually, you have to go beyond these cozy places and find your own way out into the big, cold world. I can't tell you which lists of "good companies"—stores or manufacturers—to follow once you're out there. That decision depends on the criteria each person wants to emphasize. What I can do is walk through a couple of examples, to show how many balls you may have to juggle and why they sometimes just won't stay in the air.

Try gassing up your car. We all hate the giant oil companies; they rake in obscene profits, they want to wreck the Arctic National Wildlife Refuge, and they leave a dangerous, polluted mess behind when they finish drilling. Moreover, the oil itself probably comes from dubious countries—like Russia, Venezuela, and Saudi Arabia—that use our money to make trouble for the United States. Nevertheless, we have to get our gasoline from some of these companies. (Of course we also can cut back on our fuel use, which chapter 4 will discuss.) So the challenge is to distinguish awful oil companies from slightly less awful ones.

BP desperately would like to be seen as "slightly less awful." It has been touting its image as a different kind of oil company since 1997, when it became the first Big Oil to acknowledge that climate change was a serious problem and pledged to reduce its carbon emissions 10 percent below 1990 levels by the year 2010, an incredibly steep drop by world standards. In 2000, it began a multimillion-dollar marketing campaign to rebrand the initials BP—which used to stand for British Petroleum—as "Beyond Petroleum." The company installed solar panels at its gas stations, while then-CEO Sir John Browne trotted off on the environmental lecture circuit. In a sign that the slogan wasn't just words, the company gave the Lawrence Berkeley National Laboratory in California $500 million, spread over ten years, to create an Energy Biosciences Institute to conduct research into biofuels, and it is even doing some research itself into the most cutting-edge alternative sources. Should a conscientious driver therefore look for BP stations?

Now here are some more facts to consider: do you want to buy gas from a company that had to pay nearly $400 million in fines and restitution—and put in $500 million worth of pollution-control improvements—between 1999 and 2007 because of an explosion at a Texas refinery that killed fifteen people, oil leaks from a pipeline in Alaska, illegal dumping of hazardous waste in Alaska, and violations of clean-air laws at eight refineries? Also, this company supported drilling in the Arctic refuge, and its CEO was forced to resign after lying in legal documents about his four-year affair with a young Canadian man and then trying to block newspapers from writing about it. That company, too, is BP.

Activist groups have mixed reactions to BP's environmental boasts, which do seem to be a blend of hype and real effort. Certainly, other oil companies could make a claim to environmental virtue, and no one has a pristine record. Thomas Friedman, in his book *Hot, Flat, and Crowded,* cites Chevron Corp. as "the world's biggest private producer of electricity from clean geothermal sources." Meanwhile, *The Rough Guide to Shopping with a Conscience* grudgingly praises BP and Shell for their work on developing alternative energy sources and for writing codes of conduct for human rights and the environment, while criticizing Chevron for doing business in Myanmar; however, Shell largely abandoned its solar efforts after the book was published. And Shell has probably the worst human-rights record of the majors. In 2009 it finally agreed to pay $15.5 million to settle charges that it collaborated with the Nigerian military government to silence human-rights activist Ken Saro-Wiwa, a vociferous critic of Shell's environmental practices, who was hanged by the government in 1995. Shell also is accused of bribing witnesses in Saro-Wiwa's Nigerian trial and hiring soldiers who allegedly committed human-rights abuses.

In that context, BP is probably as good as it gets. Every oil company has spills and does business in nasty countries—usually without murdering anyone—and who cares about an executive's sex life? Efforts to prevent climate change and develop alternative energy are more important. By contrast, look at ExxonMobil. As late as 2006, that company was still scoffing at the very concept of climate change. For a time, it gave nearly $3 million to groups that lobbied against emissions controls, plus hundreds of thousands more to climate-change skeptics, such as think tanks.

It still invests very little in alternative fuels, even compared to other oil giants, and its CEO, Rex W. Tillerson, once referred to a particular alternative as "moonshine." And ExxonMobil has its own human-rights problems, including a lawsuit from Indonesian villagers who allege that company guards committed abuses.

Otherwise, among the oil companies, I single out Lukoil to avoid. It's one thing for my money to go to a publicly traded, multinational giant that pays some sort of royalties to Saudi Arabia, Venezuela, or Russia; it's another category entirely to fill up at a gas station that is virtually an arm of the Russian government. Lukoil—which has taken over hundreds of former Getty and Mobil stations in the United States—was established by the Kremlin's Council of Ministers in 1991, and a government oil minister, Vagit Alekperov, was put in charge. Although it was technically "privatized" during the corrupt mass privatizations of the 1990s, Alekperov told *Fortune* magazine as late as 2009 that "I am very thankful to both the President and the Prime Minister [of Russia]. They provide great support for our business." As Isabel Gorst—a Moscow-based correspondent for the *Financial Times* of London who has done a lot of research on the topic—writes in a special case study for the James A. Baker III Institute for Public Policy at Rice University in March 2007: Lukoil "has always acted in close coordination with the government, often presenting itself as a faithful servant of state." For example, Gorst's study says, after meeting with Russian leader Vladimir Putin in 2005, Lukoil executives "agreed to refrain from sharp hikes in gasoline prices which are politically unpopular in Russia. Such cooperation with the state represents a commercial sacrifice that goes beyond the conventional boundaries of corporate social responsibility."

All this is irrelevant, however, if your tank is getting scarily low and the only stations around belong to ExxonMobil or Lukoil. Some people also swear that their cars run better on certain brands, and if that means Exxon—sigh—there's no point buying gas that won't get you from here to there.

Choosing which Big Oil villain to purchase your gas from is, of course, only one decision out of many that consumers face every day. Here's another set of issues: let's say that fair treatment of workers is a high priority for you. Maybe you believe the best way to ensure this treatment is to maintain a strong union movement. Or you want to make sure jobs stay in the United States instead of being outsourced to the lowest-paying contractor overseas. Of course you want a company with a good record on diversity, discrimination, benefits, and sexual harassment. (These topics will be discussed in chapter 6 also.) Then, should you buy clothes from American Apparel?

On the positive side, as the name implies, the company actually manufactures clothing in the United States, which is certainly a rarity in the garment industry. While it has no unions, it's generally regarded as paying above-average wages. Furthermore, founder and CEO Dov Charney is a strong supporter of immigrant workers' rights, running ads that called for "a legitimate, forward-thinking immigration policy." He even has arranged for buses to take employees to immigrants'-rights rallies. True, employers who hire undocumented immigrants too often abuse them, knowing that they don't dare complain, but I've never seen that issue raised against American Apparel. (If the workers had the legal status Charney advocates, it would in fact be more difficult for him to treat them badly, because they wouldn't be scared of being deported should they file grievances against him.) American Apparel's ads did catch the attention of U.S. Immigration and Customs Enforcement, which in December 2007 warned that it would be reviewing the documentation on the company's entire work force, but ICE was looking for cases of illegal entry, not abuse.

I realize that not all liberals are in favor of freer immigration. There's a legitimate concern that a flood of cheap labor could drag down wages all around, just like a surplus of anything usually deflates that item's cost. However, I don't see why we have to pit immigrant workers against native-born workers. We can open the doors to people escaping persecution or seeking a better opportunity—and then support a higher minimum wage and a strong union movement to protect *everyone's* salary. That dual approach is exactly what the AFL-CIO called for in the mid-1990s, when it officially rejected its historic anti-immigration attitude. In fact, maybe there's no conflict at all. Aviva Chomsky's 2007 book *"They Take Our Jobs!"* argues that immigration controls, including quotas and "guest worker" programs, actually depress pay rates, because they are usually part of a broader free-market philosophy that gives business extraordinary power. "The answer to the low-wage problem is not to restrict the rights of people at the bottom even more (through deportations, criminalizations, etc.) but to challenge the accord between business and government that promotes the low-wage, high-profit model," she writes. Anyway, I have a personal bias. I'm very humbly aware that I wouldn't be alive if my father's family hadn't been able to emigrate to the United States from Poland, about two steps ahead of Hitler.

The problem with American Apparel, therefore, isn't immigration or abuse of undocumented immigrant workers. It's sexual harassment. Charney has been sued at least three times by female staffers and has been accused of behavior like being nearly nude at the office and calling employees "sluts." (One suit was dropped, one settled, and the third was pending at the time this book was published.) The company's ads—the ones that aren't about immigration—notoriously feature barely clad models, often employees who are photographed by Charney himself, in provocative poses. In response to the lawsuits, Charney has claimed the plaintiffs were performing below-par work, and has sort-of denied the allegations. However, he also defends himself by saying that a certain sexual edge is part of the culture of the company and the fashion business. (I tried to discuss this with American Apparel officials, but the company failed to answer several requests for an interview.)

As for other industries, Stewart Acuff of the AFL-CIO offered a few examples where a consumer who cares about working conditions could, with relative ease, choose between union and nonunion, or U.S. and foreign, alternatives. However, one of his examples—hotels—requires extra research, because chains may not control all the outlets that bear their name. A particular branch is most likely owned by a franchisee, who can decide whether to accept or fight a union. So Acuff checks the "union hotel guide" on Unitehere, the Web site of the hotel and restaurant industry union, where you can type in the name of the chain and the city where you plan to stay. (Sorry for leading you to another Web site.)

Then again, if you want to support small local businesses, maybe you should skip the chain motels altogether and stay at a bed-and-breakfast.

How far does an ethical consumer go in seeking political purity? When I belonged to the Park Slope Food Coop back in the early 1990s—the co-op that includes Cathy Monblatt and Stewart Pravda as members—it was boycotting General Electric Co. for selling jet engines and other goods to the Defense Department. That meant no GE light bulbs. Sylvania, the other major supplier, also was rejected, because its prices were too high. Who was left to buy from? The co-op ended up obtaining its bulbs from some obscure Polish company. Thankfully, the store finally found a reasonably priced Sylvania source. (Conflict-of-interest alert: in the course of writing this book, I decided to rejoin the co-op, which I'll explain in chapter 9.)

•   •   •

But maybe you're not that interested in the sociopolitical implications of supporting specific manufacturers and merchants. All that may seem vague and theoretical. What you care about is the actual item you're buying, and in particular, the ingredients in that item. This is the stuff that is going into or on our bodies and, ultimately, into the ground, water, and air. Shouldn't we know what these are and whether they're safe? I remember reading some place that you should never buy any product with ingredients you haven't heard of; I might amend that to say you should never buy a product whose ingredients, when typed onto a computer Word document, get underlined in red by the Word dictionary.

Suspicious ingredients are everywhere. Are you putting hydrated silica, PVM/MA copolymer, sodium lauryl sulfate, and carrageenan in your mouth? If so, you're brushing your teeth with Colgate. Leslie Crawford, the author of the *San Francisco* magazine article about the EcoMom alliance, reported her own struggles over a new couch: After learning from online research about "the foam made from carcinogenic petrochemicals; the glues, paints, and Scotchgard with ingredients that also cause cancer; and neuro- and endocrine disrupters, whatever those are," she sent the couch back. More significantly, Texas State University history professor James E. McWilliams pointed out, in an op-ed column in the *New York Times* in 2008, that the dangerous industrial chemical melamine is "a common ingredient in cleaning products, waterproof plywood, plastic components, cement, ink and fire-retardant paint," and, worst of all, fertilizer. That's the same melamine that killed at least four infants in China and sickened tens of thousands more people when it got into milk, baby formula, chicken feed, wheat gluten, and other goods. True, the Chinese products had far higher proportions of the chemical than is found in the everyday American items. Nevertheless, it's not very comforting that, as McWilliams writes, "the government doesn't regulate how much melamine is applied to the soil" through fertilizer. Nor that "the FDA [U.S. Food and Drug Administration] reported that millions of Americans had eaten chicken fattened on feed with melamine-tainted gluten imported from China."

But certainly you can trust an established "natural" brand like Kiss My Face or Tom's of Maine? Well, Kiss My Face skin lotion has isopropyl myristate, and Tom's toothpaste has xylitol, and I'll be darned if I or the Word dictionary program know what those are. The California attorney general's office in May 2008 sued four companies—including Whole Foods California—for selling personal-care products that they labeled "natural" but that the lawsuit said contained the solvent 1,4-Dioxane, which the U.S. Environmental Protection Agency has classified as a "probable human carcinogen." Meanwhile, some of the ingredients that environmentalists dislike—most notably chlorine bleach—aren't incomprehensible chemicals at all and have been used since grandma's day. One reason the tag "natural" can't always be trusted is that neither the FDA nor the Department of Agriculture has officially defined the term, although the FDA has promised to think about writing a definition—a promise it made in a statement printed in the Federal Register more than fifteen years ago.

Okay, so a conscientious consumer can read the roster of ingredients on a product's label. But that's a pain. With the tiny print—called "mice type" in the pharmaceutical industry, referring to how drug ads squeeze in all the side effects that the manufacturers don't want you to notice—it can take a good minute per item. You have to remember which ingredients are dangerous and which merely sound weird. And most nonfood items don't have to list their ingredients anyway.

Kimberly Danek Pinkson of EcoMom doesn't even try. Instead, she queries store clerks: Has the item been certified fair-trade? Did the manufacturer sign up for the Campaign for Safe

Cosmetics, a national coalition of health and environmental groups aimed at persuading manufacturers of soaps and creams to stop using chemicals "linked to cancer, birth defects, and other serious health concerns"? Similarly, *A Good Life* by Leo Hickman—another of the ethical-shopping books—proposes five detailed questions that customers should "present to clothing retailers before giving them your business," including requesting a list of all the factories in which the retailer's products are made and the wages and working conditions in each.

To be honest, my first reaction to these practices was that they were another example of advice far from the real world. What teen-aged, part-time drugstore clerk knows which organizations all the manufacturers of all the goods on all the store's shelves have joined? What cashier at Target has a list of the factories that made all the brands of clothing sold on the racks? And asking these questions can take longer than reading the stupid label. However, Pinkson recognizes the drawbacks to this kind of consumer activism and had some practical follow-up suggestions. If the clerk doesn't know the answer—which is usually the case, she admitted—ask the manager. If the manager doesn't know, ask the owners. "While this does not always provide you with the information you need at the moment of purchase, taking your questions through as many different levels of command as possible lets the stores know that these kinds of issues are important to their customers," she said. That's the same kind of tactic Stacy Mitchell is employing in trying to get her local stationery shop to stock up on recycled paper.

Probably none of this advice will do much good in helping you choose ethical and useful products on the spot. Like Mitchell, you may just have to take what you need without waiting for the perfect answer. But in a way, doing this melds the advice of Chip Giller and Alex Steffen: you're trying to put your values into daily life while also pushing for change on a broader scale.

• • •

The contradictions in the quest for utmost purity erupted in 2008 over baby bottles.

Specifically, the concerns involved a chemical called Bisphenol A, or BPA, which has been used since the 1950s to make transparent, hard, shatterproof plastic, the kind of plastic in sports bottles, baby bottles, and children's sippy cups. It also is found in the liners of nearly all soft-drink cans and canned food.

In laboratory studies, BPA, which mimics human estrogen, has disrupted the hormonal systems of rats and mice, accelerating puberty and altering their behavior. Moreover, scientists suspect that it might affect brain and tissue development in human fetuses and young children and increase the risk of cancer, diabetes, and heart disease in adults. What makes all this worrisome in daily life is that the chemical can leach out of the hard plastic, into the contents of the cup or bottle, and it does so particularly quickly when exposed to hot liquid—like, for example, warm milk in a baby bottle.

The controversy began bubbling in August 2007, when a special panel of the U.S. National Institutes of Health declared that "the potential for BPA to impact human health is a concern, and more research is clearly needed." The following April, the National Toxicology Program came out with a warning about "the possibility that Bisphenol A may alter human development." Then Canada outlawed the chemical in infant bottles.

At that point, most major stores in Canada ripped all containers with BPA from their shelves, not just baby bottles, even though Ottawa had not forbidden it in food and soda cans or in any product for people older than eighteen months. Nalgene, one of the biggest manufacturers of sports bottles, said it would stop using the chemical. Wal-Mart promised to get rid of BPA-laden baby bottles in its U.S. outlets. Chicago made the stuff illegal in baby bottles and sippy cups, and Congress and several states considered bans. Almost alone among regulators, the U.S. Food and Drug Administration for a long time maintained, as its Web site said, that "FDA-regulated products containing BPA currently on the market are safe and that exposure levels to BPA from food contact materials, including for infants and children, are below those that may cause health effects." Critics—including a special, seven-member committee that the FDA itself set up—lambasted the agency for ignoring the most negative evidence and relying on flawed studies. In 2009 the agency finally changed its Web site to say that it "takes the questions that have been raised about BPA very seriously," and the new commissioner, Dr. Margaret A. Hamburg, promised to review the issue some more.

Yet what else could consumers use? As the shelves were emptied, plenty of plastic manufacturers were happy to leap into the void with BPA-free bottles and cups. However, these products typically cost two to five times as much as the BPA-containing versions, a not-insignificant burden considering that the target audience—families—is particularly likely to be on tight budgets. One alternative children's cup, made of cornstarch, couldn't go into the dishwasher. An early prototype tried in Japan cracked easily. In perhaps the biggest irony, three companies revived their lines of glass baby bottles. These were the bottles that parents had so eagerly abandoned in the 1980s to switch to BPA plastic because of—you guessed it—the risk of broken glass.

Steven D. Lydenberg, chief investment officer at Domini Social Investment, no doubt makes a comfortable salary managing more than one billion dollars in customers' assets. He and his wife, Robin, an English professor, certainly could afford new clothes. Nevertheless, Robin Lydenberg happily buys nearly all her clothing, along with a lot of furniture and tchotchkes, at thrift stores.

Remember the cell phone, shirt, car, laundry detergent, and book I talked about at the beginning of this chapter? The next time you go shopping, think about this: two-thirds of the environmentalist mantra "reduce, reuse, recycle" has to do with buying fewer new things. After all, even if the items you purchase are made of totally organic, animal-free, and sustainable materials, and you always get them at a neighborhood co-op, nevertheless some resources and some fuel had to be consumed to create them. If you buy what were once called "used" goods, on the other hand, you're saving that much of the earth from being dug up for coltan, that much water from being diverted to irrigating cotton fields, that much money from propping up petro-dictatorships, that many chemicals from poisoning fish, and that many trees from being chopped down for paper—that is, however much of the coltan, water, money, chemicals, and trees that would have been required to manufacture a new item. For an added bonus, you're also keeping the "used" item from overloading a landfill—and probably saving yourself money.

As Robin Lydenberg explained her shopping habit, "I really want to resist consuming as much as possible. And once you've seen thrift-store prices, it's pretty hard to pay full price."

In fact, it's a sign of environmental cachet that we rarely talk any more about "used" merchandise, which sounds worn-out. We now buy much classier "vintage" clothing and "pre-owned" cars. We get great deals on somebody else's stuff from craigslist and yard sales. Even some Goodwill Industries International outlets, the staple of frumpy charity donations, have been trying to reposition themselves as shopping destinations, with Webcasts, ads, blogs, and fashion shows, according to the *New York Times.* Chip Giller's wife, Jenny Sorensen, shared maternity clothes with ten other moms-to-be during her second pregnancy, in 2008. Pinkson got her son's Rescue Heroes at a secondhand store.

Or, if we don't buy our "vintage" stuff as-is, we buy goods that have been shredded and reconfigured from their vintage form. More and more objects are made of recycled material, from birthday cards to playground mats to toothbrushes. A whole industry has developed to take apart old houses nail-by-nail in order to reuse the parts. One company, TerraCycle, founded in 2001, collects things that can't be recycled in traditional ways—used plastic bags, yogurt cups, juice pouches, computer diskettes, cookie wrappers, banana peels—and transforms them into pencil cases, waste-paper cans, tote bags, backpacks, lunch bags, bird feeders, and more, often emblazoned with the logo from the original product.

Sadly, even with vintage clothing and recycled Oreo wrappers, the world hasn't reached the environmentalists' goal of total cradle-to-grave sustainability, where everything we use is recycled right back into a second life in a never-ending circle, and it probably never will. There are too many practical limits. Recycled facial tissues just aren't as soft and fluffy as tissues made from fresh tree pulp, and that can really rub you raw if you've got a cold. I can find eight-and-a-half-by-eleven-inch pads of recycled paper but not the smaller steno notebooks I need for taking notes when I go out on interviews.

There are also too many contradictions. Should Stacy Mitchell and I buy recycled printer paper from big chains, or virgin paper from local stores? Bon Appétit Management Co. has built its business cooking environmentally sensitive meals for corporate and college cafeterias. Surely it's less environmentally wasteful for customers to take their leftovers home, rather than use up resources and energy cooking something else from scratch the next day. Yet, vice president Maisie Greenawalt laments that "there's no good green option available [for the takeout containers]. Many disposable bioplates used in the U.S.

are corn-based, and there's a huge amount of other things corn could be used for," like ethanol and food.

And there are psychological limits, a kind of yecch factor. Do I really want to put my books in a backpack made of someone's old juice pouch, even though I assume it's been thoroughly cleaned?

Just in time for the 2007 holiday season, the *New York Times* reported the story of Claire Roby, a twenty-two-year-old environmental studies major at American University in Washington, D.C., who decided that she wasn't going to get sucked into the wasteful, materialistic fervor of the Christmas gift-giving scene. All those trees chopped down to make red-and-green wrapping paper. All the packaging. All the outdoing-the-relatives. Instead, Roby gave everyone on her gift list clocks that she made from discarded electronics components and compact discs. To wrap them, she used old newspapers.

The *Times* did not report the reactions of Roby's relatives at getting a junk-parts clock instead of, say, a new video game.

"We're not going to buy our way out of our environmental problems," Chip Giller said, repeating a point commonly made by activists. No doubt it would be a lot more fun to stop global warming by buying soy underwear, a vintage dress, or designer-brand organic cotton jeans, than by taking the bus, carpooling, and turning off the air conditioner. To the degree that growing organic cotton saves a piece of farmland from the chemical pesticides that would have been used to grow regular cotton for a pair of standard jeans, yes, buying the organic jeans helps the earth. But, Giller pointed out, "that doesn't mean I think everyone should buy a two hundred dollar pair of organic designer jeans if you don't need a new pair of jeans." Owning a lot of stuff, green or any other color, doesn't save resources; it uses them up.

Such thinking gets to the real downside of the ethical shopping movement. As being green and buying vintage have become popular, it's difficult to know what genuinely qualifies as an environmentally benign product, and what's just hype. When Barney's New York sells a designer dress made of fabric remnants for $6,500, that doesn't seem to be the kind of recycling most consumers have in mind when they tie up their newspapers for special collection days. If soy underclothes wear out faster than cotton, it actually may be worse for the planet to buy five pairs of soy rather than one pair of pesticide-grown cotton. "People are looking to do something that's good for their body and the earth. I wouldn't argue that marketers aren't preying on it," said Kim Haddow, a Sierra Club spokeswoman. The Sierra Club itself stepped right into that sticky green marketplace in 2008 with a controversial agreement to endorse a new, plant-based "natural" line of cleaning products, called Green Works, from Clorox. That's the same Clorox that built its reputation on the chlorine bleach environmentalists disdain; however, the Sierra Club emphasizes that it's endorsing only the particular "natural" products, not the bleach.

And if all this isn't enough reason to be skeptical of unethical shopping, Alex Steffen of Worldchanging points to the risk that people who buy organic jeans and $6,500 "recycled" dresses will feel so smug that they will ignore the hard-core work of lobbying, letter-writing, and campaigning that Steffen says is the only way to bring about long-lasting change.

The easiest way to minimize your environmental, labor, and geopolitical damage, in short, is not to purchase anything.

Which is fine with me. Jenny Sorensen shares maternity clothes. Robin Lydenberg buys used clothing. And the day I interviewed Lydenberg's husband's boss, Amy Domini, I was wearing a blazer that was probably eight years old and a skirt twice that age.

CHAPTER THREE

CAN AN ETHICAL LIBERAL EAT MEAT?
(AND OTHER FOOD-RELATED QUANDARIES)

What should I eat?

Over and over, this was the concern I heard most often in my interviews for this book.

Jean Leung started buying organic food when her son, Jacob, was born in 1993, because she wanted everything he ate to be as healthful as possible. But staying organic became harder and harder for her. The food is expensive. It also spoils faster than standard produce, and Leung was too busy as a freelance writer and editor to keep running to the store. Furthermore, after doing some research, she discovered that Horizon Organics, the most common brand of organic milk, is distributed by a big company based in Texas. "My parents were small-business people—they ran a laundry in Chinatown—and if I can I'll go to the little local business," Leung said. Still, she hesitated about buying nonorganic milk from New York, where she lives. "Then I read an article that a lot of local dairies were in fact organic but didn't want to go through the certification." The final push off the organic wagon came when Jacob started school. "I realized that I had lost control over what was going into him. They weren't going to give him organic at summer camp."

Although Louise Heit-Radwell, a dance educator in Brooklyn, New York, has been a vegetarian since college, it's a struggle to find protein sources for her daughter, Molly, and son, Marty.

"We used to eat a lot of tofu, but there are health issues because there's estrogen in it, and boys aren't supposed to have estrogen. And soy is overprocessed," she explained. Plus, her husband, Steven, has high cholesterol, so they have to limit their consumption of dairy products. "Now I'm trying to eat more beans and legumes and lentils. I have to find things my kids are willing to eat, because I'm not cooking three different meals." To make matters worse, Molly would come home saying things like, "At school, those chicken fingers smelled so good!" Heit-Radwell sighed. "I don't want to make my kids total nuts. I'm always trying to figure out how much sugar, how often do I make white rice, do I let them eat nonorganic chicken if they're at a friend's house? Maybe I should make chicken for my daughter." But only if it's organic chicken. "I'm forty-five years old, and I've never cooked a chicken."

One day Jessica Philips (not her real name) found herself in Trader Joe's supermarket, staring at the egg cartons. "One carton said organic free-range. One carton said organic cage-free. Some just said cage-free with DHA" (an additive in chicken feed that's supposed to improve infant brain development and reduce the risk of heart disease in adults). Philips, a Los Angeles lawyer and mother of three, asked the store's customer-service manager about the egg distinctions, but he could explain only some of them. She finally chose the free-range. "I'm a vegetarian," she said, "and it seemed to me that free-range meant a better treatment of animals." A few days later, checking her refrigerator, Philips realized that she had previously bought yet another carton of eggs, this one labeled cage-free and free-roaming. "There is only so much time you can spend on this," she groaned.

During a fifteen-year career doing public relations for Greenpeace and other liberal advocacy groups, Nancy Hwa of Washington, D.C., has considered becoming a vegetarian. "I feel guilty. I know that eating low on the food chain is better for the environment," she said. But she also wants to continue cooking the traditional recipes she learned from her mother, who was born in China. "There are a lot of Chinese dishes that wouldn't taste the same if they didn't have pork." Her compromise: she eats meat just three or four times a week.

Most mornings, Cathy Monblatt and Stewart Pravda like to have organic blueberries with their cereal. They also prefer to shop at the local farmers market. However, if it's not the growing season, the couple knows the berries won't be available at the farmers market. Should they get imported berries from another store? Should they wait until spring and substitute raisins meanwhile? "Buying organic berries, for the most part I know they're coming by air from South America," Pravda admitted. "Flying that in is not really sound environmentally. It's a hard line to draw." That's not the only tough line. "The other week I stood for a while," he said. "I just couldn't decide. Organic blueberries were four dollars a box. Nonorganic were two dollars a box."

For Carie Carter, rabbi of the Park Slope Jewish Center in Brooklyn—the synagogue I belong to—food juggling begins with one clear requirement: "If it's not kosher, I'm not going to eat it." The next steps are more complex. "If it's kosher but animals are not treated humanely and workers are treated poorly, I'm not going to eat it." However, that's almost impossible to know unless conditions are so bad that they make news, as happened with the big kosher meatpacker Agriprocessors Inc. in 2008. (Chapter 6 will discuss Agriprocessors more fully.) On top of all those factors, Carter has been making more efforts to buy organic food since her daughter, Noa, was born in 2007. Organic produce is fairly easy to find, but kosher organic chicken is a problem. So Carter ends up getting nonorganic kosher chicken from a company that at least hasn't had any bad headlines.

Organic. Free-range. Cage-free. Barn-roaming. Free-roaming. Local. Natural. No preservatives. No antibiotics. No added hormones. No added steroids. No animal byproducts. Not genetically modified. Grass-fed. Vegetarian diet. Family-farmed. Certified humane-raised. Sustainable. Dolphin Safe. Fairtrade. Vegetarian. Vegan. Kosher. Halal. Low-calorie. Fat-free. Reduced-fat. Trans fat-free. Sugar-free. Caffeine-free. Glutenfree. Low-cholesterol. No-salt.

How sanitary are the conditions in which the food was grown, raised, processed, packed, and shipped? Where does the food come from? Is it in season? How many pounds of greenhouse gases did it take to grow, package, and transport the food? If it's from a developing country, were the local farmers compensated according to fair-trade criteria? How are the workers treated? Do they get proper training and safety equipment? Are they unionized? If animals are involved, how are they treated? Are they allowed to go outdoors? How much space do they get? What are they fed? What kind of fertilizer is used? If the product includes fish, is the species endangered? Are the fish likely to contain traces of mercury? Were any at-risk habitats damaged to grow the crops or raise the animals? Is the packaging recyclable?

Where did you buy your food: At a farmers market? Through a community-supported agriculture program? At a food co-op? At a health-food store? At a small, corner deli? At a bakery, a butcher shop, a fruit-and-vegetable stand, or some other specialty store? At a regional grocery chain? At a national-chain supermarket? At a discount warehouse or big-box superstore? Through online delivery? At a take-out restaurant? Did you grow it at home?

Do you have allergies? Are you vegetarian or vegan? Are you trying to lose weight? Are you on a special diet for medical reasons? Do you follow religious dietary laws? What culturally traditional foods did you eat growing up?

What tastes good?

No wonder Jean Leung, Louise Heit-Radwell, Jessica Philips, Nancy Hwa, Cathy Monblatt, Stewart Pravda, and Carie Carter feel overwhelmed. It's not just that food is a basic requirement of life; it's also that food embodies so many different aspects of our life and presents so many options and pitfalls. Plus, it's a significant consideration in the way we raise our children, affecting their physical health along with their ethical values. "Choosing food is now so complicated, between the environmental destruction, cruelty to animals, exploitation of workers, and carbon production due to transport," summarized University of Virginia psychology professor Jonathan Haidt, who said he "agonizes" over eating fish, chicken, and beef.

Haidt has plenty of company. Whether or not to eat meat is one of the two biggest food issues facing ethical consumers. (The other biggie is how strict to be about buying organic, which will be discussed later in this chapter and in chapter 7, along with other topics.) I'll lay it out on the kitchen table right now: I'm not a vegetarian, and I don't foresee that I will be in the near future. I hope you'll keep reading anyway.

Ethically, I can't dispute most of the reasons for avoiding meat. For starters, the conditions in which the vast majority of food animals are raised, in huge factory farms, are horrible, inhumane, dreadful—any synonym for "god-awful" that you want to use.

Egg-laying chickens are crammed into "battery cages" too small for them to even stretch their wings, cage upon cage stacked floor to ceiling, so squeezed for space that the chickens have been known to rub against the wire of the cage until their bodies are raw and bleeding. Their beaks and toes are partially cut off, but even so, they cannibalize each other in their jam-packed hellholes. An estimated one-tenth don't survive. When their egg production begins to slacken, they are "force-molted"—deprived of sufficient light and water—for a few days or a week, to push out one or two last batches of eggs. Then they're killed. Broiler chickens (for eating) have it a little better during their short life spans; at least they're not in cages. But they are bred to be so top-heavy that they can barely walk around their crowded, dark sheds. They live less than six weeks, breathing air that's dusty and reeking of ammonia from the wastes that pile up on the floor. Best off are cows. They get six months of grazing with their mothers on the ranch where they were born before being shipped to a feedlot. There, they are penned into a dusty shed, forced to stand in their own waste, and given a diet based on corn and animal parts—including parts of other cows—that their stomachs can't handle naturally. As for pigs, the pregnant sows are trapped in narrow "gestation crates," unable to turn around and sometimes tethered to the floor. Once the piglets are born, most of their tails are cut off, and males are castrated, all without anesthesia. After that, they are shoved into barren pens with thousands of others, standing uncomfortably all day on metal slats.

Because of the crowding and unnatural feed, all these factory farm animals are injected with antibiotics. Depending on the species, they suffer from weak bones, foot injuries, skin disease, heart attacks, diarrhea, heartburn, ulcers, liver disease, weakened immune systems, and stress.

Those conditions in themselves ought to make an ethical liberal stop and rethink his or her grocery list. We're long past the days when people could argue successfully that animals don't feel pain. In fact, many of them are more intelligent and more "human" than we realize. They form social networks. They communicate; several primates and a parrot have even managed to have complex verbal interactions with people by means of computer keyboards, sign language, and voice. More than forty species of birds, primates, dolphins, otters, and whales use tools of various sorts. Orca whales mourn their dead. One Cambridge University scientist, cited in Peter Singer's book *In*

Defense of Animals, claimed that "pigs have cognitive functioning abilities similar to that of a three-year-old human child." A committee of the Spanish Parliament in 2008 voted to extend limited legal rights to chimpanzees, bonobos, gorillas, and orangutans, including the right not to be used in circuses, films, or for medical experiments.

There are also environmental and human health arguments for vegetarianism. Meat is an inefficient use of the earth's resources: it takes about ten pounds of grain to produce one pound of beef and two to three pounds for a pound of chicken. Moreover, farm animals are responsible for 10 to 18 percent of total world carbon gas emissions, by various experts' estimates. That includes the energy required to transport them, grow their feed, and house them; the methane and nitrous oxide produced by their manure; and the infamous cow burping. (When cows digest their food in their multiple stomachs, they spit up and rechew some of it, which produces the burping.) According to the U.S. Environmental Protection Agency, cows emit about 80 million metric tons of methane annually, which comes to 28 percent of all human-related methane. That's not all. American livestock dump out 900 million tons of waste per year, most of it full of toxic nitrogen, phosphorus, heavy metal residues, and hormone residues. It's too dangerous to be used as fertilizer, so it sits in artificial "lagoons" until it leaks into the soil or other water.

Meanwhile, the antibiotics in the farm animals' food are inevitably breeding stronger forms of antibiotic-resistant bacteria, which will force us to concoct yet other antibiotics for medicines as well as feed. Some hogs and hog farmers in the Netherlands and the United States may be infected already with one such super-resistant strain, the staph infection MRSA, which until now had been confined mainly to hospitals. Cows, when given grain instead of their natural grass, produce meat with more of the unhealthy saturated fat and less of the healthy

Omega-3 fatty acids that humans need, putting those who eat it at risk of heart disease, diabetes, and some cancers. And who can forget mad-cow disease? This sickness, which wracked the British beef industry in the 1990s and infected two cows in the United States, destroys the brains of cattle that eat waste parts from contaminated cows, then causes a rare but fatal brain condition in people who eat the infected meat. The Food and Drug Administration claims to have tightened the rules so that contaminated parts can't creep into animal feed, but consumer critics say the rules aren't strong enough.

Nor is eating fish any better for the earth. Wild fish? Over-fishing has depleted stocks like bluefin tuna, cod, and sword-fish. Fish farms? Their waste run-off pollutes nearby water, and in addition, other, smaller species get ravaged to feed the farmed fish. Worst of all are industrial shrimp farms, most of which are in developing countries such as Bangladesh, Ecuador, Honduras, and Thailand. First they drain the local water sources to supply their farms; then that farm water, polluted with salt, fish meal food, growth stimulants, and (of course) antibiotics, leaks back into the nearby land and water, wrecking it for either farming or fishing. These shrimp farm owners also frequently cut down the mangrove swamps that protected the area from tropical storms and floods, provided shelter for other animals, and helped nurture native fisheries. As a result, the local economy of sustainable shrimping, fishing, and farming is destroyed.

People clearly don't need to eat animal protein to survive; all the vegetarians and vegans worldwide are living proof of that. Or, if you prefer the oft-cited Judeo-Christian interpretation, we were all vegetarians until the time of Noah, when we showed that we didn't have the moral fiber for it.

In short, it's hard to defend killing other creatures—and hurting the environment and our own health in the process—just because we like the taste of hamburger. When I asked Bruce

Friedrich of PETA if he could think of any example where an ethical person might eat meat, including fish, his flat-out answer was no. "Trading off a momentary human desire against an animal's most basic interest not to be abused and killed? That one seems pretty black-and-white," he said.

Yet all these arguments haven't worked, because there are still hundreds of millions of meat-eaters on the globe, including me. So, some animal-rights advocates push the debate up a few notches. That's where they lose a lot of us.

They start with the problem of how to get carnivores to feel guilty that we are causing pain to animals. Since humans seem to care only about other humans, advocates have to make us see animals—or, as they put it, nonhuman animals—as morally equivalent to humans. In his book *In Defense of Animals*, Peter Singer, the dean of the animal-rights movement, writes:

> We need to take a new approach to the wrongness of killing, one that considers the individual characteristics of the being whose life is at stake, rather than that being's species…Where animals and humans have similar interests—we might take the interest in avoiding physical pain as an example—those interests are to be counted equally.

To achieve their goal, the advocates need to counter the two most common justifications for distinguishing Homo sapiens from other animals: first, people have a higher level of intelligence and cognizance. We humans are aware of what is going on in the world in ways no other creatures are capable of; in particular, humans are able to comprehend the concept of death. Animals on the slaughterhouse assembly line don't realize that their existence is going to end very soon. Thus, while other animals feel pain, they simply cannot suffer in the same way that humans can.

And second, we're humans and they're not. Of course we're not going to care as much about an alien species as we do about our own species.

In response, Singer and others inevitably bring up the new-born infant/Nazi/Alzheimer's disease argument: a normal pig probably has a higher IQ than a child with developmental disabilities. A cow is more cognizant of her surroundings than a newborn human. A turkey can tell you who just won the World Series as well as an eighty-seven-year-old great-grandmother with dementia. Ha! So much for the difference between animals and people! We would never condone killing a human being who didn't have the full intelligence level of a normally functioning adult, such as a newborn, a learning-disabled child, or an Alzheimer's patient. Then how can we kill other animals that actually may be more alert, knowledgeable, and able to communicate than some humans? And so what if they're not our species? To favor humans over other creatures is "speciesism," which makes us the moral equivalent of Nazis or the Ku Klux Klan, discriminating against a certain class of living beings merely because they're different from "us." Someday, distinguishing people from cows and pigs on the basis of their species will be seen as the equivalent of distinguishing blacks from whites on the basis of their skin color. As Gaverick Matheny, a fellow in agricultural and resource economics at the University of Maryland, writes in his essay in *In Defense of Animals:*

> Most adult mammals used in lab research—dogs, cats, mice, rabbits, rats, and primates—are more aware of what is happening to them than and at least as sensitive to pain as any human infant. Would researchers contemplating an animal experiment be willing, then, to place an orphaned human infant in the animal's place? If they are not, then their use of an animal is simple discrimination on the basis of species.

Taking that thought a step further, to move animals yet closer to people, David DeGrazia, a philosophy professor at George Washington University, manipulates the definition of the word "person." Does it only apply to human beings? He asserts in one essay in Singer's book that "ordinary great apes and dolphins are borderline persons" because they act with intent, they are self-aware, they use tools, and they exhibit "the transmission from one generation to the next of novel behaviors such as building nests, using leaves for medicinal purposes, or fashioning certain types of tools." A handful of particular individual apes and dolphins should be considered full "persons," he adds, because they have learned advanced language skills. Finally, to defend the concept of calling any creature other than Homo sapiens a "person," DeGrazia cites the character Spock from the TV series *Star Trek,* E.T. from the movie *E.T.: The Extra-Terrestrial,* and angels. Don't we consider them "persons"? he demands.

Hello. If someone needs to drag in fantasy creatures to prove his supposedly scientific point, I would submit that his point is also a fantasy.

Spock and angels aside, it seems to me that you either accept the concept of speciesism or you don't, and I don't. Instinctively, to me, there's a huge difference between the most intelligent pig and my kids when they were newly born, and between that pig and my grandmother in the last stages of Alzheimer's, and efforts to claim equivalence make me *less* sympathetic to the vegetarian argument. To that instinctive reaction one could add various logical supporting arguments: My kids may have been pretty unaware at birth, but they grew up to be capable of far more perceptiveness and intellectual judgment than any pig or chimp. Drugs might be developed to help my grandmother or a child with learning disabilities gain a higher level of awareness. It's misleading to compare the average of one species (pigs, chimps, dogs, cats) with the outliers of another species (humans with Alzheimer's, humans with severe mental disabilities). Maybe someday my viewpoint will be seen as horribly prejudiced. On the other hand, just because society once discriminated on the basis of skin color and now says that's wrong, that doesn't inevitably mean we also will reach a consensus not to discriminate on the basis of species.

Any theoretical argument can be extended into absurdity. If you're going to tear down the species wall and consider all warm-blooded animals equivalent to humans, where do you stop? The vast majority of tool-using, social-networking, higher-intelligence animals, after all, are not the ones we eat. Most animal-rights advocates draw the line at insects and certain shellfish, on the basis that these creatures don't seem to feel pleasure or pain. But isn't that what people used to believe of mammals? Aren't insects living creatures, too? Ecuador's 2008 constitution grants "the right to the maintenance and regeneration of its vital cycles, structure, functions and evolutionary processes" to nature in general, which could include bacteria. A special panel of the Swiss parliament issued protections for the "reproductive ability" of plants.

Or, to take an argument from the other side to the extreme: if you want to protect animals, you *must* eat meat. If no one consumed meat, most of those chickens, cows, pigs, and turkeys that are so horribly treated in factory farms wouldn't exist at all, except for egg-laying chickens and cows for milking. Farmers certainly wouldn't raise them as pets, and there's a limited amount of space in children's zoos. Is a short, painful life in a factory farm worse than no life at all? What if it meant the extinction of the species of domestic cows, pigs, turkeys, and chickens? I guess that's a philosophical question you'd have to ask one of the more intelligent pigs.

All these arguments are silly, of course, and beside the point. You don't need to claim that Bessie the cow is equal to my Aunt Bessie to make a case for avoiding meat. You also can't claim that you're eating meat in order to be nice to the animals you eat.

Therefore, in light of the more sober arguments—the damage to the earth, the suffering of animals, the wasted resources, the risk to my health—why am I not a vegetarian? In part, I have a medical excuse: I can't eat soy or peanuts, which are staples of the vegetarian diet. However, my real reason is, I admit, ethically feeble. As Stewart Pravda put it, when I asked him, "That's just not a step I'm up to taking." Like our biblical ancestors, I lack the willpower or strength of character. After trying in my daily life to be conscientious in so many other areas—to buy organic, to reduce energy use, to recycle and purchase recycled goods, to support the neighborhood shopkeeper and also union workers and also desperate farmers and artisans in the developing world—I fear that vegetarianism is just one demand too many for me. I wouldn't be able to maintain it.

Yet I'd like to consider myself an ethical person. So would Jean Leung, Nancy Hwa, Stewart Pravda, Cathy Monblatt, and Carie Carter, as well as Jessica Philips (who eats fish and serves meat to her family) and Louise Heit-Radwell (who eats fish and lets her daughter occasionally have chicken).

The solution that many ethical meat-eaters have devised is that our meat must come with a price. We will select it carefully, choosing animals that were raised in the most humane conditions possible, with feed that's natural for them and no weird chemicals. We will aim to be as good as we can to the animals, the earth, and our own bodies. "I realize that most people are going to eat meat," conceded Paul Shapiro, senior director of the Humane Society's factory farming campaign. "For those people who are going to eat animals, we want to make sure the animals that are raised for food don't suffer."

Nancy Hwa carries a pocket guide to sustainable seafood. Cathy Monblatt buys kosher organic chicken at the food co-op "unless it's phenomenally expensive." Jonathan Haidt goes to a local gourmet shop that sells beef from farms near his home in Charlottesville, Virginia, farms with "actual cows that I can see on the grass." Journalism professor and author Michael Pollan, after laying out the vegetarian point of view for about twenty pages in his 2006 book *The Omnivore's Dilemma,* and having trouble refuting some of it, finally found a fairly comfortable zone: "What's wrong with eating animals is the practice, not the principle. What this suggests to me is that people who care about animals should be working to ensure that the ones they eat don't suffer, and that their deaths are swift and painless—for animal welfare, in other words, rather than rights."

Related to the meat question is the issue of whether to eat food that can be obtained from animals without killing them, basically, eggs and dairy products. Vegetarians eat these foods; vegans don't. One of the vegan arguments is that the factory farms that churn out eggs and milk treat their chickens and cows just as horribly as the institutions that churn out animals for meat—or worse, in the case of laying hens versus broiler chickens. That shouldn't be a problem, though, if the same rules of ethical animal-raising are applied to dairy and egg animals as to meat animals. A second count against eating dairy is the greenhouse-gas emissions that cows produce thanks to their manure and burping. But that's what cows do. Even if we never ate their flesh or drank their milk, they would poop and burp methane. The only way to halt these emissions is to eliminate all cows, which gets back to the extremist argument that eating meat and dairy is what saves the species. (Anyway, it turns out that cow-plop can be used to produce energy, and chapter 4 will delve into that.) So I have no problem with eggs and dairy.

The real problem is determining whether our ethical efforts make any difference.

In practice, ethical meat-eating has come to mean looking for meat with labels like "free-range," "organic," "grass-fed," and "cage-free." Unfortunately, the laws aren't a great help in discerning how animals were treated, or, for that matter, learning much at all about most of the food we consume. The FDA and the Agriculture Department focus on traditional nutrition and safety, which are nice, but don't go far enough.

Here's what the laws require: The label on packaged food must name every ingredient, along with the amount of sodium, protein, various vitamins, and other nutrients that a person would get from a single serving. It also must disclose the percentage of the recommended minimum daily requirement of each nutrient that a serving would fulfill, assuming a daily diet of two thousand calories. The amount of unhealthful trans fat must be specified, and ingredients that cause the most common allergies—such as milk, eggs, wheat, peanuts, and tree nuts—have to be listed clearly. Next, there are a few rules about whether products can make health claims, such as "may reduce the risk of coronary heart disease." The label must state the country of origin of any beef, lamb, pork, fish, chicken, goat meat, peanuts, pecans, macadamia nuts, ginseng, and "perishable agricultural commodities." Carol Tucker Foreman, the longtime official of the Consumer Federation of America, considers the nutrition-labeling rules "generally good, with loopholes" and says the safety labeling offers "some protection but with big loopholes."

As for ethical concerns, the Agriculture Department has a definition for "organic," a definition that took twelve years to write, that was heavily lobbied by large farms, that many small local farmers consider too rigorous to comply with, and that animal-rights groups dismiss as little better than factory conditions. To be labeled organic, produce must be grown without synthetic fertilizers, herbicides, or pesticides. Processed organic food may have no more than 5 percent nonorganic ingredients. Organic food also may not intentionally contain any genetically modified (GM) ingredients, defined as ingredients in which a gene has been altered so it develops a characteristic it doesn't normally have. (This is also known as genetic engineering, or GE, and is discussed later in this chapter.) Animals, meanwhile, have to be fed a diet free of antibiotics, growth hormones, and animal parts; they must get a bit more space than they would be allowed in conventional factory farms; and they must have "access" to the outdoors. However, "access" is never explained. "You could have birds confined twenty thousand to a shed, with a door open for five minutes a day that leads to a ten-square-foot gravel pit," Shapiro, of the Humane Society, scoffed. Even if the door were open longer, that doesn't mean any animals actually would *go* outside. In his book, Pollan describes walking through a jam-packed, ammonia-fumed organic chicken shed to the door leading to the "access" area, standing by the open door, and waiting for liberated organic chicks to follow him into the fresh air. Of the roughly twenty thousand chickens, not a single one did.

What many consumers forget, Foreman said, is that "organic was envisioned primarily as something that was environmentally friendly. That's all it means. It doesn't mean animals are treated well. The general rule is that you must never assume that organic food is safer or more nutritious than other food."

Wait a minute. Is Foreman saying that Jean Leung shouldn't even have tried to feed her son organic milk and produce, or that Cathy Monblatt shouldn't bother paying extra for organic chicken?

In fact, very little research has been done on whether organic food is more nutritious than nonorganic food, or even—amazingly—on whether the pesticide levels in most foods are actually dangerous. Still, it's widely accepted that children and pregnant women, at the least, ought to avoid pesticides. That's because pesticides are known to cross the placenta during pregnancy and also to cause neurological and reproductive-system damage in young children. Furthermore, most government-approved tolerance levels are for adults and don't account for the fact that children's developing immune systems may not be able to get rid of contaminants as easily.

Most scientists agree that organic farming and animal husbandry are much better for the environment than nonorganic, for a host of reasons, including energy savings and biodiversity. With organic practices, toxic chemicals and growth hormones won't seep into the water or ground, and less soil is lost. Since no antibiotics are used, the risk of breeding super-resistant bugs is reduced. The hormone-free, antibiotic-free feed is definitely healthier for animals, which thus ought to make their meat healthier for the humans who eat it. And in practice, farmers who go to the trouble of getting certified "organic" generally employ other animal-friendly methods.

At any rate, the organic label is a gold standard compared with most of the other health or animal-welfare terms floating around, which are either marketing ploys or very loosely regulated. "Free-range" or "free-roaming," according to the Agriculture Department, means that "the poultry has been allowed access to the outside," so it's just as vague as "organic," but without the benefit of banning artificial hormones and antibiotics; moreover, the label applies only to poultry. "Cage-free" isn't defined by the government at all, although it's generally understood to mean that egg-laying chickens can walk around inside their shed, but not necessarily outside. (That's why Jessica Philips chose free-range eggs over cage-free.) "Dolphin Safe" is a trademark established by the Earth Island Institute to set standards for catching tuna in ways that don't harm dolphins. Similarly, "fair-trade" is a certification by a nongovernmental international organization, essentially requiring that farmers raise their crops in an environmentally sustainable manner and treat their workers decently. "Grass-fed" beef graze on grass, their natural food, and therefore don't need antibiotics. "Wild" fish were caught in their natural habitats, as opposed to being bred in fish farms; however, what you really want are "sustainable" fish, whose species aren't at risk of extinction. "Natural," to Agriculture, means "no artificial ingredients or added color, and [the product] is only minimally processed." The FDA doesn't have a definition for natural, although a spokesperson told me that "the agency has not objected to the use of the term on food labels provided it is used in a manner that is truthful and not misleading and the product does not contain added color, artificial flavors, or synthetic substances." And "no hormones added" is pointless for poultry, because the USDA doesn't allow the hormones anyway.

(I saw a slickly misleading commercial for Perdue Farms chickens in 2009, in which company chair Jim Perdue—obviously picking up on animal-rights PR—bragged that his chickens are cage-free and get no added hormones. All that means is that they are standard factory-farmed broilers. The only chickens for which being cage-free makes a difference are the ones that lay eggs, not the Perdue type that we eat.)

Faced with this void, some stores and consumer groups have developed their own labeling systems. Hannaford Brothers Co., a grocery chain of 167 stores with headquarters in Maine, in 2006 created a "Guiding Stars" program that rates food with one to three stars, based on nine nutritional factors like vitamins, minerals, and dietary fiber (all good) and saturated fat and cholesterol (bad). Two years later, Hy-Vee, an Iowa-based chain of 225 stores throughout the Midwest, came out with a more complex rating, called NuVal, that uses a scale of one to one hundred to analyze thirty nutritional factors. The Marine Stewardship Council and the Monterey Bay Aquarium have lists of sustainable seafood.

How about kosher meat? Even non-Jews often consider kosher meat a bit more ethical than other types because the laws of *kashrut,* or kosher food preparation, require what are supposed to be humane methods of slaughter. The animal must be killed with one smooth cut to the throat, using a knife with no nicks, so that the death can be as quick and painless as possible. Kosher carnivores also can feel a little better knowing they're not eating those intelligent, abused pigs or the factory-farmed shrimp that are destroying tropical coasts.

And keeping kosher isn't just about the kind of knife that's used. Many Jews say it makes them stop and think about the animals they're eating. According to some scholars, the rules spiritually connect the killing of animals for eating with the killing of animals for ritual sacrifice, in order to remind people of God as the source of their food. Another view is that the dietary laws represent a compromise with the original vegetarian lifestyle in the Garden of Eden, which imperfect humans ultimately were unable to maintain: okay, we can eat meat, but we can't gobble all flesh down indiscriminately.

There is, as well, a concept in Judaism known as *tza'ar ba'alei chayim,* or the prevention of cruelty to animals. However, this never has precluded observant Jews from using animals for heavy farm work or from eating them, and it has not traditionally been incorporated as part of the kosher laws.

With the burgeoning of vegetarianism, animal rights, environmentalism, and the consumer movement in recent years, more and more Jews became troubled by the idea that their dietary laws seemed to care about animals only at the moment of death, not throughout their life. Nor did the laws of *kashrut* talk about how to treat the workers who handle the animals, though other Jewish laws do. In 2007, Conservative Judaism's official Rabbinical Assembly set up a six-member commission of rabbis and lay people to write a *hekhsher tzedek,* or a voluntary kosher certification that would add workers' pay and safety, environmental impact, corporate behavior, and animal welfare to the traditional laws. "Over the last twenty years, the observance of *kashrut* was increasingly seen as related to ritual trivia. Broccoli was questionable because of the potential of microscopic bugs existing," explained Morris Allen, the rabbi of Beth Jacob Congregation in Mendota Heights, Minnesota, who spearheaded the drive for the *hekhsher tzedek*. "Is it appropriate for us to call something kosher if it meets the ritual demands of the Jewish people, but is produced in a way that people are exploited? Is that what we want to say about ourselves?"

In the committee's guidelines, which were formally approved in 2008, the animal-welfare section seems like a contradictory mix of ethical and business-pleasing criteria. It promises that companies "will be favored for the Hekhsher if they adhere to the Humane Farm Animal Care Standards," referring to the standards of the nonprofit and respected Humane Farm Animal Care organization, which certifies humane treatment of farm animals. These standards require that animals be able to "engage in their natural behavior," with "sufficient space, shelter and gentle handling to limit stress" and a diet free of added hormones and antibiotics. Sounds great. But the *hekhsher tzedek* also tells companies to follow guidelines endorsed by a number of industry groups, such as the American Meat Institute, the National Cattlemen's Beef Association, and the National Chicken Council. Bruce Friedrich of PETA scoffed that "it's no better than industry standard. All of the standard mutilations without pain relief are allowed, as are cramming hens into cages and calves into crates." For that matter, Shapiro and Friedrich are only marginally impressed with kosher ritual in general. "In its ideal, it is" more humane, Friedrich allowed, but then he pointed to scandals like the abuse of workers and animals at the meatpacker Agriprocessors (the one that Rabbi Carter cited) as an example of how the laws aren't always carried out in practice.

However, the *hekhsher tzedek* isn't the end of the story. Some Jews who share Shapiro's and Freidrich's concerns have taken the next step, to produce or seek out organic kosher food. A leading supplier is a company called KOL (for Kosher Organic-

Raised Local) Foods, founded in July 2007, which sells grass-fed, organic, local, kosher meat through six "buying clubs" in Philadelphia, Washington, D.C., New Jersey, Maryland, and the New York City metro area. For all of Shapiro's and Freidrich's disdain, these efforts are a lot better than the ethical vacuum that existed before.

So, yes, an ethical liberal can eat meat—carefully. And, I think, with some inevitable guilt.

One more note on animals. We don't just eat them. We wear them, we test cosmetics on them, and we occasionally put parts of their bodies in products like glue. Should the bar be higher for these uses, which are arguably more frivolous than using animals for food?

(We also take medicines that are tested on animals, but there's no choice in that case. U.S. law requires that drugs must be scientifically tested for safety on animals before they can be tried on humans, and unless you're going to raise the "species-ism" claim, I can't imagine any valid argument against that precaution.)

Plenty of alternatives to animal-ingredient and animal-tested goods are available. Instead of leather and fur, you can wear clothing made of cotton, linen, polyester, wool—depending on how strict your no-animal-parts standards are; wearing wool is more or less morally equivalent to eating dairy and eggs—and even my hemp hat and the soy underwear that the *New York Times* found. You can buy shampoos, make-up, and household cleansers that weren't tested on animals. But are they, in fact, any more ethical?

Consider cotton. Nice, natural, washable cotton. No animals have to be skinned to produce a cotton shirt. However, buying that shirt could help prop up the police state of Uzbekistan, one of the three biggest global sources of raw cotton. That shirt also contributes to severe environmental problems. Cotton is very water-intensive—Uzbekistan has drained the Aral Sea to feed the industry—and standard growing methods require a lot of pesticides. "While occupying just 2.5 percent of the world's croplands, cotton uses a tenth of all the world's chemical fertilizers and a staggering quarter of all the insecticides," writes environmental consultant Fred Pearce in his 2008 book *Confessions of an Eco-Sinner*. Genetically modified and organic cotton don't need pesticides, but the former raises other environmental concerns that this chapter will analyze a little later, and the latter is expensive. (Chapter 7 will discuss this.) So do you really want a cotton shirt?

Another nonanimal alternative is the imitation leather called "pleather," made from—oops—petroleum. That petroleum base obviously adds climate-wrecking greenhouse gases to the atmosphere and increases our dependence on oil-rich dictators. Forget it, then? Bruce Friedrich insists that the ethical scales still balance in favor of pleather versus animal skins like genuine leather. "It takes toxic chemicals and petrochemicals to produce leather," he pointed out. "It requires exponentially more of them to raise animals, to water and till the crops that you then feed to the animals, truck the animals to the factory farm, truck the animals to the slaughterhouse, take them to the cannery, and treat them with petrochemicals and other chemicals. Wearing petrochemical clothes requires a lot less chemicals than wearing leather." The *Wall Street Journal,* in analyzing the carbon footprints of six common items in October 2008, found that manufacturing a pair of leather Timberland hiking boots produced 121 pounds of carbon emissions, about four times as much as a bottle of liquid laundry detergent and 17 times as much as a six-pack of beer. "By far the biggest contributor is the shoe's raw material"—leather—the article said, largely because of the methane from cow burping.

Luckily, it's easier to be ethical in regards to the other major animal-welfare issue, avoiding products that are tested on animals. These "cruelty free" items have become so mainstream that I was able to find an assortment of not-animal-tested brands of shampoo, skin lotion, face cream, lip balm, conditioner, and the like—including Burt's Bees, Alba Botanics, and Nexus—when I randomly checked national-chain drug stores in my Brooklyn neighborhood as well as suburbs I happened to visit in southern California. That's not even counting the cornucopia of items available at natural-food stores.

I just wish it was easier to tell when something actually is free of animal testing. There's no uniform labeling system. A product might proclaim itself "100% vegan," or "100% cruelty free," or "never tested on animals," or any other variation. The print is probably tiny, and it could be hidden on any part of the label. Some manufacturers use the "leaping bunny" logo of the Coalition for Consumer Information on Cosmetics, which ought to simplify matters. However, the logo is often so small, and the sketch so abstract, that a shopper could miss it easily; the first time I saw one, I didn't realize it was a rabbit. And apparently some manufacturers don't care to publicize their ethical policies. Although Revlon is listed on PETA's Caring-Consumer Web site as a company that doesn't test on animals, and Peter Singer cites it as a pioneer in eliminating animal testing, I checked six Revlon products and none of their labels said anything about being animal-free.

You might think there's some logical correlation between eating animal-based food and using animal-based goods—if people are vegetarian, then of course they won't wear leather—but the relationship is as inconsistent as anything else humans do. For example, a lot of people avoid eating meat because they believe it is unhealthy for their bodies, not out of concern for animal welfare. So if they're less concerned about the healthiness of what goes on their skin or in their hair, they're not going to worry if animals were harmed in making those products. Jessica Philips, the Los Angeles vegetarian, admits that she wears leather shoes mainly because "I find them more comfortable, more durable, and more available. Wearing leather is where I hit the serious hypocrisy." On the other hand, I'm not a vegetarian, and I would find it a lot easier to eschew animal-based shampoos than meat. Probably that's because I can't really tell a no-animal shampoo from an animal-tested one, but boy, does tofu taste different from steak.

Unlike the case with food, giving up other animal products can be a gradual process. You can vow never to buy anything made of leather again. But meanwhile, gee, do you really have to throw out the leather jacket you already own? Doing that won't bring back to life the animal it came from, and it looks so good on you . . . (Answer: it depends on whether you feel embarrassed or cool when you wear the jacket.)

Now, get ready for purists to pounce: Are genetically modified foods really evil? And in any case, should we learn to accept them, because they're unavoidable?

Except in organic food, manufacturers are free to use manipulated genes without telling consumers. That's because back in 1992, when the first GM food—a tomato—was created, the FDA decided that a GM tomato still was recognizable as a tomato and that its nutritional value was substantially unchanged. Hence, there was nothing to say on the label.

Over the years, GM farming has spread throughout the United States, South America, Canada, China, South Africa, and even Europe, the last holdout. While today, ironically, there are no genetically engineered tomatoes and very few fruits and vegetables, the odds are high that the canola, corn, sugar, and soy you or your meat ate was genetically modified, as was the cotton in your clothing.

The advantages of this technology are that it can increase crop yields and, depending on the type of crop, reduce the need for pesticides. That, in turn, decreases soil erosion, soil damage, and pollution. Genetic engineering also allows farmers to employ what's called no-tillage planting, meaning that they don't have to dig up the ground with heavy plows, which is better for the soil. And, despite consumer groups' fears, only a handful of GE-related health problems have been reported in all these years. When Monarch butterfly larvae were fed pollen from GM-treated corn, in a test at Cornell University in 1999, they all died or were severely underweight. The following year, some GM corn called StarLink that was intended for animals accidentally got mixed in with regular corn for humans and was processed into tacos; seventeen people reported allergic reactions after eating the tacos. But that's about it for the side effects.

Scientific proof of harm is so minimal that even a strong consumer activist like Gregory Jaffe, director of the biotechnology project at the Center for Science in the Public Interest (the advocacy group that Michael Jacobson runs), says, "The current crops are safe to eat, and they have some benefits to the environment and farmers, and we should support those." And *The Rough Guide to Shopping with a Conscience* is forced to concede that "There is nothing concrete to suggest that the current generation of GE food is more harmful or less healthy than any other foods, and the American population, as the biotech industry is always keen to remind us, has been eating it for years with no measurable side effects." The direst warning the book can dredge up is that things could change in the future. It cites critics who argue that "there have been no proper 'human feeding trials,' in the U.S. or elsewhere, to rigorously screen the health of GE consumers. Furthermore, not all scientists are convinced that the current laws...are enough to rule out potential increases in the levels of plant toxins or reductions in the levels of nutrients."

So, genetically engineered food seems to be good for the environment. The practice has been used for over a decade without causing widespread, noticeable health problems. Why, then, are many people nervous about it?

Partly it's that the technology is still new, and so much isn't known. No studies have been done on the long-term human health impact. In light of China's recent history of lax food regulation and contaminated medicine and milk powder, the idea of that country in particular messing with the genes in its crops is hardly reassuring. Another concern is political, the threat that big corporations will control even more of our food supply. Because GM seeds are patented, farmers must buy the manufacturer's specific seeds every planting season, rather than saving seeds from last year's harvest, as humans have done since agriculture began. The StarLink experience also raises fears about cross-pollination. When plants are grown outdoors, it's almost inevitable that some of their pollen will drift into non-GM crops—including organic ones—or even into other types of GM plants, possibly creating "superweeds" resistant to all known herbicides. How would those genetic changes affect animals that eat the new, wild plants? Can we trust the organic label? As well, a few critics may be confusing genetic modification with cloning, since the FDA in 2008 declared that "cattle, swine, and goat clones, and the offspring of any animal clones traditionally consumed as food, are safe for human and animal consumption" and don't even need to be labeled. And clones of any sort give most people the willies. (Fortunately, the impact should be limited: the technology is so expensive that it's likely to be used only for breeding prized animals, not slicing the clones into chops.) Hovering over all these concerns, I think, is the idea that there's just something inherently creepy about eating food in which the genetic coding has been manipulated.

But if there is honest debate on both sides of the safety question, one issue seems clear-cut: people ought to know when they're eating these unnatural genes. Fully 95 percent of those surveyed by *Consumer Reports* in fall 2008 said that if food products were going to be made from GE animals, which the FDA was pondering at the time, they should be labeled. Jaffe of the CSPI, for his part, would like to see better regulation to catch "the one in one hundred where the benefits don't outweigh the risks."

The sole instance where a genetically altered food is often labeled—and where there is strong evidence of potential harm—is milk from cows treated with recombinant bovine somatropin, or RBST (also known as RBGH, for recombinant bovine growth hormone). This is a genetically engineered hormone that is injected into cows to stimulate milk production. The hormone clearly does its job; by most accounts, RBST cows produce about a gallon more per day than before they were injected. The FDA in 1993 approved the milk without requiring any special label, saying that tests had proved it was safe and, therefore, as with GM tomatoes, milk is milk.

Consumer groups protested that the FDA had misread the tests. RBST milk is indeed different—dangerously so—they asserted, because milk from treated cows exhibits elevated levels of a growth factor that has been linked to a higher risk of cancer. Over the next fifteen years, lawsuits and challenges broke out among states with a lot of RBST dairies that didn't want labels, states that let non-RBST dairies label their milk "hormone-free," the FDA, and Monsanto, the sole commercial manufacturer of the hormone. Supporters of labeling claimed that people have a right to know what they're drinking; opponents retorted that a label would be misleading and would give the dairies that called their milk "hormone-free" an unfair marketing advantage. (Yes, that argument implicitly acknowledges that customers don't want added hormones, thereby undercutting the RBST dairies that made the argument.) While as much as one-third of the U.S. dairy herd was getting the hormone, Canada and many European countries banned it. Finally, the FDA announced that companies could label their milk "from cows not treated with RBST," but they couldn't say "hormone-free" or "BST-free," since all milk contains naturally occurring hormones, including natural BST. All that may be moot, however, because by 2008 the largest bottler and a number of other major buyers—including McDonald's—had refused to carry the milk, the big store chains were offering alternatives clearly labeled non-RBST, and Monsanto was trying to sell off the product line.

I am delighted to report one piece of good news: the quandary that has plagued Jean Leung, Stewart Pravda, Cathy Monblatt, and many others—buying local versus buying organic—is not as irreconcilable as it first seems.

Both approaches are beneficial for the environment. If you buy local, you reduce carbon emissions because less fossil fuel is used to transport the food—and, as an added bonus, you are probably supporting small farmers and merchants. If you buy organic, you protect the earth by avoiding chemical pesticides and fertilizer, maintaining the soil, and not breeding "super-bugs." So far, so good.

The problem arises when the organic goods are grown far away, like Pravda's Chilean blueberries or the mounds of New Zealand kiwis, Florida grapefruit, Mexican avocados, and Ecuadorian mangoes at Whole Foods. It seems obvious that the farther the food has to travel to reach my plate, the more fuel it must require, thus worsening global warming, gobbling up nonrenewable resources, increasing our dependence on hostile petro-dictatorships, digging up sensitive terrain, and intensifying pollution. The biggest energy-guzzlers are foods moved by airplane rather than by ship or truck, which is how perishables usually are delivered from overseas—no doubt including those Chilean blueberries and New Zealand kiwis. (The high altitude of airplane emissions compounds their impact.) Thus, the quandary: which is worse for the earth, chugging the fuel to send organic meat and produce thousands of miles, or growing and raising nonorganic food close to home with all those nasty chemicals and soil-depleting techniques?

Home Depot faced that question around Mother's Day 2007, although not with food, according to an article in the *New York Times*. (A Home Depot spokesperson more or less confirmed the story to me.) The hardware chain wanted to sell organic roses but couldn't find any inexpensive local varieties. "And the amount of carbon that would have been emitted by shipping cheap ones from Venezuela seemed to eclipse any environmental benefit of avoiding pesticides and such," as the article put it. In this case, the chain opted for local, nonorganic flowers.

Complicating the picture is the transformation of organic farming from its hippie beginnings, helped along by Whole Foods' market power. Today, if you buy organic fruits or vegetables, you probably are giving your money to Earthbound Farms or Grimmway Farms. Those two companies, both headquartered in Central California, did more than $320 million in combined business in 2007, selling more than 80 percent of the organic produce eaten in the United States. Horizon, which dominates the organic milk-and-cheese market—and makes the organic milk that Jean Leung hesitated to buy—is just one of fifty labels of an $11.8 billion Texas-based conglomerate, Dean Foods Company, the largest milk bottler in the United States.

One surprising answer to the organic-local debate is that sometimes importing food from far away actually uses less energy and results in fewer carbon emissions than buying local. A pair of New Zealand agribusiness experts, in a 2007 report published by Lincoln University in Christchurch, New Zealand, calculated that the greenhouse gases emitted by producing and exporting dairy items from their country to the United Kingdom were about one-third less than the gases emitted when the British cultivated their own. This followed a study from the same university a year earlier that came to a related conclusion looking at more foods but fewer energy measures. (While the authors presumably had a vested interest in supporting their nation's farm industry, I have some faith in academic integrity.) Similarly, travel writer Sarah Murray, in her 2007 book *Moveable Feasts,* writes: "When a team of researchers at the UK's Manchester Business School assessed the environmental impact of 150 top-selling food items, looking at the energy use of everything from automatic picking machines to consumer packaging, they found no strong evidence that locally sourced foods were better, in environmental terms at least, than global produce. In some cases, they argued, the opposite was true." There are plenty more examples in her book.

These apparently illogical findings have two explanations. First, transportation is merely one ingredient in a food's total emissions tally, and probably not the main one. Factors like cow flatulence (remember?) can do a lot more damage. Just as cows were the major contributor to the greenhouse gases emitted by manufacturing Timberland boots, the *Wall Street Journal* found that they and their darn burping also were responsible for "the single biggest chunk of emissions" from producing a gallon of milk. For PepsiCo's Tropicana orange juice, nitrogen fertilizer for orange groves is the largest greenhouse culprit. Murray cites a U.S. study by Peter Singer and another ethicist that reported that "cooking and preparation generated 26 percent of the energy used in the food chain while processing generated 29 percent. Food transportation was responsible for just 11 percent."

That brings us to the second explanation. Among those non-transportation contributors to emissions are items like fertilizer, electric power for irrigation, heat and lights for hothouses, and refrigeration. These expenses may well be lower in countries that are thousands of miles away from their markets but climatically more suited to growing the particular food. New

Zealand farmers can raise their crops and graze their sheep and cows on rich clover outdoors year-round, while their British counterparts have to expend energy during the winter nurturing plants in hothouses and providing feed for animals. This is, in fact, the basis of global trade theory: each country should produce what it is most efficient at producing and import anything else from other, more efficient producers.

Admittedly, all these defenses of long-distance food may sound too good to be true. In that case, here's another way out of the local-organic quandary: it's widely acknowledged that the majority of the small, local farmers at farmers' markets are organic or almost organic, even if they lack the official USDA organic certification. Whenever Just Food, a type of produce-buying co-op, contracts with regional farms to bring fresh vegetables into New York City, it works only with farmers who follow standard organic tactics—such as rotating their crops, utilizing pests as natural pesticides, and using compost instead of chemical fertilizer—but it doesn't require the USDA seal. At my local farmers market, the stands offer a mixed variety of claims: animals that are "pasture fed," "grass fed," "heritage," "grass finished," and fed "certified organic grains"; produce that is "organically grown"; and organic baked goods. Said Carol Tucker Foreman, the veteran consumer activist, "Most of the people who sell at these farmers' markets are people who may not have taken the steps to be organic, but they are not corporate farms."

If they're using organic methods anyway, why don't the farmers get certified by the Agriculture Department? "Certification is expensive and time-consuming," explained Paula M. Lukats, Just Food's program manager. According to Agriculture guidelines, applicants for certification must provide, among other information, "a history of substances applied to the land for the previous 3 years" and an operating plan that has a monitoring system, a record-keeping system, and "practices to prevent

commingling of organic and nonorganic products and to prevent contact of products with prohibited substances." A farmer
who hasn't been organic for the previous three years probably
will have to spend the next three studiously obeying the rules
before even requesting certification, shelling out hundreds of
thousands of dollars in the process. Then the farmer "must
keep accurate post-certification records for 5 years concerning
the production, harvesting, and handling of agricultural products that are to be sold as organic."

But if the farmers aren't certified, how can we consumers trust that they really are following all those nice, almost-
organic, pesticide-free, soil-preserving practices they profess to
use? Foodies say that a local farmer has a strong incentive to be
honest, "the gaze or good word of his customers," as Michael
Pollan puts it. Lukats inspects farms that want to be part of her
organization.

To say you're buying local, however, you first have to define
"local," and that can swing anywhere between one hundred and
five hundred miles from home and even, in a pinch, three thousand. The locavore movement, dedicated to eating local food,
limits "local" to one hundred miles. Bon Appétit Management,
the environmentally sensitive catering company, tries to buy its
food within 150 miles of the restaurant it's serving, or at least
within continental North America. My nearby farmers market
is part of a New York City-wide program called Greenmarket,
which considers farms local if they're within a two hundred-
mile radius of its headquarters in Poughkeepsie, New York. But
since Poughkeepsie is about eighty-five miles from my particular market, the farmers actually could be trucking their goods
nearly three hundred miles to get to me. Just Food will contract
with farms as far as 250 miles away, Lukats said, because "that's
about what you can drive into the city and back in a day." The
Park Slope Food Coop claims to get most of its produce during
the New York growing season from farms no more than two

hundred miles away. However, it officially defines local as
five hundred miles, using math similar to Lukats's—its truck-
ers can drive twice as far as Lukats' farmers, because they don't
have to get home the same day—and it will reach thousands
of miles to Florida, Peru, Ecuador, and Guatemala for things
like oranges, strawberries, bananas, and cantaloupe. At a Manhattan Whole Foods, one day in November, the only "local"
organic produce—red cabbage—was labeled as being from
"Florida and New York."

These outlets stretch their geographical boundaries, of course,
in order to expand their menus. My farmers market doesn't sell
oranges because those are not grown within two hundred miles
of Poughkeepsie. Presumably, the food co-op could refuse to
carry them, too. But since members want the fruit, the co-op
at least tries to get them from Florida (one thousand carbon-
creating miles) rather than California (three thousand miles).
Thus, finally, we come to one irrefutable advantage of buying
imported organic versus buying local: variety. Buying imported,
you can have exotic fruits like kiwi and the out-of-season blueberries that Cathy Monblatt and Stewart Pravda craved. When
you buy local, "you can't get broccoli when you want it. You
won't get tomatoes in June. You have to learn to eat seasonally,"
pointed out Paula Lukats.

In the end, most of the people I interviewed seem to agree
with the conclusion Carol Tucker Foreman reached: "If I had to
make the choice between buying a local [noncertified] product
or an organic product that was brought in, I would always buy
the local, because it was just picked that morning, and it does
taste different."

Now that we've devised all these wonderful plans for eating in
ways that are good for our bodies and the earth, that will reduce
our greenhouse-gas emissions, that will preserve species and
soil, that won't support petro-dictators, and that will be sensi-

tive to any animals we may consume, here comes the hard part: finding places that actually sell this stuff.

Some quests are easier than others. Whatever else it's done, the industrialization of organic farming—the Whole Foods effect—has brought a lot of healthful food, especially produce and dairy, to mainstream supermarkets. From just $178 million in sales in 1980, the organic business burgeoned to $19 billion in 2007, and three-fourths of all grocery stores now carry some organic food. (The financial collapse of 2008–2009 slowed the growth, at least temporarily.) Unfortunately, the only organic produce on the shelf might be packaged lettuce and precut carrots—from the giants Earthbound and Grimmway, of course. While few supermarkets sell strictly organic meat, they probably carry some of those other, wholesome-sounding labels that may or may not actually mean anything: no antibiotics, no added hormones, no growth stimulants, certified humane-raised and -handled, and the like. New laws in California, Arizona, and Florida that bar the most restrictive cages and crates for breeding pigs, laying hens, and veal calves should increase the availability of cage-free eggs and free-range or organic meat in those states.

Once you leave the supermarket, you've got a wide variety of places where you can get produce, meat, and bread made with minimal chemicals and processing, even if not certified organic. Not only that, but many of these alternative markets keep the prices of their otherwise-expensive, organic-style food within reason through cooperative membership, volunteer labor, or reduced bureaucracy. The catch: shopping at these venues is not as quick and easy as a single "load the cart, load the car" trip to a supermarket. Each has a limited selection, so you will have to schlep from one to another. You may have to donate your time and labor. And if you stray from absolute purity—that certain chocolate bar you love, the animal-tested shampoo that just works better than anything else you've tried, or my weakness, diet soda—you're going to find yourself in the big, bad super-market occasionally.

The closest to one-stop shopping is probably a food co-op, which, as the previous chapter mentioned, often carries more than food. However, there's no guarantee that it sells natural products, although all 130 co-ops in the Iowa-based National Cooperative Grocers Association (NCGA), the major trade group, do. "Food co-op" merely means a business that is owned and governed by its members. The NCGA co-ops range in size from $1 million to more than $100 million in annual sales, and the rules for membership and working also vary. (The NCGA is obviously not a comprehensive grouping, since my local co-op isn't included.)

Friends of mine joined the Park Slope co-op for all sorts of reasons: the diversity of organic, grass-fed, and other hard-to-find food; the low prices; the quality of the produce, whether organic or not; even as a way to meet potential dates. I also know people who say the co-op saves them the hassle of reading labels; they can trust that most of the products aren't from companies with the most egregious labor and environmental records, tested on animals, or genetically modified or irradiated, since this co-op is one that follows natural-ingredient policies. Nevertheless, despite a roster of ten thousand items, even Joe Holtz, a founder and one of the top administrators, admitted that "my family cannot buy everything from the food co-op." Every week he heads into a local supermarket for special yogurts, quick meals, and ice-cream bars for his two teenagers.

For another choice, the United States has more than 4,600 farmers' markets, according to the Department of Agriculture. Each market sets its own rules, including how it defines "local." In the height of the season at a relatively large site, like my neighborhood market, you can get turkey, chicken, fish, pork, beef, lamb, and eggs; mushrooms, potatoes, pickles, zucchini, peppers, tomatoes, lettuce, asparagus, and onions; breads, muffins, and cookies of all kinds; apples and strawberries; even milk, ice cream, and wine. It almost seems like enough for a week's worth of meals. But that's the biggest problem: my local market is open only once a week. (In New York City, a handful operate two or more days.) You can't just dash in if you run out of milk. If you're a religious Jew, you can't dash in at all, because the sole market day is Saturday, the Jewish Sabbath. You also can't buy sugar, salt, flour, and other staples—let alone nonfood stuff or my diet soda—and in winter the offerings shrink drastically. Smaller markets, of course, have even less.

The new kid on the block is community-supported agriculture (CSA), which essentially cuts out the "market" part of "farmers market" by bringing eater and farmer directly together. When consumers buy shares in a CSA like Just Food, they are buying a guaranteed amount of a local farmer's output, typically paying around $500 to $800 a season. It's so direct, in fact, that CSA members usually pick up their food right at the farm. By 2008, the United States had about 1,500 of these programs.

This is only for people with time, patience, and a huge appetite for vegetables, however. Among the negatives: the farmer chooses what you get each week, depending on what's ready to harvest, which means you may drive home with a whole load of tomatoes and no spinach, whether you want tomatoes or not. And even if you purchase a half-share rather than a full membership, the take-home probably is more than a single person can shovel down in a week. Paula Lukats, the Just Food program manager, conceded with a touch of embarrassment that she gives away 50 percent of her own allotment. If all of that doesn't scare you off, remember that the share is about 99 percent vegetables and available only during the growing season. (Some CSAs separately contract with fruit, egg, or dairy farms or buy a limited amount in winter.) Lukats said that approximately half the people who sign up drop out during their first year.

Theoretically, there's one more choice: if you have the space, the time, the appropriate weather, and a halfway-green thumb, grow your own. For that matter, you don't need much space; there are hundreds of matchbook-size farms, some of them selling their crops through farmers' markets, in New York City, Philadelphia, Milwaukee, San Francisco, and other cities. Even First Lady Michelle Obama planted an organic garden at the White House in 2009 (well, with a lot of help from the White House staff and some local fifth-graders). Now you'll see for yourself how hard it is to do those environmentally beneficial things, like fighting off bugs and weeding without pesticides.

"Food," said Greg Jaffe of the consumer group CSPI, "is cultural, not just food. You have religious rules. How people want their diet to be, their health to be; how they want their lives to impact the world around them." We know the basics that our parents and schools taught us when we were kids, and despite all the fancy labels we see today, those basics still hold: Eat a balanced diet with lots of fresh fruit and vegetables, minimal carbohydrates, and some low-fat protein. Avoid overly processed foods with ingredients we've never heard of. We can turn the process of acquiring our food into a fun experience, by chatting with farmers at the farmers market or visiting a CSA farm. We can agonize. We can splurge and then feel guilty. We can go to extremes: If I eat an omelet, have I tortured the hen that laid those eggs? If I eat a grilled-cheese sandwich made from milk from a cow that burped methane, have I really caused the polar ice caps to melt?

CHAPTER FOUR

ENOUGH GREEN, ALREADY!

In the decades since the first Earth Day, in 1970, the environmental movement has become as mainstream as apple pie
(organic or not). Conservatives and liberals, Christian fundamentalists and atheists, businesses and consumer groups—even
oil companies—all at least pay lip service to concepts like clean
air and water, reforestation, biodiversity, and energy conservation, although their motivations may not coincide. (Some fundamentalists, for example, see environmentalism as part of God's
directive to Adam and Eve to be stewards of the earth, while businesses jump on energy conservation as a way to save money.)
Carpool lanes and recycling bins are ubiquitous. There's general agreement that we should increase our use of nonpolluting,
renewable, low-emission, alternative energy sources like solar,
wind, hydropower, geothermal, and biomass. Only a few hold-
outs in the scientific, political, and business communities still
deny that human activity contributes to climate change, and
two-thirds of the respondents in a Marist College Poll in April
2009 predicted that "global warming will be a major problem"
for future generations. Maybe the surest sign of how we're all
environmentalists now is that former Vice President Al Gore's
documentary *An Inconvenient Truth* won an Academy Award
in 2007, placing it in the popular pantheon along with *Titanic*
and *Gone with the Wind* and giving Gore the chance to hobnob
on national TV with heartthrobs like Leonardo DiCaprio. With

such settled unanimity about the goal, you might assume that the ethical liberal doesn't suffer any tremendous inner debate over steps to protect the environment.

But it turns out that being green is as complicated as any other juggling act. And after you think some more about it, that's not surprising. Since virtually everything humans do must be fueled in some way, as soon as we take a step in any direction, we're setting off a string of energy dominoes.

Let's say it's time to cook dinner: Don't keep opening and shutting the refrigerator. Put the lid on the saucepan while you boil water. Turn the lights off if you leave the kitchen. Did you fully defrost the roast before you started cooking? Don't keep opening the oven to check on that roast. Turn the oven off a few minutes earlier than the recipe calls for—and I do hope it's a gas oven, not electric, and the newest energy-efficient model, of course. When the meal is over, put your leftovers in tin foil, not plastic wrap. Use the microwave for quick reheating. Don't use the microwave for long-time cooking. (Oops! You can't use tin foil in the microwave.) Don't run the dishwasher until there's a full load. Don't keep the water running if you wash by hand. And by the way, what kind of soap did you use?

This chapter is not going to pile on more lists of 101 or 1,001 things people ought to do to save the earth. There are 1,001 too many lists already. Instead, I'll write about the topics I would look for in a "green" book: a few basic explanations (how is a Prius different from a plug-in?), some policy analysis, and an effort to answer a couple of tough questions that even committed enviros have trouble juggling.

Any discussion of environmental problems or solutions has to start with cars. Transportation is responsible for almost one-third of U.S. greenhouse-gas emissions. In addition, cars are a major contributor to air and water pollution, resource depletion, physical damage to the earth, and geopolitical instability, because of the gasoline they burn, the raw materials that go into manufacturing them, and the roads that are paved for them to drive on. Even Alex Steffen of Worldchanging, who is skeptical that anything people do in daily life will be very effective in halting climate change, allowed that "the single best thing you can do to reduce your impact is to live in a more compact community" that doesn't require driving to work and shopping. If we want to take better care of the environment, the biggest, quickest, one-shot way we can accomplish that is probably by changing the way we travel.

And we do change. Sure, we do. When gasoline prices are high, we are all conservationists. We combine errands, we carpool, we use mass transit, we walk, we take vacations closer to home, we talk about buying smaller cars with better fuel efficiency. We can't imagine ever reverting to our old, gas-guzzling ways. Then, when prices drop, as they inevitably do, we go right back to wasting gas.

I don't want to be cynical. I truly believe it's vital for Americans to scale back our energy use, and then be a model for the aspiring middle classes in India, China, and other energy-profligate developing countries. But it seems kind of pointless to keep repeating these facts and recommendations. We all know the steps we should take, since we take them every time prices shoot up, yet we Americans seem incapable of being fuel-efficient without the incentive of four-dollar-a-gallon gas.

Experts offer plenty of explanations for our perversity. At heart, we're lazy, short-sighted, and selfish. Or, to put it in economists' terms, a rational human being, acting in financial self-interest, will calculate that the most rational thing to do is to enjoy the immediate, personal benefits of driving comfortably and quickly wherever he or she wants to go, regardless of the broader or long-range cost to society. Then there's the cultural mythology: we Americans still see ourselves as pioneers, and speeding down an open highway is the modern equivalent of Daniel Boone charging into Kentucky. Christian Weller, the economist with the Center for American Progress, calculated that the main influence on driving habits is whether someone has a job, because "79 percent of people drive themselves to work."

In practical terms, American society doesn't easily accommodate a nonautomobile lifestyle. Jobs are in corporate parks, miles from homes or malls. Downtown stores have been boarded up. The rare bus in the suburbs runs only once an hour. "When you have kids in three different schools," said Carroll Muffett of Greenpeace, "you're going to do more driving." Not only that, but many local zoning laws insist that all new housing include two parking spaces per residential unit. Your family is going to own two cars, whether you want to or not!

With all these factors pushing us into cars, I think the only thing that will dramatically change our habits is money—specifically, a gas tax high enough to hurt. A permanent summer-of-2008 panic. The basic idea, as envisioned by many environmentalists and economists, is that the tax system would establish a very high minimum price, perhaps $4.50 a gallon, which was the peak at which people panicked in summer 2008. If the market rate rose to that level or above, the tax rate wouldn't change. However, if the market price dropped below that—say, to $3 a gallon—a tax of $1.50 would kick in to bring the price at the pump up to the legal minimum. (The $2.4 billion federal subsidy for manufacturers of no-gas cars, announced in 2009, might lower the purchase prices but wouldn't be enough to drastically change our driving habits.)

I know my tax proposal may seem extreme. Most troubling, it would hurt low-income people who need to drive to work. But we Americans have proved that we can't be trusted to control our petroleum addiction without a huge financial incentive, and the harm done by wasteful driving is much bigger than the harm of high gas prices. Moreover, it's hard to give much credence to our kvetching when we pay less than half of what

Europeans pay for fuel. For people who truly can't afford the tax, experts have devised rebates that could piggyback onto existing rebates and credits like the federal Earned Income Tax Credit. There's one more advantage to upping the gas tax: the extra $1.50-per-gallon revenue would now go to the U.S. Treasury, rather than to the big oil companies and hostile OPEC nations.

Of course, I realize that it's easy for me to preach. I live in New York City and can take the subway almost everywhere.

Aha, but you've bought a hybrid! Very nice. However, a hybrid does not automatically absolve its owner of all environmental responsibility.

First, here's the basic technical explanation. Hybrid cars have both a conventional gas engine and an electric motor, but they run primarily on the gas engine. While there are several variations, hybrids typically use the electric motor only to start the car and maybe to get it up to speed, then combine it with the gas for extra oomph. Despite the heavy use of old-fashioned petroleum, the technology saves fuel because the gas engine is smaller than in a traditional car, and the electric motor can be charged by energy that's usually wasted, such as the kinetic energy that dissipates as heat when braking. With less gas being consumed, carbon emissions are lower, though not eliminated. For example, I used the Nature Conservancy's online carbon footprint calculator to compare my hypothetical hybrid with my hypothetical small and midsize cars. Assuming that I drove 12,000 miles a year in all three cases and responsibly checked my air filter and tire pressure every month, I had an annual footprint of 4.7 tons with the hybrid, 6.8 with the small car, and 7.9 with the midsize.

Although Toyota's Prius has become synonymous with the concept of hybrid, plenty of other models exist (or were due on the market at the time this book was printed), from Audi, Cadillac, Chevrolet, Chinese companies, Ford, Honda, Mazda,

Mercedes-Benz, Porsche, and Saturn, as well as more from Toyota. Altogether, some automobile experts foresee eighty-nine different types of hybrids on American roads by 2013, including luxury models and sports utility vehicles.

At this point, an environmentalist has to question the definition of green. A hybrid SUV? A $106,000 hybrid Lexus (base price, without options)? While the first Prius and the Honda Insight get more than 40 miles per gallon, and a newer Prius is supposed to enjoy 50, the $106,000 Lexus LS 600h hybrid ekes out only 22 on the highway, 20 in the city. And remember, these vehicles still swill petroleum and produce greenhouse-gas emissions. How much worse off would the earth be, I wonder, if I drove a conventional-engine Honda Civic getting 34 miles per gallon on the highway, for one-seventh the price?

Moreover, does "green" apply only to the car itself? What about corporate behavior? For most of 2007, Toyota joined the Big Three American auto makers in a lobbying effort to block Congress from significantly raising fuel-efficiency standards. Honda did not. (In the end, Toyota and the Big Three largely failed, and Congress hiked the standards by 40 percent.)

The big rival to hybrids in the petroleum-avoiding derby has been biofuel, or fuel made from plant sugar, which for Americans mainly has meant corn-based ethanol. (Brazil does the same using sugar cane.) Starting in the 1990s from the Midwestern corn belt, the fuel zoomed across the country as gas prices and worries about energy independence skyrocketed, and by the mid-2000s, ethanol blends accounted for about 6 percent of all gas sold in the United States. This was—apparently—a miracle solution to the concern about relying on oil from hostile foreign governments. No imports were required, because corn grows abundantly in the United States. No exotic new automotive designs were needed; a blend of nine parts petroleum to one part ethanol creates a fuel that most conventional cars can use. Distilling sugar from fermented corn is fairly easy. Furthermore, any carbon gases emitted while burning this fuel should, in theory, be compensated for by the carbon dioxide that the corn and sugar had sucked out of the air while they were growing. It seemed like such a miracle solution, in fact, that Congress in 2007 ordered annual ethanol use to about double, to 15 billion gallons, over the next eight years. European governments had similar goals.

Then the backlash began. Global food prices shot up higher than a corn stalk at harvest time as ethanol and food companies fought over the same crops. Forests, grassland, and environmentally sensitive marshes were hacked and drained in order to plant corn, which ended up releasing far more climate-choking emissions into the air than the fuel could save. The tens of thousands of workers cutting sugar cane in Brazil, meanwhile, labored under horrendous, even slave-like conditions, without proper safety gear, breathing in pesticides, and dying of dehydration and exhaustion. For all that, it takes a lot of energy to produce ethanol, and cars get lower mileage than with petroleum. The cure was worse than the disease.

There had to be alternatives to the alternatives. In fact, the U.S. law mandating ethanol also sets a target of 21 billion gallons of noncorn biofuels by 2022. So the search for a second generation of hybrids and biofuels was launched.

Hybrids, for example, could cut emissions much more and get higher fuel efficiency if they used less gas, or none at all. As this book was being written, GM, Toyota, Ford, BMW, Renault, and a private, California-based company called Tesla Motors all were scrambling to come out with ever-more-electric cars, perhaps as early as 2010. (The Chinese automaker BYD already was selling a super-cheap model domestically.) GM's Volt would reverse the standard hybrid equation by relying mainly on an electric motor, using a conventional gasoline backup just to charge the battery. Tesla actually had gone all the way, producing a limited run of a two-seat sports car that drove solely on electric power. However, at more than $100,000 apiece and with fewer than one hundred on the road, the cars were clearly a rich person's toy, and Tesla was trying to design a more customer-friendly five-seat sedan for "just" $60,000. Even if GM and Tesla, starved for cash, can't stay in business long enough to actually produce their autos, other companies undoubtedly will jump in.

Still, electric cars aren't a free ride. Although they may liberate drivers from reliance on a handful of oil dictatorships, they replace that freedom with a reliance on two not-always-friendly nations that control the supply of crucial electric-auto ingredients: China, the main source of rare earth ores like neodymium, needed to make magnets and other parts for hybrid motors; and Bolivia, which holds almost half the global supply of the mineral lithium, used for powering the motors. (Not to get into a detailed discussion of geopolitics right here, but China and the United States have a complex relationship of intertwined and competing trade and diplomatic interests, with Americans relying far too much on the Chinese to buy our Treasury bills and sell us cheap goods, while Bolivian president Evo Morales is one of Latin America's strongest critics of U.S. foreign policy.) A more immediate problem with electric cars is that they usually can go only fifty miles before they must be recharged. This brings us to the inconvenience of recharging the electric battery, particularly in the no-gas version. The most common method is to plug it into a wall outlet at home or at a special charging station, like a cell-phone battery; hence the term plug-in. But just how does that outlet obtain its electricity? (Probably the same way most American buildings do, from dirty coal, which will be discussed in a moment.)

As for biofuels, who said that sugar was the only plant-based ingredient that could run a car? Just as environmentalists were losing their appetite for corn-ethanol, scientists turned their attention to cellulose, derived from nonfood plants like reeds and wild grasses. Venture capitalists poured in hundreds of millions of dollars, and the federal Energy Department funded six cellulose-ethanol companies. This approach creates a different set of problems, however. It's a lot tougher to make fuel out of cellulose than sugar, because cellulose—the fibrous stuff that holds plants together—doesn't break down easily. Since some of the plants being used are invasive species, they might run rampant and push out native plants. Furthermore, cellulose doesn't solve the basic dilemma of supply and demand: after all, if demand grows bigger than the existing wild supply, other land inevitably will be converted to the newly desirable grass—including environmentally sensitive marshland, rain forests, and cropland—bringing us right back to all the negatives of corn-ethanol. So biofuel researchers dug deeper, investigating algae, crop wastes like corn cobs, the seeds of an exotic Caribbean fruit called jatropha, and molecules that would be bioengineered to make hydrocarbons, many of which promised to produce more fuel per acre than sugar.

For drivers who can't wait, who want something even greener, and who are famous, a handful of hydrogen-powered autos are becoming available. Based on technology used in the space shuttle, these vehicles have fuel cells that combine hydrogen with plain old oxygen from the air, creating electric power to drive a motor. Advocates say hydro-cars can go further on a tank than electric models, refuel faster, and—most important—emit no greenhouse gases. On the other hand, the act of actually producing the hydrogen releases greenhouse emissions and uses up more energy than the hydrogen provides to the car itself. The biggest roadblock, though, is that you can't get these vehicles. The technology is so cutting-edge and expensive that the earliest models are just for lease, not sale, and are available only in Southern California, where special refueling stations can be found. Plus, there are long waiting lists. Hopes for mass production stalled in 2009 as Congress and the White

House argued over R&D funding for the vehicles. To create the proper buzz for this elite mode of transportation, BMW, GM, and Honda sought out celebrities, including Jay Leno, Brad Pitt, Angelina Jolie, Magic Johnson, Placido Domingo, and Cameron Diaz. (The *Los Angeles Times* reported that as soon as actress Laura Dern got her hydrogen car, she gushed, "I've got to show Steven Spielberg. I've got to show Meg Ryan.")

More creativity has been stimulated by the X Prize contest of 2010, sponsored by Progressive Casualty Insurance Company and a private foundation, which promised $10 million to whoever developed a vehicle that could get at least 100 miles per gallon and win a series of races simulating real-world conditions, Among the entrants: cars that run on solar power, biofuel, hydrogen-hybrid, and compressed natural gas, along with boring old electric autos.

A few daring souls have tried tooling around in cars fueled by used cooking oil; mixing vegetable oil or animal fat with alcohol apparently makes a tolerable form of biodiesel. One of them, author Greg Melville, wrote an op-ed essay in the *New York Times* in June 2008, describing how he paid about $2,000 to buy and install a grease-power conversion kit in his Mercedes diesel station wagon and then drove all the way from Vermont to California smelling "like the back of a garbage truck on a July afternoon." Melville claimed he got twenty miles to the gallon of grease and emitted less than half the carbon gases of regular diesel, while paying absolutely nothing for his fuel. Amazingly, however, he had trouble finding enough fast-food joints to refill his tank.

Joseph Ayala is an immigrant from El Salvador and, by day, a truck driver in New York City. He's also a cooking-fuel entrepreneur: in 2004, he created a company, called Vorco, to collect leftover oil from local Chinese, Japanese, and Italian restaurants. (All that calamari and stir-fry create a lot of grease, according to Ayala.) With another driver, he gathered about 2,500 gallons a week from 250 restaurants, which he then sold to biodiesel manufacturers in upstate New York, Long Island, and Philadelphia. Understandably, Vorco has been buffeted by volatile energy trends. Gas prices skyrocketed, competitors swarmed in, and restaurants that used to pay Ayala thirty cents a gallon to cart away what they considered garbage started to insist he take it for free; some even hinted that he should pay *them* for the raw material. Then gas prices plunged, so the biodiesel manufacturers he sold to demanded discounts.

In any case, Ayala pointed out, I couldn't drive my Pontiac Vibe on his fuel. My car isn't made for diesel, and New York has no biodiesel stations.

Yet more ideas abound for how to design an automobile's fuel tank, what goes in it, and how to get the whatever into it. Multibillionaire corporate raider-oilman-Republican contributor T. Boone Pickens has touted natural gas, which is relatively clean and is found in the United States, and in which he conveniently happened to have big investments. Honda, for one, makes a couple thousand Civics powered by the gas each year. To get around the dilemma of using dirty coal for charging clean electric batteries, Tesla's chair took a stake in a second company, called SolarCity, with the idea that it could power a charging station or the car owner's home via solar panels. (More on solar later in this chapter.) Another company, Better Place, began setting up a series of charging stations where it might also provide the replacement batteries. And car makers are still trying good old engineering solutions, like designing more fuel-efficient gas engines and seeking lighter-weight steel.

Great. There are feasible, more-or-less green ways of getting around in an automobile. But here's the question: if you own a conventional gasoline-powered car that gets pretty high gas mileage and is in good shape, should you trade it in for a hybrid or other alternative vehicle?

The hybrid certainly would shrink your carbon footprint and use less gas. Yet dashing out and buying a new car, no matter how wonderfully fuel- and carbon-efficient, seems to run counter to a different green value, the "R" of reuse. Think of all the electricity, aluminum, steel, plastic, rubber, glass, and other material that had to be dug, manufactured, and used up to make that spiffy new hybrid, while your perfectly drivable old model rusts in a junk yard, maybe half-scavenged for the most popular parts. Alternatively, you could sell or trade in the old car, so it can still be used. But if someone else is driving it, wasting gas, and polluting the air, how is that any better than you doing the polluting and wasting?

In fact, I couldn't find any consensus on this issue among people who consider themselves environmentally conscious, in part because the calculation is so amorphous. (The decision is a lot easier, of course, if the old car gets lousy mileage.) The car-owner has to consider the number of miles typically driven in a year, the miles per gallon of the old and prospective cars, the number of years the old car was owned and the new car is likely to be kept, the amount of energy that went into making the vehicles, and the prices of both. Even then, no one knows for sure.

Nancy Hwa, the veteran PR specialist from Washington, D.C., clearly doesn't pick up and dump vehicles frivolously. She drove her parents' Ford Escort until it gave out in 1997, then bought a Honda Civic (25 miles per gallon city, 35 highway) that she was still using when I interviewed her eleven years later. Back in 1997 she didn't have a green choice, because the first mass-market hybrid, the Honda Insight, wasn't introduced until 1999. Now will she dump the Civic and buy a Prius? "I'm planning to drive this car until it's absolutely dead. If a car runs great, it would be more wasteful to trade it in and buy something new," she declared. Similarly, Kimberly Danek Pinkson of the EcoMom Alliance argued that she's really helping the environment by keeping her gas-guzzling Nissan SUV, bought in 2001 when she lived in the snowy mountains near Lake Tahoe. "That one pretty much sits in my driveway," she said. "That way I figure I'm driving it less than someone else." She mainly uses a 1987 Audi.

Actually, it's Pinkson's Audi that may be doing more damage. A 2004 report of the California State Legislature projected that in 2010, "about 30 percent of cars are 12 years old and older. These cars account for 25 percent of the miles driven by cars, but they are responsible for 75 percent of the pollution from cars." In other words, autos like Pinkson's Audi are causing triple their share of pollution and ought to get off the road. "If you can afford to buy a more fuel-efficient car than your existing car," Carroll Muffett of Greenpeace recommended, "then you should buy it."

Pablo Päster, an engineer and vice president at the environmental consulting firm ClimateCheck, tackled the trade-in question on his environmental Web site AskPablo in April 2008. He came to the same conclusion as Muffett, the opposite of Hwa and Pinkson. Looking at the weight, gas efficiency, and expected life span of a 1986 Mercedes W126, a Hummer H2 (no model year specified, but newer than the Mercedes), and a brand-new Prius, and using generally accepted estimates of how many British thermal units are required to manufacture each pound of a car and burn each gallon of gas, Päster emerged with the following calculations: for the Mercedes, he writes,

> over the next 116,000 miles, your car's greenhouse gas emissions will essentially break even with the emissions from the production and use of a Prius. I'm guessing your 22-year-old car probably has over 200,000 miles on it. If you're lucky, you can get another few years out of it. So if you can afford a new Prius, you are better off switching now. And think of the fewer hassles of owning a new car.

Also, the Mercedes probably emits more smog-causing nitrogen oxides than the hybrid. Trading in the Hummer, meanwhile, poses the quandary of having the new driver tool around gobbling up all that gas and emitting all that carbon. The problem could be solved, Päster notes, if "you are feeling bold and have the car scrapped." But doesn't scrapping it waste all those raw ingredients? Päster doesn't say.

That's not the end of the trade-in debate. As Muffett and Päster point out, there's also the tiny matter of affordability. A new car means a sizable down payment and monthly installments. Another Web site, Edmunds, works on that issue. It can calculate how many months it would take for the gas savings of a more fuel-efficient new car to recover the purchase cost, using the standard data (the local gas price, the number of miles driven per month, the price of the new car, the trade-in value of the old, and the miles-per-gallon of both). To help make trade-ins cost-effective, the United States and nearly a dozen European countries have offered "cash for clunkers" plans, which pay owners a couple thousand dollars to turn in their old gas-guzzlers. The U.S. plan was so successful that it used up its entire $1 billion initial appropriation less than a week after it started, in August 2009. (These programs usually resolve the replacement-driver quandary by scrapping the old car.)

But—one more twist in the argument—a couple thousand dollars of government incentives may not go very far toward a $20,000 Honda Insight, let alone a Lexus or Tesla. Moreover, Christian Weller noted that new-car buyers can't always wait months for a payoff in fuel savings. His conclusion: "I'll keep my gas-guzzler until it croaks."

Travel of all sorts, not just car trade-ins, seems to be one of the few areas in which even the most environmentally and ethically pure admit to problems with juggling. While a bike, subway, bus, or your feet may get you to work and shopping,

many people would like to explore a wider universe occasionally. Isn't it also a good liberal value to visit other countries, to
understand different cultures? Or to go to all those parks that
we hope to preserve, to appreciate nature's beauty and diversity
in person? And for heaven's sake, is it unethical to take the kids
to grandma's house? Yet achieving these heartwarming goals
undeniably requires using fuel and emitting greenhouse gases
that we otherwise wouldn't. A lot of environmental activists are
so conflicted about this that they feel they have to justify what
they shouldn't have to justify.

What green believer could object to hiking and camping,
for example? Kimberly Danek Pinkson, for one. She considers
her family vacations a weakness. "I love to go camping with my
son," she said, "and that means we're driving a lot to go where
we're camping." Stewart Pravda might drive 150 miles round-
trip to hike at the Delaware Water Gap in Pennsylvania or in
New York's Bear Mountain State Park. "I feel guilty going on
trips," he confessed. On the plus side, his 1997 Saturn gets 31
miles per gallon. On the minus, it's not a hybrid.

To add another ball to the juggling, some people's environmental work actually requires them to expend environmentally
damaging greenhouse gases. Chip Giller of Grist said he trav-
els a lot for fund-raising, and because he lives on an island off
the coast of Seattle, his trips are inevitably in super-carbon-
emitting airplanes. "No matter how I work on the rest of life to
reduce my carbon footprint," he sighed, "it's counteracted by
the amount I travel."

Bruce Friedrich of PETA tries to reduce the number of business trips he takes. Interestingly, the key factor isn't distance;
it's the social impact of the trip. "Attending an animal-rights'
conference where everybody in attendance is already an animal-rights activist or attending a vegetarian festival where everybody is already vegetarian, that's probably not worth the
environmental impact. You could have a PETA table of ani-

mal-rights literature that is similar to many other tables of animal-rights literature," he said. By contrast, he will continue to go to about ten Speak Up for Animals conferences around the country every year, even though most of the attendees already are active, because "we find that everybody who comes profits significantly from having been there. They become more effective advocates." (I'm sure another reason Friedrich considers the conferences worthwhile is that PETA sponsors them.) He also looks for the most energy-efficient modes of travel; for example, he now spends three and a half hours taking the train from Washington, D.C., to New York, rather than hopping a forty-five-minute flight. Friedrich added, "It's one of those difficult situations that's never going to be black or white."

Gas-guzzling travel isn't always quite so noble. Eco-skeptics snicker at the case of England's Prince Charles, a devoted environmental advocate who's been warning about global warming since 1990—and who left a trail of nearly 53 tons of unnecessary carbon emissions by taking his private jet on a 2,200-mile tour of Europe in 2009, rather than flying commercial. The purpose of the European tour? Promoting green causes.

Even when people stay put, they need heat, light, and power. Throughout much of history, humans got their energy from an assortment of coal, petroleum, wood, animal fat, animal waste, and the damming of water. The modern world has altered that mix, and since the 1990s the three main nontransportation power sources for the United States—providing nearly 90 percent of the nation's electricity—have been coal, natural gas, and nuclear fuel. Environmentalists would like to shift to a different power mix, with more renewable sources such as wind, solar, hydroelectric, and biomass. (Remember those cows?)

But every one of these sources, from the ancient to the high-tech, has drawbacks. Anyway, as an individual, you have only a limited amount of control over where your local utility gets its power. You may be able to select renewable "green" energy. (This doesn't mean that the utility stretches an electric wire straight from your house to a wind farm; it just means that the utility must obtain some of its total capacity from renewable sources.) And you might be able to set up wind or solar capability in your own home.

Herewith is a quick primer.

Coal: Yes, the coal of sooty Dickensian cities, locomotives trailing black clouds of smoke, and miners trapped underground is still heating our homes and cooking our food. In fact, it provides almost half the electricity Americans use. The United States has plenty of it, it's cheap, it's efficient, and it frees us from the risks of relying on oil dictatorships. Other countries, most notably Poland, India, and China, are heavily powered by coal as well.

If the skies aren't as dark as in Dickens's time, that's partly because coal is cleaner now, and partly because we have more fuel alternatives than the Victorians did. In the United States, amendments to the Clean Air Act in 1990 forced the coal companies to find new blends and install chemical scrubbers to cut in half the emissions of sulfur dioxide and nitrogen oxide that cause acid rain. More efficient burning methods also reduce carbon emissions. Nevertheless, coal remains dirty and dangerous, and it is the single largest U.S. carbon emitter. Mining companies routinely dump tons of rock and dirt into valleys, forests, and streams when they blast off the tops of mountains to reach the coal seams inside. Fly ash and other byproducts from burning the coal sit in more than one thousand huge dumps, where they can leach toxic substances like arsenic, lead, mercury, and selenium into the water, ingredients that can cause cancer and birth defects. (President Barack Obama in 2009 announced a goal of tightening the minimal federal regulations.) Moreover, mines are still hazardous places to work: every year approximately two dozen Americans die, and thousands more are injured, from explosions, gas leaks, fires, structural collapses, and flooding. Worldwide, the death toll goes into the thousands.

Coal could be a lot cleaner. With federal subsidies, the industry is researching ways to capture the carbon emissions and store them deep underground or undersea as liquid or gas. That's not as simple as it sounds, because the CO_2 gas has to be blocked from bubbling up to the surface or polluting groundwater. While this has been done on a small scale, estimates are that it will take into the 2020s to come up with an affordable, mass-production method. Even then, environmentalists say carbon-capture would still be too risky and require too much energy. In a more limited approach, Duke Energy of North Carolina is building a gasification plant to turn coal into gas, which would help the environment mainly by using one-third less coal but could be combined with carbon-capture.

Natural gas: Natural gas emits only about half as much greenhouse gas as coal and is found right here in North America. It provides about 20 percent of U.S. generating power, roughly the same as nuclear. What's not to like? Well, it is a fossil fuel—albeit nicer than coal—which means it has to be dredged up somehow, and eventually we will run out. It's plentiful in North America only if you accept the industry's estimates and you're willing to dig in shale, sands, and a lot of environmentally delicate places. Another concern is that prices swing more wildly than those for any other fuel. Last resort, it's probably the best of the traditional bunch.

Nuclear: Jim Riccio, Greenpeace's nuclear policy analyst, couldn't contain his scorn. "The nuclear industry calls it 'green' energy!"

In a nutshell, that's the debate. Is nuclear energy a good, renewable energy source? It doesn't emit greenhouse gases. It's nonpolluting. The planet has plenty of uranium—the key ingredient—as well as other possible fuel sources, like the radioactive mineral thorium. Famously, one of Riccio's erstwhile colleagues, Greenpeace cofounder Patrick Moore, has been proselytizing for nuclear power since 2000. In 1971, Moore had sailed into the Aleutian Islands to protest U.S. nuclear tests, but now he says that opponents are confusing nuclear reactors with nuclear weapons. His argument is that if greens want reliable energy on a large scale, nuclear and hydroelectric power are the only alternatives to polluting, nonrenewable fossil fuels like coal and oil.

The rest of Greenpeace and the environmental movement are almost apoplectic at the concept of considering nuclear energy green. How can something deadly—especially in terms of potential radiation leaks from nuclear fuel—be environmentally benign? In fact, there have been at least two significant accidents already. Radioactive gases escaped after a series of mechanical failures and human error at the Three Mile Island nuclear plant in Pennsylvania in 1979, although the amount was too small to cause any injuries. Much more catastrophically, when the cooling system failed at the Chernobyl facility in Ukraine in 1986, several dozen people were killed directly, millions more were exposed to radiation, and whole swaths of territory were closed off to human contact for years. Nuke supporters retort that safety features have improved since then, and after all, the United States has suffered no major accidents since 1979.

Potential leaks are not the only negative. Even half a century after the first nuclear plant went online in 1957, the United States still hasn't come up with a safe way to store the spent fuel rods and high-level waste that can stay radioactive for tens of thousands of years. For now, the dangerous residue languishes in temporary storage pools and casks around the country. Actually the United States in the 1980s did devise what seemed like a safe solution—storing the stuff in the Yucca Mountain in Nevada—but Congress delayed and delayed because it lacked the political will to force Nevada, or any other locality, to take the hot potato, and then scientists found safety concerns with water flow in the mountain. Most foreign countries that have nuke plants, like Switzerland and France, are struggling with the same political dilemma. A further danger is that terrorists might get their hands on nuclear material and turn even the tiniest shred into a "dirty bomb."

Nuclear power has mundane problems, too. If we want it to provide more of our energy, we'll have to build more plants, and each one takes at least a decade and multibillions of dollars. Because no new facilities have been constructed in the United States since the 1970s, the nation lacks certified contractors to do the work. Only two companies in the entire world make certain key reactor parts, such as containment centers, and they've got long waiting lists. (After all, even if the United States hasn't been in the market for these parts, countries like France, Belgium, and Sweden have been building new plants.)

Despite the hurdles, plans for about three dozen facilities are on the drawing boards. Depending on whom you ask, there's a good likelihood some of them will be built, with support from local communities and more than $20 billion in federal loan guarantees and tax credits. Alternatively, the plans are just pieces of paper, and financing is hard to come by.

Hydroelectric: So what's wrong with water? Hydroelectric power has been around since the Industrial Revolution and is the most widely used alternative fuel, accounting for about 7 percent of American energy generation. It's clean, nonpolluting, and renewable, and it's a big component of my green power in New York.

Now, about a hundred entrepreneurs worldwide are trying to expand this concept from rivers to the oceans, by installing underwater turbines to tap in to the movement of waves, currents, or tides. Another approach—still theoretical—is to use warm, surface seawater to boil a second liquid, which would then power a generator. In yet a different pilot project, a grocery store and parking garage in New York City began getting power from the tides of the East River in 2008.

But green as water power is—literally in some cases—it isn't always good for the environment. No one really knows how the ocean turbines would affect marine life and ecology—along with fishing boats and surfers. And Mother Nature might not cooperate: the New York City turbine had to be redesigned after a storm snapped the blades. As for old-fashioned river-dam hydropower, it can wreak ecological and animal havoc. Environmentalists have been fighting for years to shut down dams on the Snake River in Washington State that have destroyed the breeding patterns and population of one of the world's greatest runs of wild salmon. Even the famously secretive and development-minded Chinese government now admits that the construction of the humungous Three Gorges Dam, by dramatically changing the courses of several rivers, has flooded some areas, deprived others of needed water, triggered landslides, increased water pollution, and put fish populations at risk.

Biomass: Garbage isn't just garbage. If the methane from manure and natural waste is a major contributor to climate change, it also can be a major source of fuel; in fact, it's one of the most common sources in state alternative energy programs. Typically, the waste is either heated or broken down by bacteria in special containers, producing a mix of gases (including the infamous methane) known as bio-gas, which can then be used like natural gas to run an electrical generator. The carbon dioxide that's released in the process is the same that would have been released anyway through decomposition—at least, in theory. As a bonus, any liquid left from processing can go back to the farms for fertilizer. Our ancestors knew this, when they burned peat and dried animal dung for fuel. Some enviros are uneasy, however, about the theoretical justification and the carbon emissions in biofuel processes.

Solar: Solar energy is like the cute little girl at Mommy and

Daddy's dinner party. Everyone thinks she's adorable, but no one expects her to add much to the conversation.

So with solar. In the abstract, no one is against a flexible, unlimited fuel supply that doesn't pollute and doesn't produce carbon emissions. It can be generated in big industrial configurations, known as concentrating solar power (usually through arrays of solar mirrors and dishes that concentrate the sun's rays to heat a liquid that drives an electric generator, just like any steam-generated electricity) or on a single rooftop (with photovoltaic panels that use particular materials, mainly silicon, that can generate electricity directly from sunlight via a process occurring naturally in those materials). There's also solar thermal power, for hot water.

Sure, skeptics scoff, but how about nighttime, winter, cloudy days, and all the other times when there isn't much sun? And it's true that some places will be able to obtain more of their energy from solar power than others; that's just the way geography is. Nevertheless, every spot on earth gets some sunlight. Consider that Germany, which enjoys fewer than 1,600 hours of sunshine in a typical year—less than half the amount in warm, sunny San Diego, California—has more installed solar power than any other country. (That impressive installation rate is largely thanks to government subsidies, not the level of sunlight, of course, but subsidies don't make technology work. They only make it affordable.) Anyway, for the times when there isn't enough sun, virtually all solar-using homeowners worldwide have access to conventional power as a backup.

The biggest problem for solar is cost, not sunlight. (This will be discussed more thoroughly in chapter 7.) Setting up a rooftop solar-panel system typically runs $20,000 to $45,000, some of which can be offset by federal and state tax credits. Depending on electricity usage, size of the home, and the specific state's tax breaks, a solar customer might save $1,000 a year in utility bills. Unfortunately, it's a circular problem. The best way to bring down solar's cost is to get more people to use it, because economies of scale will enable manufacturers to churn out each PV panel more cheaply. However, people won't use the technology because it's expensive. At the time that the federal government passed its biggest sets of tax credits, in fall 2008 and again in winter 2009, solar was providing less than one-tenth of 1 percent of U.S. energy needs, according to the Solar Energy Industries Association, the Washington, D.C.-based industry trade group.

Finally, solar triggers the classic NIMBY complaint: "not in my backyard," also known as "you're ruining my view." One common NIMBY target—for other alternative fuels as well as solar—is transmission lines. The nation would need a huge new network of power lines to transmit the solar (or other) energy from the areas where it's most plentiful to the rest of us. Such a network could cost $100 billion, and the lines are—well—ugly. What's surprising is that NIMBY protests sometimes come from greens. In addition to the transmission lines, they fret that solar mirror arrays, which are often set up in the desert using steam turbines, can disrupt wildlife habitats and strain the meager water supply. (The critics usually don't object to individual rooftop panels.) Those aren't trivial complaints, but gee, if even solar power isn't green enough, what is?

Wind: Wind shares a lot of solar's attributes. It's renewable, clean, nonpolluting, non-carbon-emitting, and plentiful, in the right locations. As with solar, individuals can put the apparatus (a turbine or small windmill) on their roof, and the apparatus sends electricity straight into a battery or circuit box. The cost might be similar to that of solar or up to double, with the same tax breaks.

Availability is the main difference. If everyone gets enough sunlight to provide power some of the time, most people actually don't get enough wind. The ideal setup is a long, flat roof with few other buildings nearby, regular wind speeds of at least nine miles per hour, and a half-acre of open land. Cities are just about the worst place to try installing a wind apparatus, because trees and the varying building heights cause turbulence that make a turbine operate inefficiently. Best of all are the wide-open spaces in the center of the country, particularly in the Great Plains, plus less-populated areas along the seaboards. And even the luckiest-positioned wind-farmers will need a conventional power backup for more than half their needs.

Accordingly, wind is most likely to be harnessed in big industrial farms with turbines the height of a 20-story building, which will then transmit energy—through those tacky transmission lines—to less-windy locations. And it works: wind has been growing faster than any other power source in the United States. T. Boone Pickens, in addition to promoting natural gas-powered cars, promised in 2008 to invest $10 billion to build the world's largest wind farm, in Texas, although he shrank that to three or four small farms after the global economy began to collapse.

So wind is the perfect environmental answer? Sigh. Nope. The hulking turbines can be noisy and an eyesore, which naturally brings up NIMBY. Protestors led by the Kennedy family fought for eight years (and still going, as this book went to press) to block a wind farm five miles off the coast of Cape Cod in part because, they said, it would ruin the milieu. (Okay, they had more serious concerns about disrupting fishing, too, but they raised the milieu argument a lot.)

Then there's the bird issue. Numerous birds and bats have been killed by the huge, spinning arms of turbines and windmills. The Humane Society doesn't know exactly how many, "because it's hard to retrieve bodies," said John Hadidian, the society's director of urban wildlife programs, but he's sure there are "fairly high mortalities." This point is a bit too fine even for Bruce Friedrich of PETA. "We are at the eleventh hour" in terms of climate change, he burst out when I asked him. "We are watching species extinction unlike anything that's ever been seen before in modern history. We need to get serious about wind energy and solar energy and pure renewable sources." By easing the threat of climate change and lessening the need to destroy animal habitats in order to dig up fossil fuels, Friedrich added, wind energy "probably helps exponentially more animals than it harms." For his part, Hadidian suggested attaching a device to turbines and windmills that could scare birds away, such as a strobe light that would make the blades more visible, or "fine-tuning the noise these things make." Europe ameliorates the problem with slower-moving blades.

Perhaps no place on earth is as fossil fuel-free as the wind-blown Danish island of Samsø. According to an article in *The New Yorker* in July 2008, the hardy people of that island produce all their energy from renewable sources, with enough left to sell. They have eleven large land-based wind turbines, a dozen small ones, and ten offshore. Biomass plants burn wood chips and straw from "fallen trees that previously would have been left to rot" and from "wheat stalks that would previously have been burned in the fields." Also, some farmers run their cars and tractors on canola oil that they grow and press themselves. (Hmm, how much energy would it take to pack up all my stuff and move there?)

Meanwhile, those of us not living on Samsø are inundated with advice. Lower your thermostat in winter. Raise your thermostat in summer. Keep your thermostat away from outside walls. Keep your furniture away from outside walls. Turn off lights if you leave a room even for a minute. Use motion sensors to turn off the lights automatically. Use CFL bulbs for those lights. Insulate your home. Plant a garden on your roof. Use power strips on your electricity-eating gizmos. Unplug the gizmos. Wash your clothes in warm-cold water. Follow all the dinner instructions at the beginning of this chapter. And I've left out the 988 other pieces of advice for everything from your toilet to your TV, your laundry to your laptop; you can find them in any how-to-be-green book. One episode of the TV show *Law & Order* featured a Manhattan family that tried to avoid having any carbon footprint whatsoever by shutting off the electricity hookup to their apartment, never using the elevator even though they lived on the ninth floor, buying only locally grown food, and even eschewing toilet paper. (The mom ended up murdered when she sneaked out to a local bar to use the bathroom and its toilet paper, so maybe the zero-footprint bit was going too far.)

I'm sure these are good ideas that would truly help mitigate the severity of climate change, save fossil fuels, save trees, save animals, preserve a lot of natural landscapes, and keep our water and air clean. I'm even sure that most of them, individually, aren't all that hard to do (except the toilet paper ban). I'm also sure that we would go crazy if we tried to remember and follow even a quarter of them. (For one thing, how are you supposed to fit a garden along with the solar panels and the wind turbines on your roof?)

So we pick and choose, and we all have different reasons for choosing which green steps we take and which we ignore. In my case, I have trained myself—with great effort—to turn my computer off when I am leaving the house for a few hours or absolutely, positively going to bed for the night. However, I insist on keeping it on all the rest of the time, no matter what else I'm doing, because flashes of brilliant insight can hit me at any moment and I must rush to the keyboard to preserve them. (Yes, I know I could write my brilliant ideas on paper, but trees have to be cut down to produce the paper, and petroleum must be pumped to manufacture the plastic for my pen . . . Okay, there really is no environmental excuse for leaving my computer on.)

But wait: would it in fact be better for the environment if I left the computer running all the time, rather than forcing it to warm up whenever I restart it? The book *A Good Life* sniffs that "In reality, computers should not be in the home at all; as a PC warms up it gives off potentially harmful, volatile organic compounds that later cool and find their way into household dust." And the authors of that book undoubtedly wrote their manuscript with a quill pen.

Jessica Philips agonizes about bringing individual water bottles to the park for her son's birthday party. Conscientious environmentalists know that gallons of oil go into making, filling, shipping, and refrigerating each bottle, all of which is wasted if the bottle is tossed. One year, Philips tried reusable cups instead: she gave the kids cups shaped like soccer balls, which they could take home as party favors, and then filled the cups from a couple of huge plastic kegs of water. "It was a pain in the neck, lugging those kegs from the car," she said. "And the kegs have to go in the trash anyway. I don't think I would do it again." Yet she's not happy about reverting to the individual bottles. "I did have a little bit of a drum in my head about using all those bottles."

Nancy Hwa confessed that she just can't do without air conditioning in muggy Washington, D.C. To minimize her sinning, "I try to keep the temperature relatively high, 78. In springtime, when it starts getting warm, I use the window fans as long as I can. I keep my shades drawn during the day, because the living room gets a lot of afternoon sun." Nevertheless, there's no getting around it: "I feel guilty."

I feel guilty. That's what I kept hearing, and this was from people who already are far greener than average, people who buy recycled goods, ride mass transportation, and eat organic food. I heard it in the tortured justifications over using gas to go camping or emitting carbon to fly to an environmental conference. It was part of the debate over vegetarianism. We know we can't do everything, yet the constant drumbeat of Web sites, books, magazines, TV shows, and lists makes us feel as if we're never doing enough. *A Good Life* hits its readers with page after page asking: "Is it OK...to dry-clean your clothes?" "Is it OK...to have a lawn?" "Is it OK...to use tampons?" (*Tampons?*)

One way some people try to assuage their guilt is with carbon offsets. Essentially, consumers buy offset credits equal to a certain amount of carbon emissions, and the companies and organizations selling the offsets give the proceeds to alternative energy, reforestation, and other environmental projects that, they hope, will keep out of the air the same amount of greenhouse-gas emissions that the original purchasers are trying to offset. For instance, TerraPass, an offset company headquartered in San Francisco, might use some of its income from selling offsets to help a dairy farmer pay for biomass equipment, said Erik Blachford, TerraPass's CEO. Or a bank might agree to make a start-up loan to a wind farm if the entrepreneur could show a steady income stream from offsets. Probably the classic example is tree-planting. Carbonfund, a Washington, D.C.-based non-profit, finances programs that plant trees in Nicaragua, China, and Louisiana.

Customers most often offset their driving, but they can apply the credits to almost anything that uses fuel, including their home, airplane flights, and special occasions like weddings. The organizers of the 2007 Academy Awards gave each performer and presenter an offset supposedly equal to the emissions from one year in the life of a celebrity, an amount that must be so huge that it would replant the entire Amazon rain forest five times over. The offset companies have online calculators to help customers figure out how much carbon dioxide is emitted by the activity they're offsetting and then translate that into dollars—for example, $30 annually for the typical American car, according to Carbonfund; $50 at TerraPass. However, people can buy more or less than their specific emission.

To skeptics, the concept reeks of a rotten lunch, not a free one. At a public hearing held by the Federal Trade Commission in early 2008, panelists questioned whether the money was just paying for green projects that would have happened anyway. Critics also wonder how much of the offset income goes to administration and profits rather than emissions reduction. Tree-planting comes in for particular scorn, because it could take decades for the trees to grow big enough to soak up much carbon. Another concern: a profligate energy-guzzler would feel so virtuous about getting an offset that he or she would negate the whole thing by buying a new SUV. The most famous example of binge-offsetting may be Al Gore, who in 2007 revealed that he bought offsets to compensate for the fact that his ten-thousand-square-foot Tennessee house used about twenty times as much electricity and natural gas as the average U.S. home. (In fairness, the former vice president gets a lot of that household energy from wind, solar, geothermal, and biomass sources.)

Of course, Blachford and Carbonfund's president, Eric Carlson, dispute most of these criticisms. Is the money being wasted on projects that need no help? "We don't just go in there and buy random credits," Blachford said. "You get into it with the farmer; you have to do a real financial analysis. We routinely see projects that we decide not to pursue, if we think there's some question about whether this would have been done anyway." How much money actually reaches a project? Blachford said 80 percent of a customer's fee, and Carlson said 90 percent; however, both companies include administrative costs like monitoring, publicity, and some salaries in their effectiveness percentages, so it's impossible to know the real answer. Is tree-planting an inefficient offset? Blachford actually thinks so—and TerraPass doesn't sponsor any—but Carlson, in defense, pointed to the side benefits of reforestation, like "clean air, clean water, and habitat restoration." As for the supposed SUV-driving offset-waster, Blachford and Carlson claimed that they've never seen such a phenomenon and that it doesn't make sense anyway. In annual surveys, TerraPass customers are sixty times more likely than the general population to bike to work, nearly twenty times as likely to own a hybrid, and seventy times more likely to install solar panels, Blachford said, so why would they suddenly switch lifestyles and buy an SUV?

The consensus among activists seems to be that an offset is like chicken soup: it can't hurt, but it doesn't substitute for real medicine, or, in this case, real reductions in energy usage.

Do you still feel guilty about the fuel you're consuming? You can follow Alex Steffen's philosophy—which the author Thomas Friedman shares—that any actions we take in daily life are insignificant compared with the size of the climate crisis, and it's much more important to be out lobbying and petitioning than counting kilowatts. Consumer pressure really can make a difference. In 2002, environmental groups criticized Dell Inc. for not doing enough to get its computers recycled. Today, Dell is considered a leader in reducing its carbon footprint, and it runs a tree-planting program with Carbonfund.

So don't go crazy about using electricity. In fact, use lots of it to send letters, write e-mails, and make phone calls to politicians.

CHAPTER FIVE

BEYOND APARTHEID AND TOBACCO: REDEFINING SOCIAL INVESTING

During the 1970s, officials from five Protestant denominations started raising questions about the church investments they were overseeing. "They wondered whether it really reflected their values to be, on the one hand, making money for future pensions, versus having money in companies that were doing things that made them uncomfortable," recalled Laura Berry, executive director of the Interfaith Center on Corporate Responsibility (ICCR), a New York-based shareholder activist organization representing about three hundred religious institutions. In particular, the Protestant officials felt uncomfortable investing in companies that did business in apartheid-era South Africa. Some of them said, "We all own positions in GM. Let's talk to GM about pulling their investments out of South Africa." When GM turned the group down, they filed resolutions for a shareholder vote.

From moral qualms like that grew a $2.7 trillion movement known as socially responsible investing (SRI), accounting for about 11 percent of all U.S. investments today, according to the Social Investment Forum, a trade group. (Warning: any dollar figures cited in this chapter are from late 2008, unless stated otherwise, and these figures change minute-by-minute.) This movement includes mutual funds, venture capital, bank deposits, separate accounts for the super-rich, and big institutional and pension funds. The basic idea is the same one behind buying recycled paper or boycotting Wal-Mart—that is, use your money only to support companies and products you believe are making the world a better place. You can do it by shopping, and you also can do it by investing.

The earliest SRI groups, like the churches in the 1970s, avoided companies involved in the gambling, tobacco, alcohol, and weapons businesses, as well as South Africa. Since then the criteria have mushroomed to embrace just about every liberal cause an activist can name, plus a few conservative and religious ones, from avoiding companies that use sweatshops to shunning banks that pay interest, from halting climate change to fighting terrorism, from boycotting companies that don't provide health care to seeking out those with independent boards of directors. Regarding South Africa, at least, SRI seemed to work. By the mid-1980s, some one hundred U.S. cities, states, counties, and universities had voted to end or restrict their investments in the country, and an equal number of American companies had shut down their South African operations. The international pressure and isolation intensified, until apartheid was dismantled. In 1994, Nelson Mandela was elected the country's first black president, in its first multiracial election.

In many ways, ethical investing is easier than ethical shopping, because it's more flexible. Anyone with a car must buy gasoline, but no one has to invest in an oil company. Surely it's simpler to stop buying a stock than to stop eating steak. Moreover, less effort is involved. You don't need to go from store to store reading ingredients. After you've made your initial investment decisions, the stocks can just sit there, largely unchanged, for years. (In fact, experts advise against constant in-and-out trading.) Best of all, it would seem that no juggling is necessary. Ethical investors can find plenty of funds that screen out companies based on *all* their values: no tobacco, no weapons, no Sudan, no nukes, no labor violations, no environmental problems, whatever.

Sorry, but you can't avoid juggling. If the perfect company doesn't exist in the shopping mall, what makes you think it exists anywhere else in the business world? If you were to insist on 100-percent purity—if you filtered out every company with even a dollar's worth of involvement in tobacco, nuclear power, Pentagon contracts, business connected with Darfur or Myanmar, or alcohol, plus any recorded complaints of environmental spills, labor troubles, discrimination lawsuits, or use of sweatshops overseas—how many companies do you think would be left? Just as with shopping, investors have to select which ethical criteria to put first and which to drop.

Actually, investment juggling may be even *tougher* than the shopping version, because cost plays a much bigger role. The main point of shopping is to acquire an item; acquiring it cheap is a nice but secondary benefit. However, the main point of investing is to make money, and ever since SRI began, financial pros have debated whether ethical screens inherently cut into profits. The classic credo is that investment decisions should be based purely on business factors, such as the company's balance sheet, competitive environment, quality of management, potential liabilities, and new-product pipeline. An investor who looks at anything other than straight bottom-line considerations—does the company use recycled materials? does it allow human-rights organizations to monitor the conditions in its subcontractors' Asian factories?—is by definition not putting profits first and therefore cheating himself or herself. By the same token, any money that a company diverts from its core business—for example, to buy recycled paper that costs more than regular paper or pay above-market wages to workers in its Chinese sweatshops—is money that's not going to the bottom line and therefore is stealing from investors' deserved returns. Thus, those who believe in this classic approach will argue that socially responsible investors are going to have to do one more bit of juggling: you have to choose between ethics and returns.

Now, if you're still interested, and you've got some spare cash, let's see if we can find the perfect stock or mutual fund.

As of July 2008, Calvert Group oversaw $6 billion in twenty-one SRI funds, including large-company stocks, midsize companies, small companies, international stocks, bonds, an index fund, alternative energy, and funds that specialize according to risk. You might think that was enough variety. Nope. "There are always investors that say, 'You should consider this issue and that issue,'" said Paul Hilton, Calvert's director of advanced equity research. "If we try to respond to every one-off issue, there wouldn't be anything to invest in." Nevertheless, two months after Hilton and I talked, Calvert announced a twenty-second SRI fund, a Global Water Fund that would seek "utility, infrastructure, and technology companies active in managing water resources." That's not to be confused with companies that use water as an energy source, such as hydroelectric companies; they would be part of the Global Alternative Energy Fund.

Calvert's repertoire illustrates the variety but also the limits of social investing, just how far it can be tailored to match the wide range of humanity's ethical concerns. Typically, a collection of SRI funds starts with the Grand Old Bans, the "sin stocks" that originally inspired the founding churches of the ICCR: no tobacco, liquor, gambling, or weapons. While not every SRI manager applies all these screens, they are the closest thing to a common denominator. "They're part of our tradition," said Joseph F. Keefe, president and chief executive of Pax World Management Corp., which has about $2.7 billion in SRI money. In 2006, Pax actually shed bans against alcohol and gambling stocks, arguing that those taboos were tied to the narrow religious and temperance origins of SRI, while Pax is, as Keefe put it, a "secular fund" with an emphasis on environmental sustainability. Nevertheless, Pax still avoids tobacco and weapons, which it sees as more directly related to sustaining life. "Those products, if used as directed, will kill you," Keefe explained.

Once the boozers, smokers, gamblers, and gun-makers are gone, SRI funds usually look at corporate track records in a half-dozen areas often grouped together as ESG—or environmental, social, and governance issues—which involves a mix of screening out "bad" companies and seeking "good" ones. The most common concerns are their U.S. labor relations, employee benefits, environmental record, treatment of workers in countries where wages are low, product safety, impact on the local community, management structure, and shareholder rights.

Standard liberal causes in the main, but governance, or the G in ESG, seems like an oddball. These are hard-core business matters, the kind corporate raiders used to raise before launching ferocious bids to take over a company, topics like having stockholders vote on the pay of top executives, or appointing board members who aren't chummy with the CEO. Although they may be admirable business ideas, why should someone who cares about climate change waste time on management structure? "Good governance strategies will take care of the environment and society," Laura Berry of the ICCR replied. Consider the issue of whether the chief executive of a company should also be the board chair. If an SRI shareholder raised questions about the dumping of pollutants in a local river, a board chair who hadn't been running the company while the dumping was going on probably would be more willing to investigate than an insider would be. "It is almost impossible for a board to have courage if the top manager and the chair are the same person," Berry said.

Over time, certain issues wane—especially if companies have mended their ways in response to pressure—and new ones appear. (The name of this philosophy also has shifted; some funds now call it sustainable and responsible investing, managing to keep the initials, or just sustainable investing, forgoing the initials.) In recent years, the environment has burgeoned as a priority, particularly climate change. Obviously, no one shuns South Africa any more. Berry said that shareholder efforts to drop food giant Nestlé, because of how the manufacturer aggressively marketed powdered infant formula in developing countries in the 1970s and 1980s, also have pretty much ended; however, many consumer boycotts continue.

While the first church groups targeted classic liberal causes, and most SRI funds still lean leftward, the concept can be adopted for all sorts of issues. Sarah Steelman, the Republican treasurer of Missouri from 2005 to 2009, wanted to create a "terror-free fund," to avoid companies that have a financial relationship with countries on the federal government's list of state sponsors of terrorism—which at the time we talked, in 2008, consisted of Cuba, Iran, North Korea, Sudan, and Syria. "We are engaged in a war," Steelman told me. "The economic sanctions that are placed on those countries mean an American can't do business in those countries. Then why are we putting literally billions of dollars in taxpayer money into companies that do business with those governments?" She used those guidelines on a $26 million account that her office directly controlled, and a number of other states also have considered "terror-free funds." However, Steelman was less successful in persuading the $6 billion Missouri State Employees Retirement System to do likewise, even though she was a trustee; then she lost a primary bid for the Republican nomination for governor, and her term as treasurer ended.

If churches can do SRI, why not mosques? The huge pools of petrodollars and the wide migration of Muslims around the world have led to a mini-boom in mutual funds, hedge funds, and banks that operate on Islamic principles. Some of the rules are standard church-SRI fare—no casinos, tobacco, alcohol, or pornography—to which they add no pork and no investments that involve charging interest. Luckily for these investors, the no-interest rule translated to a rejection of the super-risky debt gimmicks that got the rest of the financial world in trouble in 2008 and 2009.

"Group Danone is the largest purveyor of organic dairy products in the world," Amy Domini began. That would certainly seem to qualify the company for the Domini 400 Social Index, which many SRI funds use as a benchmark to decide what to invest in. Those organic products would fit right into Domini's "natural environment" category, because they help the environment by rejecting chemical fertilizers. Not so fast. Amy Domini pointed out that "20 percent of its business is bottled water, and about half of that is to people with potable water." Thus, Danone is wasting millions of barrels of petroleum to make plastic water bottles for Americans who could easily drink their own tap water. Furthermore, in 2007 the company bought a manufacturer of infant formula named Royal Numico. (Shades of Nestlé!) Now should Danone go in the index? Domini herself said yes, but Steve Lydenberg, the company's chief investment officer, disagreed. Because Lydenberg makes the investment decisions, even though Domini runs the company, he overrules her in cases like this.

So here, in the Danone conundrum, is the crux of the SRI problem: how pure do you want to be?

If your standards are too high, you may not find any companies that qualify. But if your standards are too low, how is socially responsible investing any different from ordinary investing? Boston-based Trillium Asset Management—which runs about $1 billion in SRI money for churches, endowments, foundations, nonprofits, wealthy individuals, and one mutual fund—has some clients who insist on avoiding anything tested on animals. Unfortunately, that eliminates a whole universe of otherwise ethical-seeming, nonalcohol, nondefense, nongambling, socially beneficial stocks, such as all drug companies and much of the consumer-products industry. Similarly, investors who shun any weapons connections whatsoever must swear off U.S. Treasury bills, since investing in the U.S. government helps support the Defense Department. During the financial collapse of 2008–2009, when Treasuries seemed like the only safe haven, a no-Pentagon screen could be scarier than a loaded gun.

Each of Calvert's seven ESG categories has a checklist of, on average, three to four criteria defining what a company must do to qualify for that category. Under the "product safety and impact" tag, for example, Calvert requires that companies "produce or market goods and services that enhance the health or quality of life for consumers"; "respond promptly to correct problems with product safety"; "avoid animal testing, or when testing is legally required, reduce the use of animals"; "demonstrate integrity in their advertising and labeling"; and "maintain quality control and customer satisfaction." Or another list: to qualify for the "workplace" category, companies must "demonstrate inclusive diversity policies [with] fair treatment of all employees"; "provide strong labor codes" including "comprehensive benefits" and "a record of sound employee relations"; and "have extensive employee health and safety policies" with training and "a positive safety performance record." Now for the punch line: *all* the stocks in Calvert's twenty-two mutual funds must satisfy *all* the sub-requirements (twenty-four, if you're counting) in the checklists of *all* seven of the firm's SRI categories. "That's a lot" to demand, Paul Hilton admitted.

(I'll say. I think that if I found a company so saintly that it met all twenty-four requirements, I wouldn't just buy the stock; I'd marry the CEO.)

The strict rules have cost the funds some investments Hilton wanted, like Liz Claiborne Inc. In the early 2000s, Claiborne "really was good for human rights, supply chain management, women's issues, environmental issues," Hilton recalled. "We had a very positive relationship with the company." Other consumer advocates praised the manufacturer for joining the Fair

Labor Association set up by President Bill Clinton to enforce labor standards in overseas sweatshops. So what was Calvert's problem? Claiborne had a clothing label called Crazy Horse, "which was the source of a lot of protests from the Crazy Horse family and a lot of American Indian peoples." Calvert had to dump the stock. (Hilton didn't remember how much of it Calvert owned.) By 2007 Claiborne had gotten rid of the offending line, and Calvert could bring it back.

Hilton claims the Claiborne case is a rarity. Even with the twenty-four-item checklist, he says two-thirds of the companies he evaluates pass muster, leaving an investor plenty of choices. Still, should one line of clothing eliminate a $4.6 billion company? Should bottled water outweigh all the good organic products Danone sells? "There's no company that's going to be perfect in every single score," said Cheryl Smith, executive vice president of Trillium and also chair of the Social Investment Forum. "If they are, you haven't looked hard enough." It's the same juggling act an ethical consumer faces when shopping. Whole Foods sells organic produce but fights unions. American Apparel keeps manufacturing jobs in the United States but its CEO allegedly harasses his employees. At what point do you draw the line? If you reject any company that is less than 100 percent perfect, you'll have nothing left but a few Polish light bulbs, like my neighborhood food co-op years ago.

To me, the main issue is flexibility. Calvert goes too far in demanding that every stock meet all twenty-four sub-criteria. Domini takes a better approach in juggling the relative importance of Danone's water and organic businesses, although an investor might disagree with the final verdict. It's okay to have twenty-four criteria, or even 124, as long as there's some give-and-take. An SRI manager could require that a company meet two-thirds of the criteria, or three-fourths. Or maybe there would be weighted voting, with some criteria more important than others. In the case of Liz Claiborne, I'd be tempted to keep the stock, unless the Crazy Horse label was a major portion of its business.

However, that gets us to the other juggling problem with values investing. Each investor has a different set of values, and the trick for the Calverts and Dominis of the world is to create enough funds to satisfy most classes of investors without trying to create a separate fund for each customer. I'm not a Native American; I can't viscerally appreciate how the name "Crazy Horse" might be insulting. As a feminist, on the other hand, I would want to boycott a company making "Pimp" brand clothes. But what if that company used a union work force in the United States and had a great environmental record? What if the "Pimp" label accounted for only 1 percent of the company's total business?

Thus, the boycotts of Claiborne and Danone. Historically, the easiest, default choice for SRI funds has been to be super-pure, because the risks of angering some bloc of customers can be high. But pressured by over-juggling, the funds have begun to let a few balls drop. In the mid-2000s, acknowledging that perfection is impossible, both Pax and Calvert softened their absolute rejections of nuclear energy—and were promptly blasted for it by greens. Under the new approach, Pax will invest in a utility that already owns nuclear plants—but not a utility that is constructing new ones—if nuclear contributes just a small portion of the company's power supply. Calvert will allow similar investments in two of its SRI pools, the Global Alternative Energy and International Opportunities funds. "If that utility is a leader in wind and solar, if that utility is trying to control emissions, applying a zero [nuclear] tolerance screen is cutting off your nose to spite your face," Keefe of Pax explained.

When I asked Cheryl Smith for an example of a tough juggling act where Trillium ultimately kept its stock holding, she cited 3M Company. On the negative side, she said (reading from a 2004 report), it tests items on animals, it had a very

small amount of weapons-related sales, it had "links to genetically modified organisms"—"that could mean that some of
the ingredients in its products are genetically modified," she
explained—and it had some production facilities in a country
tied to a repressive regime. So how did 3M manage to stay on
Trillium's recommended list? "The weapons business they have
is tiny. It doesn't sell animal products. On the environment,
everything else we have, other than indirect links to GM organisms, they're very good. They're not major polluters. They've
got an excellent record for employees; they're often in the lists
of top companies to work for. They produce useful products.
There's a whole variety of ways in which that company is good."
Of course, Smith pointed out, for an absolute purist on animal testing, GM organisms, or weapons—a vegan or a Quaker,
say—even those minuscule stains might render 3M untouchable.

Apparently, it's not so easy to keep track of all these dos and
don'ts. The Securities and Exchange Commission, in a routine investigation in 2003 and 2004, found that Pax managers
had bought ten holdings that violated the firm's standards. A
couple of the companies had nonmilitary Pentagon contracts,
while another seemed to be an oil company. Keefe, who was
not at Pax at the time, said he couldn't figure out how all that
happened.

Some funds take a different juggling approach, seeking what
they call "best in class." The idea is that if you want to diversify
across the broad economy, to have a toehold in a lot of industries, your screening may have to be relative rather than absolute. If you desire any oil holdings at all, you're going to have
to hold your nose and find the least-bad, even if they might not
meet all your criteria otherwise. Keefe likens this to grading on
a curve: "We try to find companies whose performance, programs, and policies are better than their peers." Domini does
that in most industries, but it still has a total ban on tobacco
and Big Oil. This may turn out to be an easier way to juggle, but

it really just shifts the question from whether to avoid a particular company to whether to avoid an industry. Which industries do I feel so strongly about having in my portfolio that I will sacrifice some purity to squeeze them in?

Joseph Keefe was eager to brag about the stellar profits of Pax's best SRI funds. For example, he pointed out that the Pax fund that invests in junk bonds—bonds of companies in such weak financial condition that they have to pay super-high interest rates to attract investors—was listed in the top 1 percent of all junk bond funds (both SRI and standard) for 2007 by Lipper Analytical Services, one of the two main sources for the evaluation of mutual fund investment returns. Furthermore, Keefe said, the Pax balanced fund (which owns a mix of stocks and bonds) was highly ranked in 2008 by the other respected rating service, Morningstar. Of course, these ratings say nothing about the investment returns of the six other Pax SRI funds, as well as the years before and after 2007 for the junk bonds and before and after 2008 for the balanced fund.

The information Keefe is revealing—and what he isn't—exemplifies the two sides of the big debate over socially responsible investment returns. Do investors inevitably sacrifice some profits by injecting nonfinancial issues into their decisions? (And is that what all the missing Pax returns would show?) Or—as the 2007 junk-bond and 2008 balanced-fund data would seem to prove—is being socially responsible actually good for a company's bottom line in the long run?

It might seem obvious that ethical investing must hurt returns. There are just so many factors you can juggle, and if you focus on one, something else has to give. If the first thing you're looking for is a good record on pollution, then you can't be looking at profits as your first priority.

An oft-cited case is ExxonMobil. It's the biggest company on the planet, with a credit rating of gold. Even as oil prices collapsed during the devastating recession of 2008-2009, it managed to remain the world's most profitable company for the third year in a row, according to *Fortune* magazine. However, it's an oil company. It makes money by selling a product that increases global warming and contributes to a vast amount of other environmental damage. Furthermore, Exxon spent all those years lobbying against emissions controls and claiming that climate change was a myth, and it still refuses to invest more than pennies in alternative energy. No socially responsible investor could come anywhere near it; yet that investor would have missed a strong run-up in the company's stock price in 2007-2008 that far outpaced the general market.

As the chief investment officer of RegentAtlantic Capital in New Jersey, Christopher Cordaro spends his time managing the fortunes of multimillionaires. Now and then, one of these clients asks to screen out investments for ethical reasons. "It's not my place to say that's silly," Cordaro said. "My job is to understand that's important to them, and then quantify what that decision means in their portfolio. Any time you're shrinking the universe of acceptable investment possibilities, you've got to be giving something up."

Being virtuous also has overhead costs. It's a lot more difficult to determine if a company secretly dumped dangerous chemicals into a nearby lake or if its subcontractor uses child labor in a sweatshop abroad, than it is to simply read the numbers in financial reports. Managers must pore through studies by human-rights organizations that investigate working conditions overseas; records of employment and environmental violations from federal, state, and local governments; legal filings; consumer boycott lists; and more. They may need to hire experts to do this. The $250 billion California Public Employees' Retirement System, known as CalPERS—the largest pension plan in the United States—paid $1 million a year for outside research services just for one particular SRI category, the human rights records of developing countries. To satisfy a client who wanted to avoid buisinesses that harm animals, Cordaro of Re-gentAtlantic spent a couple of hours going through every company in his usual list of prospects, one by one. "We don't have a database that sorts this way," he pointed out.

On top of all that, Robert Reich, the former U.S. labor secretary, criticizes socially responsible investing from a rather unusual left-wing vantage point. In his book *Supercapitalism,* Reich argues that when ethical investors try to change corporate behavior on topics like carbon emissions or workers' rights one company at a time, they are hurting their own long-range cause. Doing the right thing, then, becomes a voluntary act for individual business managers—even a bragging point—rather than standard operating procedure. "A declaration of corporate commitment to social virtue may also forestall government legislation or regulation in an area of public concern where one or more companies have behaved badly, such as transporting oil carelessly and causing a major spill or flagrantly failing to respect human rights abroad," he writes.

That sounds very nice, but I think Reich is being way too idealistic. I'll happily take an improvement in Wal-Mart's pay scale right now, even without a national hike in the minimum wage, and I suspect most Wal-Mart workers would, too. Considering the U.S. government's lousy track record in banning offshore oil drilling, approving international agreements on global warming, or ending big subsidies to factory farms, among other leftist issues, I don't care to wait for Washington to suddenly get virtue—or courage.

More significantly, Reich goes on to raise an issue that he presumably intends as a critique but that actually spotlights the heart of the SRI defense. He argues that companies shouldn't be praised for taking ethical steps that are in their best interest anyway. "McDonald's employs more humane slaughtering techniques, which prevent costly worker injuries and yield more meat. Wal-Mart has adopted 'green' packaging for its fresh produce—transparent plastics made from corn sugars—because it's cheaper than petroleum-based packaging."

SRI proponents say that's just the point. Far from eating into returns, socially responsible and sustainable behavior helps companies in the long term, and therefore there is no conflict between values investing and traditional bottom-line investing.

Labor relations are a good illustration. It's long been established that well-treated employees are more productive than an unhappy work force. If management doesn't maintain good working conditions, it risks high turnover, strikes, consumer boycotts, and a bad public image, all of which are costly.

"We're not taking our second-pick companies," Paul Hilton of Calvert insisted. Ethical investing is "an extra diligence process. We're able to identify companies with better management and lower risk."

Besides, some of the opposition to SRI isn't really about the investments themselves; it's more of a theoretical debate about whether pension funds and hired managers have the right to use unconventional criteria when investing money that other people entrust to them. In an August 2007 report, the highly respected Center for Retirement Research at Boston College warned that in such cases, "the decision-makers and the stakeholders are not the same people. The decision-makers are either the fund board or the state legislature. The stakeholders are tomorrow's beneficiaries and/or taxpayers.... The welfare of these future actors is not well represented in the decision-making process." In other words, you can do what you want with your own money, but you have no right to play corporate scold with someone else's. When I interviewed him for this book, Steven A. Sass, the center's associate director for research, allowed that these concerns might not apply to individual investors like you and me if we're willing to take an SRI risk.

Of course, the proof of all these arguments lies in hard numbers, and both sides can trot out statistics to show that SRI does or does not hurt returns. I'll just give a sampling. (If statistics and percentages make your eyes glaze over, you can skip the next two paragraphs.)

First, a few "antis." Two professors at Dartmouth College, Karen Fisher-Vanden and Karin S. Thorburn, analyzed what happened to the stock prices of companies that joined an organization dedicated to curbing climate change, either Climate Leaders or Ceres. The professors found that the companies "experience significantly negative abnormal stock returns...suggesting that 'green' expenditures crowd out growth-related investments." From his experience, Chris Cordaro figures that ethical criteria cut his clients' profits by a half-percent to 1 percent. Using the outside research for which it paid $1 million a year, CalPERS for nearly seven years prohibited investments in twenty-seven developing countries (including China) that didn't meet certain standards on child labor and government oversight. When they eased the restriction in August 2007, fund officials estimated that the ban had cost CalPERS $400 million in lost returns.

Now, the pro-SRI side: in 2003, Marc Orlitzky of the University of Sydney in Australia and Frank L. Schmidt and Sara L. Rynes of the University of Iowa did an SRI meta-analysis, or a study of multiple studies—in this case, fifty-two studies of social investing across thirty years. Their conclusion: "The meta-analytic findings suggest that corporate virtue in the form of social responsibility and, to a lesser extent, environmental responsibility is likely to pay off." Another meta-study, commissioned by the United Kingdom Environment Agency in 2004, uncovered "strong evidence that where a company has sound environmental governance policies, practices and performance, it is highly likely to result in improved financial performance" in 85 percent of the seventy studies it looked at. Even the Center for Retirement Research report, despite its qualms, concluded that a pension fund probably would have enough choices left, after screening ethically, to sniff out good investments. "Given the large number of stocks available," the report said, "the cost [in terms of lost profits]—using traditional asset pricing models—is likely to be negligible." And CalPERS—officially—still believes in SRI. "We have found that advocating for good will have a beneficial long-term impact on share value, at least indirectly, by strengthening the foundation of the economy," Clark McKinley, a spokesman for the fund, told me. He insisted that the reason for shunning the developing countries was really just hard-nosed financial risk avoidance, not bleeding-heart social concerns.

Bottom line: does socially responsible investing hurt returns? The true answer is that the question is unanswerable, and none of these analyses means anything.

Any researcher knows that statistics can be manipulated. What period of time are you studying? What yardstick are you using for comparison? Furthermore, as with all investments, returns depend on each portfolio's quirks and managers.

Since socially responsible funds tend to favor technology companies and avoid Big Oil, they did well during the tech boom of the late 1990s and suffered when tech stocks collapsed and oil prices skyrocketed in the early 2000s. Amy Domini admitted that her main mutual fund plummeted about 45 percent after the tech bubble burst and the United States invaded Iraq in 2003. "The U.S. became a war economy. A war economy turns to weapons and gold," which her fund doesn't hold, she said. By the time I interviewed her, in summer 2008, Domini said the fund's performance had been up again for the past six months. Who knows what its returns will be by the time you happen to read this.

Maybe, in the end, all that shouldn't matter. Maybe lower returns are the price an ethical investor should be prepared to pay, just as an ethical shopper might pay more for organic food.

Wayne Silby, the founding chair of Calvert, raised that argument in speaking to a group of super-rich investors in Boston in fall 2007. As he explained to me in an interview months later, this approach is only for people who can afford a bit of a loss. "Once you have enough money, the idea of doubling your returns and so on, maybe there are social benefits that you would rather emphasize," he said. "Why is it that we're so neurotic about having double-digit returns when we could still preserve our capital and do this benefit to the world?"

CHAPTER SIX

THE PEOPLE WHO MAKE OUR STUFF

For more than two decades, starting in the 1980s, the main course of most American kosher meals came from the small town of Postville in northeastern Iowa. There, a company called Agriprocessors established a slaughterhouse that carefully followed all the ritual rules. After thoroughly cleaning and refurbishing an abandoned meatpacking plant, Agriprocessors brought in rabbis to certify that the cattle and chickens were killed in the appropriate manner, with the appropriate knives, to minimize suffering.

Then in May 2008, the federal Immigration and Customs Enforcement Agency descended. Inspectors from ICE and other government agencies claimed that nearly four hundred undocumented immigrants were working at the plant, including children as young as thirteen, many of them under dangerous conditions, without proper safety training, cheated out of overtime pay, forced to work twelve hours at a stretch, yelled at, sexually harassed, and pressured to keep working even after they were injured on the job. The Iowa attorney general ultimately charged the company with more than nine thousand violations of child-labor laws, while the state labor department issued thirty-one citations for safety problems and fined the company $10 million for breaking state wage laws. On top of that, PETA twice filmed surreptitious videos showing workers slicing animals with painful, nonkosher cuts. All this followed hundreds of citations and fines for environmental, health, and safety violations over the previous couple of years.

Within six months, Agriprocessors's chief executive was forced out and then arrested for harboring undocumented immigrants; the Orthodox Union threatened to withdraw its official kosher certification; the Conservative Jewish movement issued its *hekhsher tzedek* label regarding the treatment of animals, workers, and the environment; and Agriprocessors filed for bankruptcy.

News reports jumped on the irony of a company getting the highest religious certification for its treatment of animals while its workers were treated in the lowest possible ways. But Agriprocessors is unusual only because of its extremes, and because the public noticed. The underlying irony is all too sadly commonplace. Among the issues we liberals juggle—the ingredients in the things we buy, the energy that was used to produce them, the companies that make them, the stores from which we buy them, the means by which we travel to those stores, the companies we invest in, the impact on the planet, the impact on animals, the impact on our bodies—we almost never think about the workers who manufacture, grow, fix, ship, and sell the stuff in our lives.

Consider the Birkenstock crowd's love affair with Whole Foods. Any complaints are usually about its prices, rather than its union-busting. And when environmentalists protest the use of coal, they focus on the risk of carbon emissions, not the risk that miners will die in cave-ins.

Once upon a time, the labor movement was an integral part of the progressive political movement. Unions were a pillar of the New Deal. Folk singers such as Pete Seeger and Joan Baez sang "I Dreamed I Saw Joe Hill Last Night," about the radical union organizer of the early 1900s. Today, to write words like "labor" or "Joe Hill" in a book about left-wing activism is laughable. Unions are seen as outdated at best, corrupt at worst. The most famous labor leader in America is still Jimmy Hoffa of the Teamsters, who disappeared—presumably murdered—in 1975 and who is more often associated in the public mind with the Mafia than the minimum wage. On the campaign trail, liberal candidates view blue-collar voters as an alien species, in front of whom they have to hide their true feelings about guns, gays, God, and abortion. What happened? Why don't liberals care about working people any more?

"For a long while, the labor movement didn't do a very good job of reaching out," Stewart Acuff of the AFL-CIO answered, when I put that question to him. (He was essentially using support for U.S. unions as a rough proxy for concern for working people in general, as I've been doing to a lesser extent, which I think is fair as a starting point, though not the whole story.) "The labor movement wanted to hold itself up as an attractive place for workers to be. It took us a long time to even admit that workers had lost the right to organize and bargain collectively in this country," Acuff continued. In other words, the labor movement was damned if it did and damned if it didn't, and therefore it did little. If it tried to galvanize public support by pointing to horrible working conditions, it would be admitting that it had failed to protect workers, more than a century after the founding of the American Federation of Labor. But—as every fund-raiser and signature-collector knows—if labor leaders talked about how successful they'd been for their members, potential supporters would shrug and figure the movement didn't need their help.

Within Acuff's answer lies another explanation for the liberal-working class split. When he said that people have "lost the right to organize," he was referring to the tactics managers use to prevent unions from forming, such as firing organizers and challenging election results in court. These tactical barriers, added to the collapse of the heavily unionized manufacturing sector, have caused union membership to shrink from 35 percent of the U.S. work force in the 1950s, to 12 percent by 2006. "If we still had a union representation rate of 35 percent," said Christian Weller, the economist at the Center for American Progress who tries to buy union-made goods, "many people would look for the union label." Higher membership rates would help in two ways: more union-label merchandise would be available, because there would be more union members to make it. And more consumers would feel a kinship with those union members and their merchandise, because they, too, would belong to a union.

Instead, most American workers today look across the divide at union members and see a foreign world of privilege. About 2.6 million Americans lost their jobs in 2008, while laid-off United Auto Workers (UAW) members enjoyed a jobs bank that paid them for not working, until it was "suspended" in December of that year. The vast majority of employees at private firms have no company-sponsored retirement program or only a 401(k), forcing them to put aside their own money and trust the mercy of the stock market if they want any cushion in old age, while union contracts promise a fixed pension for as long as a retired union worker lives. Working-class solidarity? Resentment is more like it.

"Half of all workers don't have a retirement plan at all," pointed out Francis Vitagliano, a visiting scholar at Boston College's Center for Retirement Research, whom I interviewed in 2006 for a different book, about companies that drop their pension plans. Why should these people without retirement coverage feel any sympathy for unionized pilots who lose a cut of their six-figure pensions when their airlines go bankrupt? Vitagliano continued.

In part, organized labor has alienated other Americans by its own parochialism, added Carol Tucker Foreman, the consumer activist and a loyal—if frustrated—union supporter. (Her husband, Jay H. Foreman, retired as executive vice president of the United Food and Commercial Workers Union in 1996, after thirty years with that union.) "The UAW was one of the best members the consumer federation ever had," she said. "But because their industry was so unwilling to change, they ended up being perceived saying, 'You've got to buy an American car, even if it's a crummy car and even if you can buy a better Japanese car for less.'"

I think there's one more key reason liberals don't intuitively put employees' welfare into their ethical equation, and this one affects people who aren't in unions, too. Working conditions aren't merely another complication, like trying to have food that's organic plus local (which can be found together, albeit in limited varieties). Too often, worker-related values conflict with other values at such a basic level that juggling them seems irreconcilable.

For example, if you're worried about the carbon footprint from long-distance shipping, you should buy food and other goods that are grown and made close to home. However, struggling farmers, craftspeople, and factory workers in Africa, Asia, and Latin America desperately need to sell the shirts they sew and the blueberries they cultivate to American consumers in order to survive. What's more important, keeping carbon emissions low or helping starving African farmers?

Another example: if you want to preserve natural resources and limit the use of fossil fuels, you should buy as few brand-new items as possible. The environmental mantra tells us to reduce, reuse, and recycle. However, workers (both in the United States and overseas) will lose their jobs if no one purchases their output. What's more important, saving resources or saving jobs?

If you'd like to be part of a community and also get healthful, pesticide-free food, you can join a natural-foods co-op. However, at many co-ops, including mine, members do the work of stocking, cleaning, and cashiering, without pay. If I didn't join the co-op, I would presumably shop at a regular grocery store where someone—most likely a member of Jay Foreman's old union—would get paid for doing the same work that co-op members perform. Without my business, that store may hire one less worker. So by joining the food co-op, I'm contributing to the decline of organized labor and stealing a paycheck from a stock clerk, janitor, or cashier.

To make matters worse, the interests of various sets of workers—Americans and foreigners, undocumented immigrants and union members—can clash with each other. Should I support the U.S. labor movement and look for a union label on clothing, before unions disappear completely? Oh, but aren't conditions so much more dire for workers in Africa, Asia, and Latin America? Don't they need my dollars more? As a nation built on immigration, how can we shut our doors to foreigners who are no different from our own grandparents? Still, do undocumented immigrants undercut wages, thereby hurting all working people? Isn't that how Agriprocessors was able to get away with its abuse for so long, because the undocumented immigrants it hired didn't dare complain?

The foreign-versus-America debate was the one issue that infuriated Stewart Acuff of the AFL-CIO. "Would it make you feel better to buy clothes made by a fourteen-year-old girl locked in a dormitory who may or may not be abused by her employer, than it would to buy clothes by a forty-five-year-old woman making a living wage in Georgia?" he snapped at me.

When the interests of American and overseas workers collide head-on, there's an instinctual desire to protect our own, particularly in bad economic times. "The closer the impact is to people you know, the more heavily that gets weighed," said Arthur Caplan, the University of Pennsylvania ethicist. "If someone says this will impact your husband and children, that counts more than the local farmer, and the local farmer counts more than a farmer in India." Stewart Pravda saw that impact as a teenager, working in the warehouse of a coat-manufacturing company where his father was a manager. "I would unload the stuff, and each day it was from a different country—Thailand, Mongolia, Romania—whatever country was cheaper. I'm cognizant of the fact that there are really poor people elsewhere in the world that need our help," he continued. "But every job that leaves the U.S. is hard for us."

For liberals, however, there are serious political and ethical risks in tilting too sharply toward the idea of protecting American jobs. Where do you draw the line between keeping jobs for Americans, versus keeping out would-be Americans? Protectionism has some ugly cousins, including the anti-immigrant, anti-Catholic, nativist movement of the late 1800s and the right-wing America First Committee of the 1930s and 1940s that opposed the U.S. entry into World War II, with its demagogic, anti-Semitic ally, Father Charles Coughlin. Today, protectionism's most prominent supporter is the anti-Semitic, anti-immigrant Republican (and erstwhile presidential candidate) Pat Buchanan. The *New York Times,* in September 2007, ran an article about how people who used to instinctively assume that Swedish cars and German kitchen gadgets were better than American brands—that is, upper-middle-class liberals—were increasingly looking for "made in America" labels. Describing one Web site, Stillmadeinusa, created by a graduate student named Stephanie Sanzone, the article noted, "Unlike many 'Buy American' Web sites, which feature images of weeping bald eagles or quotations from Pat Buchanan, Ms. Sanzone, a Democrat, keeps her site nonpartisan."

It's bad enough to be aligning with union-busters like Whole Foods. But once you start trying to help American workers keep jobs and reduce your carbon footprint by buying local, you end up in bed with Pat Buchanan!

Well, I refuse to let right-wing politicians divide me from

any of my natural allies, and I refuse to solve my dilemmas by pitting one set of working people against another. Without being as pie-in-the-sky as the liberal dreamers I scoff at, I've got to find a way to juggle all this.

Let's start by looking at a couple of the big debates.

Debate Number One: are we exploiting workers if we buy goods made in overseas sweatshops that pay these workers just a dollar or two a day?

That question can't be answered by simply comparing salaries or working conditions. Of course working conditions, pay, benefits, safety provisions, and legal protections are far better in the United States than in developing countries. And of course, American workers need higher pay, because the cost of living in the United States is about a zillion times more than in those other countries.

By and large, reporters who have researched conditions in foreign sweatshops agree that the horrible stories we hear are true. The workers—usually young women, often children—toil sixteen or eighteen hours a day, seven days a week, under strict and sometimes humiliating supervision and the constant terror of being fired. They are verbally and sexually abused. The factories are noisy and dangerous; the company dormitories are dark, crowded, and Spartan. Their wages, paltry to begin with, sometimes are delayed or not paid at all. Nevertheless, most reporters say, it's a lot better than the alternatives of prostitution, scavenging in dumps, or starving on the family farm.

Fred Pearce, for his book *Confessions of an Eco-Sinner,* met several women who worked grueling hours in garment factories in Dhaka, Bangladesh. Some had children, left behind in their native villages, and had no idea when they'd see them again. Yet they weren't really complaining, Pearce concluded. "Back home, there wasn't enough land, and certainly not enough work, to support so many....The alarming truth was that these women, for all their pitiful surroundings, were the rich ones in their families. And it confirmed what I heard in the prawn villages around Khulna [another city in Bangladesh]— that a job in a garment factory in Dhaka was an aspiration," he writes.

The Cambodian women whom Nicholas Kristof interviewed in 2009 for the *New York Times* were even more desperate. They tried to survive by scavenging for discarded plastic cups in a dump reeking of toxic fumes, then selling the treasures for five cents a pound. "I'd love to get a job in a factory," one woman told him. "At least that work is in the shade."

But didn't talk-show cohost Kathie Lee Gifford burst into tears on national television in 1996, as news stories and consumer advocates began unraveling how her name-brand clothing was being made? Surely any ethical person would be ashamed. Some of the work was done by thirteen- and fourteen-year-olds in Honduras. Other pieces came from seamstresses less than two miles away in New York City who hadn't been paid. Abashed, Gifford vowed to raise public awareness about sweatshops. And then what happened? Wal-Mart, which had been marketing the clothes for the Gifford line, canceled its contract with the Honduran factory, and those workers *blamed* Gifford for taking away their livelihood.

To Edward Gresser, director of the Project on Trade and Global Markets for the Progressive Policy Institute, a liberal think tank, it's "cotton farmers in West Africa [and] textile workers in low-income Arab and Muslim states" who benefit most from globalization and free trade, when they can export their cotton to Western textile mills and their cotton clothing to American shoppers.

Developing-country manufacturing is one of the few topics about which even gung-ho ethical guides admit to something less than total self-assurance. *The Rough Guide to Shopping with a Conscience,* after detailing some of the awful conditions in factories that make all sorts of things for big U.S. and European companies, warns that:

> the alternative for a worker is either even worse pay from a domestic firm, or rural work. The latter, despite Western middle class idealization of 'simple' countryside living, usually involves grinding poverty and hard labor—hence the tens of millions of subsistence farmers voluntarily leaving home each year to head for the cities and factories.

The very fact that the ethical guides and I have to go through all these elaborate justifications is proof that shirts made in China, Bangladesh, Honduras, Vietnam, Cambodia, Ghana, and elsewhere aren't just shirts. I don't want my money lining the pockets of factory managers and owners who cheat workers in any country. But in the end, I have to take my cue from the people I'm supposedly helping. If the women in Bangladesh and Cambodia are thrilled to get factory jobs, then I will support them. I will not cringe at a foreign label.

Debate Number Two: are we hurting the planet if we buy goods shipped thousands of miles from developing countries?

Luckily, sometimes there is no conflict between reducing greenhouse-gas emissions and helping laborers overseas. As chapter 3 discussed, locally produced food and other items aren't always more energy-frugal than imported varieties. Some parts of the world—including impoverished parts—are simply better suited to growing bananas or grazing sheep, for reasons of climate, soil, and water resources.

But if something can be produced, at reasonable environmental cost, in a struggling foreign country and also nearby, what do you do? Take apples. With so many varieties grown right here in New York, New Jersey, and Washington State, it would seem an environmental crime to obtain apples from another country an ocean away. However, South Africa exports apples through a special program to help the desperately poor of that nation, according to *The Rough Guide to Shopping with a Conscience.* By buying this fruit, the book says, Americans "support a number of positive initiatives and 'empowerment projects' including creating opportunities for landless workers to 'become co-owners of fruit farms,' a scheme recently praised by Nelson Mandela among others." Who wants to disagree with Nelson Mandela? Moreover, those South African apples have been certified as fair-trade, so that American apple-eaters pay a little extra to ensure that South African apple-pickers are treated decently. Can we be sure of the same with New York or Washington apples?

For that matter, even if importing from overseas always cost more in emissions, two researchers from the International Institute for Environment and Development, a British think tank, argue that we shouldn't base our decisions solely on carbon. We should also consider "social and economic development aspects," write James MacGregor and Bill Vorley. Yes, they concede, fresh food from Africa probably will be shipped by air. But "an estimated 1-1.5 million people's livelihoods depend in part on the supply chain linking production on African soil and consumption in the UK." Using similar reasoning, the governments of Uganda and Kenya protested in 2007 when the British retail chain Tesco, as part of a carbon-awareness program, started slapping little stickers of airplanes on products that were shipped by air, according to *BusinessWeek* magazine. "The moment consumers look at this sticker, they would stigmatize those products," the magazine quotes the Kenyan agricultural attaché to Britain, Abraham Barno, as saying.

•   •   •

In the real world, consumers often can avoid these tough choices between unionized American workers and impoverished workers abroad, between helping the environment and helping to keep intact global supply chains, for the simple reason that there are few alternatives. Just try buying a pair of jeans with a "union-made in the USA" label.

You might start with the Stillmadeinusa Web site. It lists dozens of U.S. clothing manufacturers, churning out everything from kids' jackets and bridesmaid gowns to women's swimsuits. You want jeans? In 2009 thirteen U.S.-made brands had jeans for less than one hundred dollars a pair, mainly for adults, and seventeen more offered them at higher prices. But the site could confirm only that a half-dozen always used U.S.-made fabric, and there was no indication whether any were union shops. Moreover, these were little-known names; the site admitted that the most famous labels—Levi's, Lee, Wrangler, Gap, Lands' End, and L.L. Bean—probably are imported. When I asked Stewart Acuff what kind of jeans he and his family owned, he admitted that "we try to find union-made in America but it's very hard to do. Me and my family sometimes wear nonunion-made articles of clothing." (He wouldn't specify which articles.)

Men have a few more options when they need a suit. President Barack Obama made sure to get the tuxedo for his inaugural ball from Hartmarx, which turns out the Hart, Schaffner & Marx and Hickey Freeman labels at union plants in Illinois and New York. The company filed for bankruptcy three days after the inauguration but fortunately found a buyer that promised to try to keep the American factories humming. Christian Weller says he can purchase Ralph Lauren suits made by Teamsters members in Canada. (Nevertheless, he had to check the label of the jacket he was wearing when I interviewed him, because, he said, he had bought it in a hurry.)

Shirts and shoes to wear with the suit are another matter.

"I couldn't find a button-down shirt made in the U.S. I've given up," Stewart Pravda said. For running shoes, Acuff could suggest only that New Balance and Saucony "were the last to leave [U.S. soil], and I think they both manufacture some of their shoes in the United States." Of course there's American Apparel for high-fashion T-shirts, if you don't mind the sexual harassment and you don't care that it's not unionized. Writing for the *New Yorker*'s "Style Issue" in 2009, children's book author Patricia Marx wandered the fashionable streets of Manhattan seeking clothing and other goods made in the U.S.A. While she found more than I expected, they were often the pricier versions of mass-market cousins from overseas. "Take the Fender guitar," she writes. "Models from the firm's plant in Mexico start at five hundred dollars, whereas the varieties made in Corona, California—hand-built of superior materials—start at a thousand."

And how about buying a fuel-efficient car, or harder yet, a hybrid? Actually, a few American-made choices do exist. For the 2009 model year, the UAW Web site roster of "vehicles built by union members in the United States & Canada" included the Chevrolet Malibu and Saturn Aura hybrids, along with eight hybrid SUVs (if any SUVs really should count as environmentally friendly). Plus, the electric-motor Volt, if it ever comes to market, presumably will be made by UAW workers at General Motors. Of course, most of the major non-U.S. manufacturing centers—Japan, Germany, South Korea, France, Spain—aren't exactly impoverished countries. So purchasing a foreign-made auto doesn't necessarily mean you're either helping or exploiting disadvantaged workers.

With food, you can be as local—and limited—as your farmers market and CSA. However, to consume bananas, chocolate, tea, or coffee, you'll have to obtain them from a developing country, where the underlying crops—the bananas, cocoa beans, tea leaves, and coffee beans—probably will be picked by workers under awful conditions, then shipped a thousand or more miles. These crops aren't grown anywhere in the United States.

In short, if you want to keep your dollars with American union workers and avoid any possibility of buying items made by ill-treated, underpaid laborers in a foreign country, you can do it. But it takes a lot of extra effort and time, and your options will be narrow. You can't just stroll into your favorite boutique, looking for a shirt that catches your fancy. You will have to specifically seek out stores and Web sites that sell American-made or union-made; then, see if they have anything that comes close to what you want. And you probably will pay more.

Conversely, are there times when the choice is easy the other way, when buying made-in-America is the convenient default? Sure. One major criterion involves safety. Remember the milk, baby formula, chicken feed, pet food, wheat gluten, and other products from China that were poisoned with melamine? To the wails of countless three-year-olds, Thomas the Tank Engine toys, also made in China, were recalled in summer 2007 because of possible lead-paint contamination. Toothpaste and blood-thinner from that country have been cited as well. In a *USA Today*/Gallup poll in July 2007, 51 percent of the respondents said that when they go grocery-shopping, they "make a special effort to buy items produced in the United States." While the FDA, Agriculture Department, and Consumer Product Safety Commission are hardly perfect, they are a lot more thorough than Beijing's porous safety inspections.

The tough part is figuring out exactly where things are from. Only eleven types of meat, nuts, and perishable foods (mentioned in chapter 3) must clearly state their country of origin. For my research, I conducted a totally unscientific survey of about two dozen brands of toothpaste, over-the-counter and prescription drugs, pet foods, and toys found in my house and a couple of nearby stores. The result: three toys were labeled made in the United States and one was made in China. The rest of the items in my survey didn't say.

Another case when we often have to buy American is the service sector. Although your customer complaint may be handled by a call center in India, your dry cleaning isn't. Here, the choice may be between union and nonunion. You can patronize unionized Costco over union-busting Whole Foods and Wal-Mart. You can investigate hotels, as Stewart Acuff suggested. Do you really notice any difference in the quality of service when a package is delivered by FedEx Corp., United Parcel Service, or the U.S. Postal Service? If they're all the same to you, Acuff recommends UPS or the post office, because both are unionized, while FedEx has fought off organizing attempts.

How about Starbucks? The chain uses some fair-trade coffee. Ultra-hip leftists love its exotic-sounding, personalized concoctions. (What the hell is a half-caff double venti soy latte?) It leads the "food services" sector in ClimateCounts's rankings for its success in reducing carbon emissions and qualifies for the Domini SRI index. According to news stories, Starbucks "latte liberals" supposedly swooned for Barack Obama in the 2008 Democratic primaries (although those same stories reported that blue-collar drinkers of cheaper Dunkin' Donuts coffee preferred Hillary Clinton). So does that mean Starbucks brews a great liberal cup of coffee? Not necessarily; the Industrial Workers of the World union has filed numerous complaints against the chain for actions like blocking union drives and firing employees, some of which have been settled and some of which have been upheld by the National Labor Relations Board.

Finally, in tough economic times, the balancing act is also relatively easy. We swing toward the environmental mandate to reuse and reduce, rather than support factory workers, simply because we can't afford new stuff.

•   •   •

"These are bigger issues than buying a pair of slacks," Stewart Acuff said. As he sees it, I'm focusing on the wrong point when I agonize over what shirt to buy, whether to help a sweatshop worker in Bangladesh or a union worker in North Carolina. "This has to do with structural issues," he continued. "It's a question of political economics and what we expect from policy makers in negotiating for trade deals." Paula Lukats of Just Food, the New York CSA, gave a similar response when I asked her if Just Food was hurting farmers in Africa because it bought from local farmers only. Rather than answering me directly, she said, "I think there are a lot of things that we do in terms of our national farm policy that has impacted those subsistence farmers a lot more gravely, far more than whether I'm buying tomatoes from New Jersey." The focus on government policy also ties in with the point that Alex Steffen of the Worldchanging Web site and the author Thomas Friedman make, when they argue that anything consumers do to alter their lifestyles is a drop in the bucket and that we should use our energy for political action instead.

What all these experts seem to be saying is that the worker-versus-worker dilemma is impossible to resolve ethically, so just buy what you want, and then lobby Congress and multinational corporations, and someday your problem will be solved if working conditions everywhere are improved.

This is where the ethical-consumer guides, too, usually end up. "If shunning third-world goods is unconstructive," *The Rough Guide to Shopping with a Conscience* says, "how about using our power as consumers to demand that companies improve conditions throughout the supply chain?"

Consumers can join boycotts and write to corporate managements asking them to monitor working conditions at their subcontractors. Voters can send letters to their local newspapers, sign petitions, and urge their senators and representatives to put strong worker-protection standards in trade agreements, ban purchases from dictatorships, and boost foreign aid. "We took the first step," Acuff said to me in late 2008, "in electing Obama and a strong [Democratic majority in] Congress. Lobbying for the passage of the Employee Free Choice Act [which would make it easier for workers to form a union] and for fair trade deals is the most important thing people could do now."

Ethicist Arthur Caplan proposed a related solution: shop at the farmers market to help local growers, "then give money to a group that supports farming development overseas, or give money to politicians that support helping other countries."

These are great suggestions. Sometimes they even succeed. Nike Inc. joined the Fair Labor Association set up by President Bill Clinton to enforce labor standards overseas, after tremendous consumer protests and boycott threats in the 1990s. Similar pressure moved Gap to make much more information available about its suppliers' factories. As for juggling support for workers and the environment, it's certainly possible that going green can create jobs. The Energy Independence and Security Act of 2007 authorized $125 million in annual government funding to train people for environmental work, such as retrofitting homes to be more energy-efficient, building carbon-capture coal plants, laying mass transit lines, and designing cheaper solar panels, and the federal 2008 stimulus plan tacks on $600 million more.

The problem is that this big-picture approach falls prey to the "in the long run" trap. If we protest and boycott and exert pressure, the world will be a wonderful place in the long run...But I have to buy a shirt right now. And I'm not going to buy two shirts just to make sure that a seamstress in Bangladesh as well as a union worker in North Carolina both have jobs.

Furthermore, going green and creating green jobs isn't a purely win-win solution. Nongreen but often well-paying jobs are wiped out when power plants, mines, and automobile factories shut down. And every time Jenny Sorensen shares her maternity clothes with other moms and Robin Lydenberg goes to secondhand shops, someone in a clothing factory loses a paycheck.

So the practical solution, I think, is to redefine the dilemma. The flip side of all those conflicts between workers' rights and carbon emissions, or between two sets of workers, is that there's no wrong answer. No matter which choice an ethical consumer makes—within a defined universe of competing ethical options, of course—that consumer will be favoring a value he or she supports. I can help the seamstress in Bangladesh, or the worker in North Carolina, or save resources and energy by not buying a shirt at all; but whatever I do, I win.

I would add just one caveat: because this is an area that activists usually haven't thought much about, we need to make an extra effort to include working conditions in our list of criteria —even if it ranks at the bottom of our priorities, even if we end up buying the same sweatshop-made shirt or thrift-store jacket we would have bought anyway. After all, sooner or later, whether it's a shirt or a software program or a book, all of us are the people who make each other's stuff.

CHAPTER SEVEN

THE PRICE OF PURITY

A dozen large eggs: $2.59

A dozen large eggs, organic, cage-free, vegetarian-diet, no antibiotics: $4.79

A half-gallon of milk: $2.25

A half-gallon of milk, organic: $4.79

Twelve pads of 8½-by-11-inch lined paper, 50 sheets per pad: $6.29

Four pads of 8½-by-11-inch lined pads of paper, 50 sheets per pad, made of recycled paper: $5.29

Four seventy-five-watt incandescent light bulbs: $2.49

Two seventy-five-watt-equivalent compact fluorescent light bulbs: $8

Chicken breast filets: $2.99 a pound

Chicken breast filets, organic: $12 a pound

(These are actual prices from my New York City neighborhood, collected during shopping trips in spring and summer 2008 at a regional-chain grocery store, a specialty grocery store, a national-chain drug store, and a national-chain stationery-supply store.)

True believers will dredge up all sorts of exceptions and justifications, but the sad fact is that ethics don't come cheap.

One reason is that any deviation from standard operating procedures requires some special effort, whether it's to design a humane slaughtering system, conduct additional research, find new suppliers, or customize ingredients. And extra work inevitably equals extra cost. Socially responsible funds must hire consultants to monitor the companies in which they invest, as CalPERS, the big California pension fund, did when it screened developing countries. Fair-trade coffee growers are paid a premium as an inducement to stop using child labor and chemical pesticides.

In addition, certain ethical processes are inherently cumbersome or resource-consuming, hiking the price even further. Free-range chickens need more land than chickens shoved together in a crowded barn. Small neighborhood stores can't obtain the bulk discounts that national chains get. Union members in the United States earn more than workers in China and Guatemala. Time is money, too; keep in mind the hours you spend working at the food co-op or reading the tiny print on labels. Since organic food spoils faster than food pumped full of preservatives, you will have to go shopping more frequently, wasting time and gas. You also probably will throw away more spoiled food, wasting money.

Despite all these costs, the argument for making the ethical choice still may seem obvious. How can you weigh mere money against virtue? How can you put a price cap on the suffering of a fellow human being in a sweatshop? Isn't $9.58—the difference between twelve pads of recycled versus nonrecycled paper— a small charge to pay if it can save trees, save energy, and reduce the threat of climate change? Would you really notice the difference if your socially responsible mutual fund earned a half-percentage point less than a fund full of ExxonMobil stock? As green activists love to point out, if each of us just foreswore three $3.20 lattes at Starbucks every month, we could save the world.

But start adding up all the ethical expenses: $5 extra per week for a gallon of organic milk rather than regular; about $2.20

for organic eggs; at least $10 a month for green energy. And what about the big-ticket items, like tens of thousands of dollars for solar panels? How many of these purchases can an ordinary person afford, no matter how well-meaning and conscience-stricken?

Living the ethical lifestyle becomes particularly tough in a struggling economy. The number of Americans who regularly buy green products tripled, from 12 percent to 36 percent, during relatively prosperous 2007, but that growth stalled during the 2008 recession, according to a February 2009 survey by the consumer research company Mintel International Group. Newspapers and magazines reported a similar slowdown in sales of organic food in 2008. "When people have some savings, that is the escape mechanism" that gives them the freedom to pay extra for organic eggs or donate to the Sierra Club, said Christian Weller of the Center for American Progress.

Even in good times, a sizable portion of the population doesn't have an escape mechanism; they have no savings accounts and don't drink $3.20 lattes. Working-class, lower-middle-class, and poor people can't afford an extra $2.20 a week for organic eggs. They love Wal-Mart and other big-box stores for the low prices (or the image of low prices). Yet they are—supposedly—a key constituency of the liberal coalition. Or is a virtuous lifestyle only for those who can afford it?

I posed that question to Rob Michalak, who is Ben & Jerry's director of social mission. Ben & Jerry's is perhaps the epitome of the good liberal company. It uses all-natural ingredients, including milk with no RBST hormones and mostly cage-free eggs, and it tries to acquire these items from family farms. Its corporate mission statement talks about seeking "to improve the quality of life locally, nationally & internationally." When I did some comparison shopping, however, I found that a pint of Ben & Jerry's typically cost one to three dollars more than any other brand. It even topped Breyers (which also advertises itself as "all-natural," had no weird chemical names on its roster of ingredients, and is owned by the same corporate parent, Unilever) and Häagen-Dazs (which, like B&J, is marketed as a super-premium ice cream). So I asked Michalak how low-income people fit into the mission statement. He seemed taken aback at first. "People at different income levels will make different choices as to how they want to budget," he finally replied. "Some people may choose for this to be their indulgence."

The true believers aren't operating totally in fantasyland. Some aspects of a socially conscious lifestyle do save money. "The principles of reuse and recycling, those are principles that my grandparents living through the Depression were following," said Chip Giller of Grist. Or, in the twenty-first-century version, buying used goods through craigslist and trading whatever through Freecycle, a nonprofit with more than 6.6 million members worldwide; sharing maternity clothes, as Giller's wife did; switching off lights when you leave a room; and making your own furniture cleaner out of olive oil and vinegar.

Moreover, if you can afford the higher up-front payment, virtuous purchases are sometimes cost-efficient in the long run. CFL light bulbs are the classic example: although they might cost six times as much as incandescent bulbs at the check-out counter, advocates say they use 75 percent less energy and last ten times longer, thereby paying for themselves, through lower energy bills and fewer replacement purchases, in just a few months. True, there are complaints in addition to price: the bulbs burn out too fast, they take too long to reach full strength, they cause migraines, their light is weird, they contain dangerous mercury. Still, CFL-haters probably will have to give in, because in 2012 new federal efficiency standards will make the old incandescent types obsolete. As a possible alternative, manufacturers are starting to develop a more efficient (and more expensive) incandescent bulb.

The list of long-term ethical savings includes all kinds of things, big and small, that a consumer might not ordinarily consider. Think about napkins: a set of four cloth napkins was thirteen dollars at my local housewares store, while a package of 250 paper napkins went for around three dollars. So a family of four—eating three meals a day and buying two sets of cloth napkins, to have a spare—would earn back its investment in cloth in about six months (and that doesn't count having dinner guests). Other examples: organic food may be expensive, but "you're staying healthier. That means fewer visits to the doctor's office," Kimberly Danek Pinkson suggested. Home Depot claims to sell more than 2,500 energy-efficient and water-conservation products that can save consumers money over time. Energy experts say that efficient appliances, better insulation, and similar home improvements can pay for themselves in five years.

As more people join the virtue parade, prices should, in theory, drop through economies of scale. At least, this is what the solar industry is counting on. "Every time cumulative installations of PV [photovoltaic] power double, the cost comes down by about 18 percent," the Solar Energy Industries Association (SEIA) asserts in its promotional material. (There's more about the cost of solar power later in this chapter.)

The same result should happen if more companies seek to appeal to this growing market, thanks to good old capitalist competition. When the Sierra Club and Clorox launched their Green Works line of eco-friendly cleaning products in 2008, they were jumping into a business dominated by the Seventh Generation brand. To lure Seventh Generation customers, Green Works products are "substantially" cheaper—about fifty to seventy-five cents—according to Kim Haddow, the Sierra Club spokeswoman. Big-box chains can have the opposite effect when they drive out local merchants, leaving themselves with monopoly pricing power. Thus, if shoppers would temporarily pay the apparently higher prices of a little neighborhood store, they might save money in the long run by maintaining a check on the chains.

Of course, to the degree that socially responsible investing advocates are correct when they say ethics are good for the bottom line, then ethical companies should be able to keep costs and prices down anyway. Rabbi Allen of Minnesota, the leader in writing the new humane kosher certification, offered another solution: maybe ethical kosher companies will be too nice to charge extra. "I'm not sure [the certification] necessarily has to raise the price," he said, after some initial discussions with kosher-food processors. "It might have to change the allocation of profits. If you're paying a worker six dollars an hour in a business that made eighty-four million dollars last year, maybe you have to pay your workers a little more and take a little less profit."

All those arguments aside, advocates claim it's not fair to count only the number on the price tag, because standard products that have been in widespread use for years—particularly industrial-farm food—have hidden costs that don't show up at the cash register but that all of society inevitably pays for, even people who never buy the stuff. Our tax money subsidizes big factory farms that churn out corn and soybeans. In addition, writes *The Rough Guide to Shopping with a Conscience,* "the taxpayer also bails out industrial farming in less direct ways, such as cleaning up the massive environmental damage it causes," from messes like fertilizer runoff. Then there are the health problems suffered by agricultural workers who breathe in chemical pesticides and consumers who eat pesticide-laden fruit and antibiotic-laden meat, all of which ultimately raises medical-insurance premiums for everyone. Another guide, *A Good Life,* advises:

> We should stop thinking about price the way supermarkets do. Instead, we should think about the true cost of nonorganic produce: the cost of having to clean up pesticide run-off from

our land and watercourses; the animal welfare concerns associated with conventional farming; and the legacy of routinely using antibiotics and growth promoters when rearing livestock. In other words, food should always be seen as an investment and not simply an expense.

While most of these explanations have some grounding in reality, you can see what's happening. With each step, we're getting more and more theoretical, and farther and farther away from our actual pocketbooks.

Back in the real world, it's not too hard to be virtuous with the little things, because the amount we're "losing" is so small. Many people wouldn't mind occasionally spending a couple of extra dollars for something they believe in. It's probably less than they donate annually to United Way.

One of the first steps I took, after my research into animal treatment and my guilt-ridden debate over eating meat, was to switch to organic, cage-free eggs. Although they're nearly double the price of ordinary eggs, the dollar differential is less than $2.50 a dozen, which most of us would hardly notice in a week's grocery list. Considering what a significant impact that can make in the life of the chickens, it seemed to me a huge bargain and an easy call.

Recycled paper involved a different yet equally painless calculation. Twelve pads of the recycled version cost nearly ten bucks more than virgin paper, but how often do I buy it? Those twelve pads will last me for a couple of years, which should bring the "ethics premium" to less than fifty cents a month.

As consumers move up the price scale, the juggling gets tougher. There's rarely a clear point at which someone can say: virtue isn't worth it anymore. Jessica Philips purchases organic eggs, milk, apples, and berries, but the wallet starts to pinch with sixteen-dollar-a-pound wild salmon, when the less-healthful farmed kind is about eight dollars a pound. So she's been substituting a midrange alternative, frozen wild salmon. The first time Nancy Hwa bought organic cotton sheets, she was pleasantly surprised to see that they didn't cost much more than nonorganic. "If they were twice the price," she said, "I would think twice about it."

What about that soy underwear the *New York Times* found, for twenty-four dollars? Is that a reasonable price? But because soy clothing is delicate, it won't last as long as clothes made of other fabrics, so maybe you need to double that twenty-four dollars to account for buying replacements more often. Now is it still reasonable?

Sometimes—dare I say it?—the purists are too pure. This is especially true regarding food. If you want all-natural ingredients, no pesticide residues, no added hormones, and decent treatment of animals, you often can get 90 percent of what you're seeking from conventional, nonorganic items at regular grocery stores. If you insist on the organic label, it will cost you 10 percent to 100 percent (or more) extra, according to news reports, surveys, some "green" books, and my own experience. When WSL Strategic Retail, a marketing consulting firm in New York City, surveyed 1,500 consumers in November 2007, nearly half said that organic products are better for people and the environment, but only 27 percent felt they were worth the cost. How much purity are you willing to pay for?

Organic milk is typically about double the price of nonorganic. One of the chief reasons for buying it is to guarantee that the milk didn't come from cows injected with RBST, the genetically engineered hormone that has been linked to increased cancer risks. However, many big, nonorganic bottlers also shun RBST. So if avoiding the hormone is your motivation, you might as well save money and go for regular brands that have labels saying something like "no artificial hormones."

It's also fairly easy to separate fruits and vegetables into must-be-organic and not-necessary. Remember that the main point about organic produce is that it's grown without synthetic fertilizers, herbicides, or pesticides. The Environmental Working Group, a nonprofit that focuses on public health and the environment, created a list of produce with the highest and lowest pesticide residues, based on nearly forty-three thousand tests done by the FDA and the Agriculture Department from 2000 to 2005. According to this listing, the biggest bang for the organic buck comes from (in descending order) peaches, apples, bell peppers, celery, nectarines, strawberries, cherries, lettuce, imported grapes, pears, spinach, and potatoes, all of which tend to retain high amounts of pesticides. By contrast, it may not be worth paying extra for organic eggplant, broccoli, cabbage, bananas, kiwi, asparagus, frozen sweet peas, mangoes, pineapples, frozen sweet corn, avocados, and onions.

Even without this research, people I interviewed made similar distinctions, on the assumption that it's more important to buy organic foods when we eat the skin (peaches, apples, peppers, berries), and less so with thick-skinned foods that we peel (bananas, kiwi, mango, pineapples, onions), presumably because the pesticide residue stays on the skin. In fact, this is not exactly the reasoning behind the Working Group's taxonomy—after all, broccoli and asparagus are on the "safe" list—but it will do as a rough guideline. Louise Heit-Radwell adds a second classification, figuring that if her family eats a lot of something, like raisins, it's even more important for that to be organic. Remember, too, that if you can't afford all-organic, all the time, kids and pregnant women should get the good stuff, because scientists say they're more vulnerable to pesticides.

This whole taxonomy, of course, applies only to the people eating the food. Farm workers and the earth are harmed whether a pesticide is applied to a mango or an apple.

With so many ethical-sounding labels for meat, as chapter 3

described, consumers have lots of ways to live their values, at varying price levels. *BusinessWeek* in 2004 reported that the Agriculture Department was skeptical of the need for organic meat, because only 15 percent of the regular meat it tested had detectable pesticide residues. Most of that, the magazine added, was "from long-banned chemicals like DDT, which remain in the environment and is not a problem organic farming methods can solve." Take that opinion with a few grains of salt, however. Agriculture historically has been cozy with the big, nonorganic beef producers, and part of the department's official mission is to promote the industry.

The biggest single purchase most people ever make is their home. It's also one of their largest guzzlers of energy. Clearly, installing solar panels or a mini-windmill ought to save money, energy, and the earth in one hefty blow.

Time out for eye-rolling.

Advocates have been touting solar power at least since the presidency of Jimmy Carter in the 1970s, and while usage has grown jerkily since then, it still covers barely a closet-worth of the housing market. As of 2009, there were about 8,775 mega-watts of installed solar power in the United States, according to the SEIA. (By contrast, wind, a more recent mass-power source, provides about 1 percent of the nation's total needs, or ten times as much as solar.) The vast majority of these solar watts, more-over, came from big commercial installations, not panels on in-dividual houses. Why aren't we all doing the logical thing?

One problem for individuals is that they must own their own home or have the landlord's permission to put up panels. (Or, even harder, if they live in a co-op or condominium building, they have to get approval from a majority of other apartment-owners.) The main stumbling block, however, is the dollars.

Let's see how the financing works. For a typical house, solar panels cost $20,000 to $45,000. Subtract the 30 percent federal tax credit; then subtract any state and local incentives, which could trim the cost by one thousand dollars more. Because the panels won't meet all your energy needs, even in sunny California, you'll have to keep buying some conventional power. So add back in a small monthly utility bill. But during the times when your solar panels produce more power than you use, such as summer days when you're on vacation, you can sell the excess to the local utility in most states through a process known as net metering. That will give you credits that you can apply toward the power you buy from the utility at other times. So subtract again.

End result: depending on your usage, your local utility's rates, your initial installation cost, and your state's various rebates and net metering policy, you might save 7 to 15 percent a year on your utility bill. (If you live in the Wind Belt described in chapter 4, a home wind turbine might cost about the same and save a little more.) All this is separate from the insulation and other home-energy efficiencies that this chapter discussed earlier. Looked at another way, two articles in the *New York Times* reported that a couple of different co-op apartment buildings in Manhattan would recover their costs in ten years without the improved 2008–2009 federal tax credits or one year with full credits. Also, most experts say the solar set-up increases the resale value of a house.

That's great, but you're not selling your house right now, and you don't have twenty thousand dollars (let alone forty-five thousand dollars) to lay out for panels. The good news is that there are ways to make solar more affordable. Some companies have created what are basically panel-rental schemes: they buy, install and maintain the solar panels, and thus get the tax credits. The homeowner pays them a monthly fee—lower than the pre-solar utility bill—to use the power that the panels create. A few states, including California and Colorado, allow cities and towns to lend homeowners the money for solar installation, to be paid back as an add-on to their property tax bill. And in a handful of cities, a San Francisco–based company called 1BOG (for "one block off the grid") signs up blocs of customers to get group discounts.

Maybe some of us put our foot down at forty-five thousand dollars worth of solar panels. Others recoil at sixteen-dollar-a-pound wild salmon, or a four-dollar box of blueberries. But we're the wealthy ones, the ones who might, just for a moment, be tempted by those purchases. Plenty of people can't even begin to consider such extravagances. People for whom ordinary eight-dollar-a-pound farmed salmon is out of the question. People for whom that salmon is more than a full hour's salary. People who don't own any stocks, socially responsible or otherwise. People, in short, like the people who make our stuff, the low-income and working-class and barely middle-class, the blue-collar and pink-collar, the technicians, nurses' aides, file clerks, store clerks, and others barely making the rent.

As liberals, we supposedly care about these people and about issues like poverty, the minimum wage, universal medical coverage, housing, and equal opportunity. We donate money to Habitat for Humanity to build low-cost housing; we campaign for candidates who promise health-care reform. Bruce Friedrich of PETA became vegan in college, not so much out of concern for the animals, but mainly because he worried that diverting grain and corn to animal feed creates shortages and raises the price of food for humans.

Even when we're not specifically targeting poverty issues, we certainly never intend to hurt people in need. Indeed, in the best of circumstances, our work on behalf of other liberal causes may aid vulnerable population groups indirectly. Take climate change: it's the poor who tend to live in the lowlands that will get flooded as global warming intensifies—just as they were the ones washed out during Hurricane Katrina in 2005—so we're helping them when we reduce carbon emissions. And people of all income levels are better off if fewer pesticides seep into the earth.

But sometimes our efforts to be ethical actually make life harder for those who can't afford virtue. For example, projects to capture the emissions from coal plants and reforest land destroyed by strip-mining will raise the price of a cheap fuel—coal—that's a staple for the impoverished areas of Appalachia. The Consumer Product Safety Improvement Act of 2008 strictly limits the amount of lead allowed in toys, clothing, furniture, jewelry, and other stuff used by children younger than twelve. The concept is admirable, to prevent children from being exposed to high levels of lead, which have been proved to impair brain function. However, it's had an unintended result: thrift shops no longer sell low-priced, secondhand kids' clothes and toys, because it would be far too expensive to test the lead content in the items' zippers and paint.

While food is an area where it's fairly easy to find inexpensive ethical options, ironically it also presents probably the biggest conundrum of virtue-versus-price. In the past few decades, factory farming, subsidized corn crops, and antibiotics have given Americans plenty of cheap—albeit unhealthful—beef and chicken. Now, just as a middle class able to afford this Western lifestyle is emerging in developing countries, we American liberals declare that our mass-market food system is all wrong. Cows should be grass-fed and raised without genetically modified hormones; chickens should be free-range and organic. And if that kind of healthful farming puts the price of meat way beyond the wallets of the aspiring Asian, African, Eastern European, and Latin American middle class, well, don't those consumers want to be healthy, like us wealthier Americans? Don't they care about the future of the earth the way we do?

The new *hekhsher tzedek* certification for kosher food, requiring safer and more humane conditions, will be better for the people working at the slaughterhouses—who are probably low-paid—but how about for customers on tight budgets? "You want organic, free-range, kosher blah blah, and it will cost you four times as much," Paul Plotkin, the rabbi of Temple Beth Am in Margate, Florida, and chair of the subcommittee on kosher laws of the Conservative movement's governing Rabbinical Assembly, told me. "If you want to do it and it makes you feel good, go ahead. But if you make it a requirement, you make a product virtually unaffordable and unavailable. As long as we acknowledge a carnivorous diet as being moral, then we have to balance the need of the animal against the need of being able to bring that food source to the market at a price the average person can afford." Since the new certification isn't, in fact, mandatory for kosher labeling, some food companies undoubtedly will reject it, and observant Jews still will be able to buy less expensive, old-fashioned kosher meat without the environmental, animal, and worker-welfare guarantees. However, I'm sure Rabbi Plotkin is right in assuming that meat with the added guarantees will cost more, and Rabbi Allen of Minnesota is being unrealistic in hoping that these wonderfully ethical food processors will reduce their profits to keep prices low.

Inevitably, in any discussion of price and virtue, we have to go to Wal-Mart. Look, I hate that Goliath as much as any good liberal. I've shopped there exactly once in my life. Countless books and newspaper and magazine articles have been written about how it cheats its employees, strong-arms its suppliers, and drives rivals out of business. The company all but admitted to some of the worst practices, agreeing to pay up to $640 million in December 2008 to settle lawsuits charging that many outlets illegally denied workers their mandatory breaks and forced them to work without pay. Other lawsuits accuse the chain of sex discrimination. Plus, its supposed discounts often are exaggerated.

Nevertheless, for plenty of low-income people, Wal-Mart and its cheap prices (the genuine ones) are a lifesaver—even literally, because the chain in 2006 began selling about 350 generic drugs for just four dollars a prescription. After intense public criticism, the company also improved its skimpy health-care coverage for employees. Going beyond most green companies, Wal-Mart has set ambitious goals for increasing the energy efficiency of its buildings and telling customers the environmental and social impact of its merchandise. All these moves have turned some critics into wary admirers. Anyway, what's the alternative? Inner-city neighborhoods and poorer suburbs don't typically offer an abundance of locally owned, well-stocked hardware stores, stationery stores, bookshops, bakeries, fishmongers, and organic greengrocers.

Anti-hunger advocate Mark Winne, in his 2008 book *Closing the Food Gap: Resetting the Table in the Land of Plenty,* describes two studies comparing food choices in poorer and wealthier areas of Connecticut and New York City. In 2001, University of Connecticut students "fanned out across [low-income] Hartford and two of the city's affluent adjoining suburbs, Wethersfield and West Hartford, to inventory and analyze the contents of two hundred restaurants and small grocery stores." About twice as many suburban sites offered healthful choices like low-fat milk and vegetables, they discovered. Three years later, the New York City study showed that "only 18 percent of the food stores in [low-income] East Harlem carried low-fat, high-fiber food and fresh fruits and vegetables. On the [ritzy] Upper East Side, 58 percent of the stores stocked those items."

And if inner-city residents are lucky enough to have a few good shops nearby, they pay dearly for the privilege. "Prices at the independent corner stores that dot city streets run about 7 percent higher than those at chain supermarkets—effectively levying a 'ghetto tax,'" said an article in the *Journal of Consumer Research* in 2008. Added Paula Lukats of Just Food, when I asked how the prices for her organization's community-supported fresh produce compare with retail charges in less-well-off areas: "You can't find equivalents to compare. In a lot of neighborhoods, there's not an opportunity to eat well."

As Robert Reich writes in *Supercapitalism,* "Millions of us shop at Wal-Mart because we like its low prices...It is not as if Wal-Mart's founder, Sam Walton, and his successors created the world's largest retailer by putting a gun to our heads and forcing us to shop there."

We can't scoff Wal-Mart away—at least, not until more local merchants with quality products set up shop in the inner cities. In addition, these merchants need to accept food stamps, as my food co-op does and the local farmers' market does in the prime summer season, but not the rest of the year. Two hopeful signs are that there are about a half-dozen New York City greenmarkets in mixed- or low-income neighborhoods, and the federal government, many states, and nonprofit organizations are helping to subsidize the purchase of electronic terminals so that more farmers' markets across the country can process the debit cards that replaced paper food stamps in 2004. Another hint of optimism comes from Lukats. Right now, Just Food members are largely "a core group of younger professional folks," she conceded. But CSAs have sprouted in about a dozen minority neighborhoods in New York, including Harlem and Bedford-Stuyvesant, and Lukats said they have come up with creative ways to help members afford the annual cost. Some have held fund-raisers, while others permit payments on a sliding scale based on income. (Next, the CSAs really ought to allow members to purchase smaller shares. How many spears of asparagus can any family eat in a week?)

In 2007, my twelve-year-old son asked why our family wasn't getting our electricity from renewable sources. There was no good reason, so we began investigating. The big local utility, Con

Edison, publishes a list of green suppliers that can use its network of lines and wires, all of which seemed interchangeable, all
claiming to obtain their power from nice, clean New York State
hydropower, wind, or biomass. How could we choose among
them? I decided to base my selection on cost. It wasn't easy to
compare prices, however, because almost every company had
a different method for calculating its rates. Some charged by
the kilowatt-hour. Some charged a fixed price for each block
of kilowatt-hours. And some were brazenly up-front, adding a
"clean" surcharge to the existing Con Ed bill. Moreover, there
were different prices if you wanted 100 percent green or if you
would settle for 75 or 50 percent. I had to average a few months'
worth of our family's old bills to see how many kilowatt-hours
we used in a typical month, then slice that number every which
way. Under any methodology, going green would cost ten to
twenty dollars more a month than using traditional fuels.

To make matters even more confusing, according to a Con
Ed spokesperson, New York City gets a significant amount of its
electricity from hydropower and very little from coal even when
it's not specifically buying green, so it wasn't clear how much
difference my ten dollars or twenty dollars would make.

But having put in this much effort, and feeling excited about
doing something really solid for the environment, I was not
about to back out. On the contrary, I decided that if we were going to take this step, we should step all the way and splurge on
100 percent green. We now pay those extra dollars every month.
And yeah, I do feel less guilty when I flip on a switch.

CHAPTER EIGHT

HOW THE EXPERTS SET
THEIR PRIORITIES

So, after days and days (or weeks or months...) of research, we ethical consumers finally lay out our priorities. We have decided which values we want to emphasize and which entities we can trust—whether it's Costco or the local food co-op, Ben & Jerry's or BP—because of the way these organizations adhere to the values we've chosen to focus on.

But how did Costco, the food co-op, Ben & Jerry's, and BP reach those policies—on carbon emissions, animal products, workers' rights, or whatever else we value them for? How do they juggle their own competing demands? Why do they emphasize animal welfare over recycling, or U.S.-made over not-genetically modified? What if they can't find organic local tomatoes for a reasonable price? What if their unions, their customers, the Sierra Club, the Humane Society, and the mayor of the town where a store is located all demand conflicting actions? Similar questions apply to institutions like humanitarian agencies and consumer monitoring groups.

We ordinary consumers don't have the resources that big organizations enjoy to research the provenance of their products, nor do we share their clout to demand that suppliers change their methods. Still, our dilemmas are similar. Maybe we can learn something from the big guys' experiences.

Ben & Jerry's Homemade Inc.:
Fifteen Thousand Contented Cows

To whip up a year's supply of ice cream and other food, Ben & Jerry's needs the milk of more than 15,400 cows and the egg yolks of more than 7,000 chickens, plus literally tons of sugar and cocoa powder. Finding and tending that many animals and crops might seem hard enough. But these aren't just any cows, chickens, sugar cane plants, and cocoa beans. According to the company's three-part mission statement of product, economic, and social goals, the animals and crops must result in goods that are "the finest quality all natural ice cream and euphoric concoctions...incorporating wholesome, natural ingredients and promoting business practices that respect the Earth and the Environment," through a manufacturing process that strives for "innovative ways to improve the quality of life locally, nationally and internationally" while "expanding opportunities for development and career growth for our employees." Now try finding 15,400 cows and 7,000 chickens raised with all-natural feed, without any shots of antibiotics and artificial hormones, happily roaming the barnyard or pasture on a family-owned or fair-trade farm that doesn't use chemical fertilizers or pesticides.

In reality, the company hasn't always been able to obtain ingredients that meet all of its mission-statement values. It has to prioritize and "the definitions can evolve over time," Rob Michalak, the director of social mission, said. After some prodding, he came up with two rough sets of preferences. One was a list of ingredients ranked in descending order by how much of each is used: first dairy, then sugar, eggs, "add-ins" like brownies and cookies, and, last, flavorings. "There's a certain sort of logic to the priorities, starting with the largest ingredients and working your way from there," Michalak said. That is, it's more important for the dairy ingredients to be "the finest quality all natural" than for the flavorings.

The other set of priorities was a little harder to pin down. It consisted of values like the quality of the ingredients, the use of artificial hormones, the type of farm and its working conditions, the effect on the environment, the reliability of the supplier, and cost. So the idea is to connect the ingredients in the first list with as many qualities as possible in the second, starting at the top of both lists.

One of the few absolutes is no genetically modified ingredients, including the artificial bovine growth hormone RBGH. Getting RBGH-free milk nowadays is fairly easy, but sugar is a problem. "The U.S. sugar-beet industry is going more and more to GM-raised sugar beets," Michalak explained. "If it turns out that all the sugar beets in the United States are GM-based, we're going to have to find a different source."

Another red line is that "we won't source cocoa from any primary supplier that would use child labor or enslaved laborers." That, too, is a tough goal to meet, because nearly half the global supply of cocoa comes from Côte d'Ivoire, where it's harvested under exactly those conditions, according to investigations by governmental and human rights groups. Moreover, the typical no-shade, no-crop-rotation method of growing cocoa damages the soil and spreads crop disease. A small amount of fair-trade chocolate is available, and Michalak said Ben & Jerry's is pressing more suppliers to adhere to fair-trade standards for coffee, vanilla, flavorings, and cocoa, and in turn to pressure their own suppliers.

Supporting family farms is also a high priority; luckily, that priority often overlaps with other values, such as reducing the use of chemical pesticides.

Then, after all these criteria, Ben & Jerry's has to factor in standard business considerations like reliability of the supplier and availability.

Missing, however, are a few values that consumers might expect. The ingredients don't have to be organic, for example. Michalak said that's partly because the Agriculture Department didn't establish its organic standards until 2002, or twenty-four years after Ben & Jerry's was founded. Anyway, he added, "all-natural products were a fine standard." The company in 2006 began requiring its eggs to be cage-free, but it took four years and some pressure from the Humane Society—the exact chronology depends on whom you talk to—to switch all seven thousand chickens. Michalak asserted that once the Humane Society pointed out the horrible way chickens are treated, "we came to the conclusion that a certified humane, cage-free style of farming was the one that most reflected our mission and values." He continued: "As it turned out, there isn't enough certified cage-free [supply]. For a long time, consumers said, 'Give me cheap eggs,' so the egg industry said, 'We can do that.' Part of what needs to happen is that the marketplace needs to increase its demand [for cage-free], and part of the role we can play is to increase that demand." But Paul Shapiro of the Humane Society claimed that Ben & Jerry's is so big that it could have created the demand itself and phased in the switchover twice as quickly.

Best Companies Lists:
Who Defines "Best"?

Year after year, *Fortune* magazine ranks Wal-Mart, FedEx, and General Electric among the ten "most admired" companies in the United States. Admired? By whom? For what? Is Wal-Mart admired for putting mom-and-pop stores out of business? Is FedEx admired for fighting unions? Is GE admired for polluting the Hudson River with toxic PCBs (polychlorinated biphenyls) for three decades? *Fortune* also publishes a separate, annual list of the one hundred "best companies to work for." Regulars on this list include Starbucks and Whole Foods. Does that mean that whoever chooses these winners places a higher priority on the companies' touchy-feely ambience and organic ingredients than on their high prices and refusal to work with unions? And why aren't the "best companies" also the "most admired"?

Shoppers, investors, and job-hunters could go crazy trying to keep up with the plethora of "best companies" lists. There are the "100 best companies to work for in Oregon" (*Oregon Business*), "top 50 companies for Latinas" (*Latina Style*), "America's 200 best small companies" (*Forbes*), and "40 best companies for diversity" (*Black Enterprise*). And many more. How do you want to define "best"? Are you looking at sales, market capitalization, Wall Street analysts' opinions, overall working conditions, promotion of women, or environmental record? How about the best job prospects in a recession?

Fortune's "best companies to work for" started as a book that business journalist Milton Moskowitz and labor journalist Robert Levering wrote in 1984, called *The 100 Best Companies to Work for in America.* The two writers visited 150 businesses, interviewing about two dozen employees of varying job levels at each place. From those interviews, they developed a set of criteria that, Levering said, has remained valid ever since, for companies of all sizes and industries. *Fortune* began publishing the rankings in 1998.

The guiding criteria are divided into five categories: credibility (including two-way communication), respect (including training, resources, recognition of good work, safety, and work-life balance), fairness (including pay, benefits, and lack of discrimination), pride (the relationship between an employee and his or her job), and camaraderie between employees. The first three are grouped under a super-heading of trust, which Levering called the top priority.

When a company applies to be on the list—and hundreds do every year—at least four hundred of its employees are randomly selected to answer a fifty-seven-question survey. Their responses account for two-thirds of the firm's score, with the remainder coming from a questionnaire completed by the company itself.

Even with all that surveying, and even for a list that's supposed to be about working conditions, there are no questions about two important issues for workers: unions and outsourcing. Levering justified the first omission by pointing out that "less than 10 percent of nongovernmental employees are in unions, so [for a business] to be antiunion or whatever is not particularly noteworthy." In other words, when so few companies have unions, it's meaningless to ask employees whether their employer has a union or hampers organizing efforts. Besides, Levering continued, if conditions were so miserable that a strong union drive was underway, that would be picked up by the "trust" questions. As for outsourcing, the closest Levering could come was the true/false query: "Management would lay people off only as a last resort."

Nor does the employee survey ask about the company's role in social issues like reducing carbon emissions. Levering said that's because "we look at everything from the perspective of how it impacts employees," not how it impacts society. True, he acknowledged, a company's political reputation or environmental policy could have an impact on morale, and he suggested that the survey gets at that point obliquely by asking whether "I'm proud to tell others I work here" and "When I look at what we accomplish, I feel a sense of pride." But I think the connection is too oblique. There could be plenty of reasons besides carbon emissions why an employee would or wouldn't feel pride in the job.

In fact, that gaping hole explains how cigarette-maker R.J. Reynolds Tobacco Co. managed to make the list in 2002, albeit way down at number ninety six. "The overwhelming majority of people feel that probably the tobacco industry is one of the most socially irresponsible ones on the planet. By majority opinion, they would say it should not be included on any good-guy list," Levering admitted. "But using our methodology, [RJR employees] thought it was a great workplace. Many of the people felt as if the company was unfairly under siege and was providing a service to those who wanted to smoke." And who knows, maybe RJR gave its work force a great health insurance plan, with free quit-smoking programs. (Let's hope so.) RJR has dropped off since then, and Levering would not say why, because he never discusses the reasons companies aren't on the list.

By comparison, *Fortune*'s "most admired" roster doesn't try to take the employees' viewpoint at all. It is a hard-nosed, strictly business rating of the 1,500 largest companies in the world, based on surveys of more than 3,300 financial analysts, business executives, and corporate board members. The respondents rate the top candidates in their particular industry according to eight attributes, on a scale of one to ten: financial soundness, innovation, long-term investment, people management, quality of management, quality of products or services, use of corporate assets, and social responsibility.

Aha! So this survey includes the issue of social responsibility that the "best companies" list ignores. But how does the magazine define social responsibility? Does that mean that a "most admired" company cannot have been sued for sexual harassment or cited for pollution? Actually, there are no specific criteria for the attributes. Each respondent defines it the way he or she wants. "It's intentionally done that way, because the task that we put before an executive [respondent] is already overwhelming," explained Mark A. Royal, a senior consultant with the Hay Group, the consulting firm that coordinates all the surveying. "We're asking an executive to provide eight or nine data points on ten companies. If we had a battery of questions underneath each of those attributes, we'd probably have our response rate fall off a cliff." As it is, only about one-third of the ten thousand busy executives who get the questionnaire bother to respond. And for Hay or *Fortune* to try to come up with a list of criteria would be close to impossible, added Melvyn J. Stark, a vice president of Hay. "Social responsibility for ExxonMobil, we can immediately think of what we want to," he said. "What would social responsibility for Heineken be?"

Royal and Stark claimed that the eight attributes are equally important and that corporations tend to get pretty much the same score for all of them. "The attributes at some level are part of an interactive system," Royal said. Nevertheless, the consultants implied several times that "people management" edges out the others. As Stark put it, "At the end of the day, if you don't have good people doing the right things, you can't sustain profits."

Hmm. Isn't "people management" very similar to the concept of management that cares about its workers, or, to put it another way, similar to describing a "best company to work for," from the worker's point of view? But if "most admired" overlaps so strongly with "best companies to work for," then how do you explain the presence of Starbucks, FedEx, and Wal-Mart as admired companies? Well, remember that management, not the AFL-CIO, is doing the voting in this survey.

Meanwhile, *Working Mother* magazine has a more narrowly focused "100 best companies for working mothers." Its annual survey looks at seven basic areas that affect working women with kids: child-care benefits; compensation, including adoption reimbursement and family health coverage; corporate culture, especially promotion of women and sympathy to work-life issues; family-friendly programs such as assistance with elder care or special-needs kids; flexibility of work schedules; maternity-leave policies; and representation of women in the upper managerial ranks. Within those areas, the surveys ask more than five hundred specific questions.

The questions and the scoring change over time, based on the magazine's reporting. "Years ago, when very few companies offered on-site child care, it was something that a lot of working moms wanted," recalled editor-in-chief Suzanne Riss. "Now we're finding that private child care is improving, and a lot of working moms don't feel the necessity to have it connected with their jobs." But one priority doesn't shift: "The Number One thing that working mothers say, in every survey we've done and every survey I've seen, is flexibility."

So how do we, as readers and consumers, juggle all these lists? To find the absolutely perfect company, I suppose you could create a giant questionnaire with all the questions from every "best" survey.

Park Slope Food Coop:
Competing Pressure Points

"We have to be able to stand up in front of a general meeting every month and say why we did something," pointed out Joe Holtz, general coordinator of the Park Slope Food Coop, the one to which I belong in Brooklyn, New York. Holtz has nearly fifteen thousand members to answer to—the co-op claims to be the largest member-owned-and-operated co-op in the United States—and they expect ethical purity, as each of those fifteen thousand defines it.

The Park Slope co-op has been juggling the pressures of purity since it was founded in 1973, so it presumably has figured out a way to keep the balls in the air. For starters, the fifty-six paid staffers must follow a mission statement like that of Ben & Jerry's in selecting the ten thousand items the co-op carries. According to the statement, purchasing decisions should emphasize "organic, minimally processed and healthful foods" and support "non-toxic, sustainable agriculture" and "local, earth-friendly producers" while avoiding "products that depend on the exploitation of others." Also, the co-op strives "to reduce the impact of our lifestyles on the world we share with other species and future generations." Following that is a supplementary list of about a dozen and a half specific environmental qualities to consider, some of which are total bans, some of which are only preferences, and some of which are bans except that existing products are grandfathered—with another exception, that the grandfathering disappears if suitable replacements are available. This list covers such concerns as chlorine bleach, toxic inks, petroleum-based ingredients, animal testing, manufacturers' environmental records, and recyclable packaging. The co-op is supposed to "maximize" its offerings of organic and cruelty-free products, "seek" products that are recyclable rather than disposable, and "avoid" toxic substances. (I think this means that toxics are an absolute no-no but the other two examples aren't.)

The member pressure comes on top of all these written guidelines, and it comes in two forms. Because this is a store, albeit nonprofit, the co-op has to move items off the shelves. Therefore, Holtz said, the staffers need to think about issues such as "Do our members want it? Is it reasonably priced? If you take this item away, will people not want to belong?" For example, the co-op carries a particular rice cake from Australia, even though shipping it soaks up gallons and gallons of fuel, because "it's very popular, and nothing like it is produced in the U.S.," Holtz said.

But if failing to carry an item could mean lost sales, carrying the "wrong" items could alienate the kind of consumer activists who tend to join co-ops. Passionate vegans, vegetarians, environmentalists, parents, supporters of a boycott against Company A, opponents of that boycott, and advocates of assorted other causes all have eagle eyes, noses, and mouths to spot any lapse. Too much sugar? Not whole-wheat? Petroleum-based? Imported? Factory-farmed? Contains bleach? Members can raise objections every month at the general membership meeting. Because it's the kind of full-bodied co-op where members must contribute their labor, the Park Slope co-op probably induces an especially strong level of activism. If you're going to spend nearly three hours every four weeks unloading crates of cauliflower, you're probably going to want a say in what kinds of cauliflower the organization offers.

Holtz and his fellow staffers acted to preempt potential complaints in 2006, when they learned that the giant organic dairy supplier Horizon was feeding its cows as much as 40 percent grain rather than grass, which is more healthful for both cows and human customers. "We just knew that our members would start to hear about this," Holtz recalled. The staff quickly found organic replacements for almost all its Horizon fare.

Finally, there are also standard logistical, business considerations, like minimizing the number of distributors.

With all these issues to juggle, the next question is: who does the juggling? This isn't an anarchist collective. The paid staffers like Holtz handle the mundane decisions, but some topics are so hot-button that the staff won't dare make a decision on their own, and they bump it to a membership vote.

One issue was whether to stop offering flimsy, disposable, plastic shopping bags. You might think that would be a no-brainer. Manufacturing the bags wastes petroleum, and then after one use they're often discarded, only to get caught in trees, litter the streets, plug up waterways, and pile up in landfills. Certainly, no organization that vows "to reduce the impact of our lifestyles on the world we share with other species and future generations" would have these things around. Well... Until May 2008, the Park Slope co-op actually did provide members with an endless supply, virtually for free. (Shoppers were supposed to pay on an honor system, a nickel for two bags.) As a coordinator responsible for the co-op's ongoing functioning, Holtz fretted that "if we take away plastic bags, will this alienate some people, who will say it's too inconvenient? The co-op will be weakened." Members at a general meeting ultimately made the decision to trash the bags.

When the membership voted to stop selling bottled water,

around the same time as the plastic-bag decision, the two-year-long debate was so passionate—and the co-op such a well-known institution—that the *New York Times* wrote about it. Supporters of a ban pointed to the two million tons of plastic that go into making a year's supply of American water bottles, the waste of energy, the carbon emissions, the reliance on petro-dictators, and the environmental despoiling. Opponents talked about free choice. And if bottled "spring water" was forbidden, what about bottled distilled water? Or seltzer?

"Every product," Holtz told me, "is a different set of nuances."

Médecins Sans Frontières (Doctors without Borders): Disaster Triage

Médecins Sans Frontières. Aren't these the dedicated, selfless doctors who jump into every catastrophe—flood, war, famine, cyclone—bringing desperately needed medical help?

Not quite *every* catastrophe, but close. An annual budget of $750 million and a field staff of two thousand, augmented by about twenty-five thousand locals from the countries where the disasters occur, allow MSF to reach a lot of trouble spots. Nicolas de Torrenté, executive director of the U.S. arm, says the organization can accomplish "at least half" of the work it would like.

That means it has to reject about half. How the heck do devoted doctors decide which people they won't help?

Triage starts with the definition of the group's mission. MSF is "a medical organization that does humanitarian work, if people are in an acute need as a result of a crisis. Historically, that has been war, but by extension it applies to other types of crises where there's massive disruption in normal life," de Torrenté explained. "Life is at stake."

This definition automatically eliminates one set of demands: long-term development projects. MSF only does emergencies. Ironically, the basic mission also can block MSF from helping disaster-struck countries that are in pretty good shape and, presumably, able to take care of their people's needs themselves. Three other key considerations are that MSF must be able to independently assess the need, deliver the care directly to the people who should receive it, and monitor the results. Finally, the organization takes into account the risks to its own staff.

Despite all these carefully defined criteria, de Torrenté admitted, "There is an element of arbitrariness in this, absolutely." There is also a lot of internal debate over whether or not to adopt a more expansive mission. Sometimes the staff has stretched the definition of "emergency" or "medical" in order to get involved in a country. Other times, it has refused to intervene in what would seem clear examples of response-worthy disasters.

One occasion when the definitions pretty much disappeared involved Niger in 2005. With the United Nations estimating that more than one-third of the population was desperately short of food, MSF wanted to expand an existing nutrition program. The catch: the country was "relatively democratic for Africa, relatively stable." Moreover, the starvation was caused partly by long-term problems like poor soil, poverty, and illiteracy, and remember, MSF doesn't do long-term. Ultimately, those in favor of intervention won the day by arguing that "if you have such mortality rates, it's not normal. If we dig a little deeper, we can find the crisis," de Torrenté said. The "crisis" they came up with was market manipulation of the country's crops, which de Torrenté conceded was certainly not a sudden emergency. A couple of years later, MSF stretched its definition of "crisis" even further by joining an international effort that was lobbying to alter the patent laws in developing countries to allow cheaper, generic versions of brand-name drugs. While access to medicine is certainly connected to MSF's mission, it's difficult to call a patent lawsuit a humanitarian crisis.

At the other extreme, MSF deliberately halted famine-relief efforts in Ethiopia and North Korea, because it feared that its aid was being used as a political tool. Mind you, de Torrenté expects that many times "there's going to be some diversion" of aid, as governments try to take credit for donations or siphon off a percentage to their supporters. Many of these places, after all, are not parliamentary democracies with strong social-welfare systems or traditions of public accountability. When this sort of thing happens, the MSF staff will look the other way, up to a point. "It's not our preferred method, but we can work with it," de Torrenté shrugged.

Other humanitarian organizations face the same dilemma. Oxford economics professor Paul Collier, in his book *Wars, Guns, and Votes,* writes that "on average, 11 percent of [development] aid"—that is, aid meant for roads, hospitals, schools, and the like—"finds its way into the military budget." It was even worse in Sudanese refugee camps in the 1990s, according to a report by Human Rights Watch. That report, "Civilian Devastation: Abuses by All Parties in the War in Southern Sudan," noted that nongovernmental organizations "estimate that up to 80% of food has been stolen by the militaries."

But sometimes the corruption and diversion just go too far. MSF reached the breaking point in Ethiopia during the famine of 1984–1985, de Torrenté said, when "the government used the aid to do forced population transfers," herding 3.6 million starving peasants to resettlement camps under military control.

North Korea presented a different kind of abuse. After devastating famines in the 1990s, the United Nations and other groups poured in with assistance. But MSF finally pulled out, according to de Torrenté, because "we were not allowed to directly see the people we were trying to help." In a book published by MSF in 2004, *In the Shadow of 'Just Wars',* research director Fiona Terry describes how North Korean authorities staged phony tableaus to persuade visiting donors that their aid really was going to kids who needed it. There were "sick children in spotless rooms with new blankets wrapped around their shoulders for the foreigners to see, and unused kitchens that supposedly produced meals for dozens of children." But then the visitors "spotted malnourished, filthy children dressed in rags scavenging for grain along the railway tracks, or hidden away in state orphanages in deplorable conditions. Requests to the authorities to assist these outcasts were met with the claim that they did not exist."

When Cyclone Nargis first hit Myanmar in spring 2008, it looked like another case of a dictatorship manipulating international assistance. Although MSF managed to reach tens of thousands of people, its director of operations, Bruno Jochum, warned in a May 16, 2008, press release that "The aid effort is hampered by government-imposed restrictions on international staff." Among other restrictions, he said, sanitation and water specialists were not allowed to travel to the disaster area. According to news stories, the country's ruling generals blocked foreign workers from monitoring the distribution of their aid, stole relief supplies, and pushed survivors so deeply into the devastated Irrawaddy Delta that international relief workers couldn't get to them. By July, however, conditions had improved, and MSF said it had full access to the victims who needed help.

Thus, in the end, more than 460,000 Burmese who might otherwise have died got food and medical assistance from MSF. And perhaps the generals who might otherwise have been overthrown got some undeserved goodwill from their desperate citizens. If you're thinking of donating to MSF, is that a worthwhile trade-off?

Alan Dershowitz:
The Only Supporter of Israel in the Room

Alan M. Dershowitz has been called a torturer and a fascist by students and left-wing activists. The liberal Huffington Post has redacted his columns and even refused to run one altogether in 2007, he claimed.

Yet Dershowitz—a professor at Harvard Law School, a noted civil-liberties and criminal-defense lawyer, and the author of more than two dozen books—is no conservative extremist. Among his books is *Supreme Injustice: How the High Court Hijacked Election 2000,* in which he asserts that the court's controversial 2000 decision *Bush v. Gore,* which handed the White House to George W. Bush, was "the single most corrupt decision in Supreme Court history." He then aimed his pen at Christian fundamentalists in *Blasphemy: How the Religious Right Is Hijacking the Declaration of Independence.* (Yes, Dershowitz seems to favor subtitles about metaphorical political hijackings.) His courtroom record is eclectic but with a definite bias toward civil liberties and unpopular cases; he has defended football star O.J. Simpson on murder charges, heiress-turned-left-wing-activist Patty Hearst on armed robbery, junk-bond king Michael Milken on insider trading, and human-rights icon Anatoly Sharansky on trumped-up Soviet accusations of treason and spying. When I interviewed him in September 2008, Dershowitz said two of his primary concerns were "getting Barack Obama elected and maximizing free speech on college campuses." Why would liberals condemn someone who is obviously on their side on so many key issues?

One word: Israel.

Of all his causes, Dershowitz is probably best-known for his support of Israel as a Jewish homeland. After citing Obama and free speech in our conversation, he concluded, "I would say right now my top priority is probably Israel, because I think it is being singled out for unfair treatment around the world, and I always try to defend the underdog."

His reasons go beyond an intrinsic sympathy for the underdog, of course. And Dershowitz doesn't support all of Israel's actions blindly; for example, he opposes the civilian settlements that various Israeli governments have tolerated, or even encouraged, in areas the Palestinians claim.

To start with, "I make the Woodrow Wilson case, the case of self-determination," Dershowitz said. "Israel is not a colonialist state. Jews have the right to their own nation." This is the historic Jewish homeland, the land of the Bible, the land of King David and King Solomon. Jews have lived in the spot that is now Israel for more than three thousand years, and Jews everywhere, every day, pray to return to Jerusalem. Centuries of persecution in Europe—including Russian pogroms, the Spanish Inquisition, and, worst of all, the Holocaust—prove that Jews cannot rely on the kindness of strangers for temporary lodging. American liberals sympathize with Kurds, Irish Catholics, Native Americans, Tibetans—and, yes, Palestinians—who yearn for self-rule in a land of their own. So why, Dershowitz asks, are Jews less worthy of sympathy?

Dershowitz's other major point is that Israel largely has managed to maintain liberal-democratic institutions even while battling against never-ending attacks that seek to wipe out its very existence. The minute Israel officially became a state in May 1948, five Arab nations invaded. Arab countries attacked or prepared to again in 1967 and 1973. Terrorist groups still shoot deadly rockets into Israeli cities and send suicide bombers to murder as many Jews as they can in buses and pizza parlors, and then applaud these murderers as "martyrs." Dershowitz argued that "no country in history, faced with comparable threats, has ever had a higher standard of human rights, a higher standard for the rule of law, more concern for the rights of civilians among its enemies." Unlike any other country in the Middle East (or much of the entire world, for that matter), Israel is a fully functioning democracy, with vigorously contested elections, strong opposition parties, a free press, an independent Supreme Court that regularly strikes down government policies, and a slew of human-rights and peace groups that don't have to fear their members will be thrown in jail for speaking their minds—including when they support Palestinian causes.

In some ways, Dershowitz asserted, even Arabs arguably are better off in Israel than in their own lands, especially Arab women, whose rights are severely restricted under harsh Islamic *shari'ah* law. "Palestinians are no paragons of support for women's rights or gay rights," he said. "What happens to gays in Palestinian territories? They seek support in Israel."

Such full-throated defense of Israel is as out of place at a liberal pot-luck supper as a can of beer would be at a black-tie dinner. Most leftists share Dershowitz's desire to defend the underdog—but for them, the underdogs are the Palestinians, because they live in more dire conditions and lack a formal state of their own. Thus, the default attitude of left-wing activists is: look at the horrible way the Israelis treat the Palestinians. Or worse. Ultra-radical lefties compare Israel to apartheid-era South Africa and even Nazi Germany, label the entire stretch of land between the Jordan River and the Mediterranean "Palestine" with no spot for Israel at all, or advocate a single "Jewish-Palestinian" state that of course would soon become solely Palestinian because of the much higher Palestinian birthrate.

Among respectable intellectuals and liberals—those who should be Dershowitz's colleagues—some of the ugliest slanders of historic anti-Semitism have returned. In their 2007 book *The Israel Lobby and U.S. Foreign Policy,* two academics from the most ivory of towers—John J. Mearsheimer of the University of Chicago and Stephen M. Walt of Harvard—claim that pro-Israel lobbying groups "control" U.S. foreign policy. *Time* magazine columnist Joe Klein accused American Jewish neoconservatives of having "divided loyalties" between the United States and Israel, implying that they couldn't be trusted to be patriotic Americans. One of the very first steps a union of British university lecturers took after it was formed in 2007 was to boycott all Israeli academic institutions. Two years later, under pressure from a pro-Palestinian student organization, Hampshire College in Massachusetts voted to drop a particular investment fund, a move that was widely seen as pulling its money out of companies doing business in Israel. Although the college claimed it was divesting for broader reasons, more than eight hundred professors, students, and alumni signed a statement specifically supporting the Palestinian group's boycott of Israeli investments, and Hampshire's action carried particular weight because years ago it had been the first U.S. college to divest from South Africa.

Speaking of boycotts, among the "high-profile boycotts" listed in the nice green book *The Rough Guide to Shopping with a Conscience* are "Companies doing business in Israel," alongside such genuine villains as "Companies doing business in Burma" and ExxonMobil. (True, the book states that "inclusion of a campaign here doesn't suggest endorsement from Rough Guides." But the mere fact of including Israel alongside those standard Bad Guys clearly declares that it's an appropriate liberal target.)

Fortunately, Dershowitz is a tough bird, a veteran of hard-fought courtroom and classroom debates. He claimed to be unruffled when he went to Yale University to speak about Thomas Jefferson and his book *Finding Jefferson* in 2007, and "all the questions were about Israel. They were set up. [The questioners said] I'm a torturer, a McCarthyite." How did that make him feel? I asked. "Like I'm right," Dershowitz replied.

Bon Appétit Management Company:
Make Them Ask for Cheese

Maisie Greenawalt really would prefer to serve nothing but healthful foods like homemade granola at the restaurants that her employer, Bon Appétit Management Company, runs at four hundred colleges, businesses, museums, theaters, and ballparks across the United States. A subsidiary of the British food-service conglomerate Compass Group, Bon Appétit tries to combine gourmet and environmentally sensitive cooking.

Its menus even cite the names of the local farms that provide some of the ingredients: Spiced apricot-glazed Grimaud Farms duck satay with a stuffed Riverdog Farms corno di toro chile at Yahoo corporate offices. Grilled Lark Farm heirloom tomato and zucchini with house-made ricotta and Santa Monica Farmers' Market butter lettuce at the Getty Villa.

"We'd rather not have in our college cafes all of the sugar cereals available at every meal," Greenawalt sighed. "But college students like to eat Cap'n Crunch at dinnertime."

Sugary cereals are just one of the compromises Bon Appétit has to juggle as it tries to nudge its clients toward meals that are good for their bodies and the planet, and also delicious, while satisfying their unshakeable whims. Actually, delicious comes first. "Because that's what we are: a food company," said Greenawalt, a vice president. As Greenawalt tells the story, Bon Appétit was founded in 1987 by two catering-company executives who believed food should look as wonderful as it tastes. After a while, however, "they realized that food doesn't taste the way we remembered." Biting into a tomato used to be like biting into a crisp, juicy apple. When did tomatoes become as mealy as mush? The founders blamed global trade, which forced farmers to breed their crops for traits that would hold up in long trips, such as slow ripening, rather than freshness and taste. Bon Appétit thus began to seek local providers, not out of environmental concern, but for quality control.

Today, the company focuses on ten criteria, including the use of high-quality ingredients, sustainable seafood, local suppliers, no antibiotics, no added hormones, no trans fats, no high-fructose corn syrup, and no premade or convenience food. Most of all, it is almost zealous in its hatred of carbon emissions. Even cheese is frowned upon.

Cheese? What could be more wholesome and vegetarian? And how do you run a couple hundred college cafeterias without pizza? Bon Appétit executives retort that cheese usually comes from cows, which gobble up to ten times their weight in grain and contribute to global warming through their burping. (Yes, grass-fed cows would solve the grain problem, but Greenawalt said the supply is way too low.) When I met with her—not for a meal—Greenawalt pulled out a handy carbon calculator to provide an example: four ounces of grilled chicken has a lifetime cycle of 579 bad carbon "points," while five ounces of cheese has 1,290.

Not that cheese is totally banned. That heirloom tomato and zucchini at the Getty Villa comes with homemade ricotta, after all. "If you really love cheese, and a Brie from France makes your heart sing, even though it's imported, then eat it," Greenawalt said. "But do it consciously. We want a guest to consciously order cheese," to think about what this hunk of burping, grain-eating cow product is doing to the earth. For example, a menu might not list cheeseburgers; customers would have to request the added cheese.

As for the other criteria, Greenawalt said that avoiding trans fats and buying sustainable seafood are the easiest vows to obey. California—a major market for Bon Appétit—bans trans fats in restaurants anyway. "It's not a taste people crave. It's not like cheese," Greenawalt explained. For seafood, the company follows the Monterey Bay Aquarium list. However, there's a catch: the vast majority of seafood Americans eat comes from far away, most of it carried by oil-gobbling airplanes in order to arrive fresh. Another Bon Appétit executive, in an article in the *Los Angeles Times* in April 2008, said that as an alternative, the company was increasingly buying fish that are frozen immediately after being caught, which allows them to be transported more slowly—and carbon-cheaply—by boat.

At the other end of the priority ranking, shunning high-fructose corn syrup is probably the hardest to carry out, Greenawalt admitted, simply because the stuff is so pervasive. Ironically, buying local—the firm's founding principle—also presents tough challenges. Typically, only about 30 percent of ingredients come from within 150 miles of a particular restaurant, which is how Bon Appétit defines local. A secondary definition expands this perimeter to cover all of North America except Hawaii, but that doesn't always work, either. "People want bananas. People want coffee. People want cocoa. People want Thai lemongrass," Greenawalt noted.

How does a commercial business force its customers to be healthy? It can't, especially not a business that's built on food as a source of pleasure. "We don't want people to either feel punished or forced to give up their favorite food," Greenawalt said. "When you get into more of the carbon issues, things like reducing beef and cheese, that becomes a balancing act. How can I offer the options to my guests that they want? If you're going to have beef, let it be natural beef with no antibiotics and no added hormones."

That compromise between its own vision of the perfect meal and its customers' tastes explains why Bon Appétit still dishes out Jell-O salad with shredded carrots at one corporate restaurant in Utah. "If you have a chef that has a real palate, they don't like Jell-O," Greenawalt explained. But when the company tried to remove the dish, "the [Utah] people revolted. Not that there's anything wrong with Jell-O," Greenawalt—the businesswoman now, not the gourmet—added quickly.

Each of these companies, experts, and organizations faces juggling quandaries on a far grander scale than the typical individual. Sometimes the juggling is literally life-and-death, as in the case of Médecins Sans Frontières; sometimes it affects millions of people, as with Ben & Jerry's. Yet the issues themselves may not be that different from the ones that, for example, customers of Ben & Jerry's, the food co-op, or Bon Appétit confront in daily life. How important is it to me that my milk is organic? If I have a limited amount of money to donate to charity, should it go to help typhoon victims in an emergency, or to build schools in a stable but poor country? Do I dare speak up and make a scene if I disagree with my friends' criticism of Israel?

It's kind of nice to think that when I mull over my everyday decisions, I have so much in common with these big, famous entities that have the power to do so much good in the world.

MY CHOICES

At what age do humans become ethical? When do we develop the first sense of right and wrong, the earliest stirrings of a sense of justice? Most experts think it happens at around five or six, just as children are starting to assert their independence from their parents. "At age five, a child becomes aware of the effect of his actions not simply on the response of others, but on their feelings, too. This is the origins of responsibility, and a prerequisite to conscience," Dr. T. Berry Brazelton (one of the country's most renowned child-rearing experts) and Dr. Joshua D. Sparrow write in their 2002 book *Touchpoints Three to Six*. Before that point, if a kid obeys his or her parents' rules—Don't hit! Don't leave your little brother behind!—"it's not necessarily because he understands, or agrees with them, but more likely because he wants to avoid punishment," said Dr. Steven P. Shelow in the 2005 edition of the American Academy of Pediatricians' *Authoritative Guide to Caring for Your Baby and Young Child: Birth to Age Five*. Dr. Benjamin Spock, the guru for generations of parents, gives the example of stealing: "Small children of 1, 2, and 3 take things that don't belong to them, but it isn't really stealing. They don't have any clear sense of what belongs to them and what doesn't.... Stealing that means more occasionally crops up in the period between 6 and adolescence. When children at this age take something, they know they are doing wrong."

By this birthday, too, children seem to have discovered a built-in gyroscope that alerts them to ethical imbalance (or maybe it alerts them only when the imbalance doesn't require them to give up something themselves). Almost from the minute they can form sentences, our kids waylay us with unanswerable questions about social issues: Why is that man on the sidewalk asking for money? Why doesn't he have a place to stay? Why can't he stay with us? Years before I was aware of the feminist revolution, I noted in my diary that all the examples in my fifth-grade math book were about boys. How come there weren't any girls?

All these values emerge from a mix of sources, some of them more widely shared than others, some tilting more leftward or rightward than others, including family, religion, school, friends and colleagues, TV, books (ahem), newspapers, the local community, society at large, and maybe something innate in human wiring. When we rebel against one source—say, family or religion—it's because of the values we've absorbed from another, like friends or society. If the University of Virginia psychologist Jonathan Haidt is right about the five basic psychological systems and the difference between liberals and conservatives, we liberals teach our kids a lot about being fair and avoiding harm to others, and less about respecting authority, staying pure, and feeling loyal to a group. The writer Caleb Crain even argued in an essay in the *New York Times Book Review* in 2009 that if you consider the kind of behavior kids are usually taught, "Marxist principles have been dripping steadily into the minds of American youth for more than a century." Parents tell their offspring that "no individual owns the sandbox and that it is better for all children that this is so," and urge them "to view the blandishments of corporate America [as portrayed in TV commercials for candy and toys] through a lens of harsh skepticism."

Since the 1970s, mainstream America has been inculcating two liberal values in particular, preserving the environment and fighting discrimination. Is there any middle-class child older

than kindergarten age today who doesn't know about recycling or who hasn't heard of Martin Luther King Jr.? (Coming up fast is another lefty virtue: healthful—even organic—eating.)

Whether we act on these values, however, depends on a whole other set of criteria, including individual personality, an inherent human desire for immediate gratification, our relative weighing of risk versus reward, and, of course, practical matters like cost and time. As sociologists well know, people tend to overestimate their willpower and self-discipline—in other words, their ability to live up to their values. In a famous study at Cornell University, 83 percent of the 250 students surveyed confidently predicted that they would buy a daffodil at the school's "Daffodil Days" fund-raising event to benefit the American Cancer Society, yet when the event arrived, only half that many managed to fork over the cash for one lousy flower.

For my lifestyle, before this book, I never sat down and specifically asked: what are my most important ethical values, and how can I live my everyday life in accordance? But if you read over my "before" list in the Introduction, the emphasis is glaring: instinctively—like kindergartners since the 1970s—I have focused on the environment. One of the first measures I can remember taking, back in the 1980s, was to switch from throw-away paper to reusable cloth napkins. When I said earlier that I'm not a vegetarian because it was one demand too many on my brain, what I really was saying was that more strictly environmental demands like recycling and reusing were more important. If I wanted to make animal welfare my priority, I could have said that searching for recycled paper was one demand too many.

So okay, the environment is my Number One issue. But why? If I had to spell out a justification, I'd more or less agree with Wood Turner of ClimateCounts, when he says, "If we're not thinking in a very comprehensive way about how we're facing climate change, the many other issues that we're facing as a society don't amount to much." To put that in the most hard-nosed—and not-very-liberal-sounding—terms, the earth and the human race will survive even if millions of people and animals lead miserable lives. It's not so clear, however, whether the earth (and we humans) could survive the combined onslaught of climate change, deforestation, water and air pollution, soil depletion, rising ocean levels, melting polar ice caps, and mass species extinction. Before we can worry about the treatment of sweatshop workers, the pain of battery chickens, the pesticides in our children's bodies, or the rights of women under extreme *shari'ah* rule, let's make sure those workers, chickens, children, and women have a planet to live on.

As it happens, there are side benefits to focusing on the environment. Because it's such a multifaceted cause, it overlaps with a lot of other causes, and thus I sometimes can get a twofer. For example, if I contribute to a campaign to preserve old-growth forests, I simultaneously would be saving the habitats of any endangered species that live in the forests. Usually the worst-polluting factories are located close to poor and minority neighborhoods, so if I work on a campaign to force those factories to reduce their emissions, maybe I can help the health of local residents. I've even made the environment part of my family's religious observance. Every Friday evening, Jews traditionally put aside money for *tzedakah,* which roughly translates to "charity." Our *tzedakah* money always goes to saving the Amazon rain forest.

It's also relatively convenient to devote yourself to a multifaceted cause like the environment, because there are lots of ways to do it. You can bike, walk, take mass transit, buy a hybrid car, buy a carbon offset, put in solar panels, put in more insulation, buy green energy, buy energy-efficient appliances, buy CFL bulbs, turn off your computer more often...and those actions apply to just one environmental issue, saving energy. Now make another list, citing various ways you could fight pollution.

The long journey that became this book hasn't changed my gut decision to make the environment my priority. However, the research I've done and the people I've interviewed certainly have affected the way I think about that priority and have given me new ideas about how I might live accordingly, while also opening my eyes to other important causes. As a result of what I've learned, I can no longer shop, run my computer, or eat the way I used to.

Most of the changes I need to—want to—make won't be easy. I will have to push myself.

At the same time, I don't have answers to every contradiction, and I'm not even going to try to follow all the advice that I've found. A person can't do everything. There may be *250 Tips for an Eco Lifestyle* and *100 Everyday Ways You Can Contribute to a Healthier Planet,* but luckily there are 6.7 billion people on that planet to help share the load. In fact, one of the most disturbing things I encountered in this project was widespread guilt. Here I was, talking to people who are deeply concerned about poverty, workers' rights, animal welfare, pollution, climate change, trees, democracy, and all the rest—people who are doing far more to make the world a better place than the average consumer—and they kept telling me how *guilty* they felt because they sometimes bought imported blueberries. Virtually everyone except the professional experts seemed to fret over some presumed ethical-lifestyle sin.

For that, in part, I blame all those one thousand-ways-to-be-perfect lists. Of course there's always more I could do, and no doubt the list-makers think they're inspiring us and providing helpful hints. Yet the sheer length of the lists just as easily could make people give up. Kim Haddow, the Sierra Club spokeswoman, raised a similar point about the widespread warning that Americans must reduce our carbon output 80 percent by the year 2050 in order to reverse climate change. "When people hear the eighty percent, it's paralyzing," she said. "But if you break it down as two percent [a year] for the next forty years, people think they can do that. I can take the train to work one day a week."

So here are some of my promises and priorities, some ways this book has altered me and some ways I hope to continue altering my lifestyle to be more in tune with my ethical values. You may disagree. Heck, I might change my mind after I think about things further or do more research. And it may certainly turn out that some vows are bigger than I can handle.

Looking back at my "before" list, I think my major ethical shortcomings involve food. It's such a huge aspect of everyday life, yet my list is so embarrassingly short. When I started this book, pretty much all I did on the organic/animal welfare/preservatives front was buy organic pre-cut carrots (because Costco carries them) and—usually—milk without RBST hormones (because it's so commonly available).

How could I not care what my family was eating? Mainly because the subject of food bores me; plus, I had no time to do any research, because I was putting my effort into all those environmental causes. Anyway, it wasn't as if I was filling the larder with candy bars. We had the standard healthful provisions: fresh fruits and vegetables, cheese, skim milk, orange juice, whole-wheat bread, turkey burgers instead of hamburgers and the leanest ground beef when we did have beef. It's just that virtually none of this was organic or additive-free. If I bothered to investigate organic alternatives, the 100-percent price differential scared me away fast. I also was vaguely aware that there was some debate as to which fruits and vegetables really need to be organic and that a lot of foodies consider Horizon—which supplies most of the organic milk and cheese in supermarkets—no better than the big nonorganic conglomerates. In which case, why spend twice as much for a meaningless label?

Yet I claimed to care about the environment. Didn't I realize that organic farming was so much better for the planet? Actually, no. I thought about it only in terms of its effect on the eater's health.

Once I started this project, I knew I'd have to include issues like factory farming and the exact meaning of "organic," which are important to many liberals, no matter how boring I found them. So I began researching. The results shook me up and led to my first lifestyle decision inspired by this book: I will eat more in accordance with my values.

I'm still not ready to become a vegetarian and may never be. However, there are plenty of other ways I can improve my culinary habits. As I mentioned in chapter 7, after reading the descriptions of hens crammed into battery cages, rubbing their skin raw and pecking each other mercilessly in a desperate fight for breathing room, I knew I couldn't contribute to such misery any more, and I've switched to cage-free, organic eggs. The next move has been phasing in organic produce and more healthful dairy and meat. Largely because of the price barrier, I'm focusing only on the fruits and vegetables on the Environmental Working Group list. I'll make sure the milk I purchase is free of RBST, since that's the main human health concern, but organic isn't necessary.

Water is a problem. I doubt that I drink enough ordinary bottled water to worry about BPA-containing bottles. (Sorry, I just find water boring and tasteless.) Anyway, it usually takes a lot of scientific data to persuade me to toss out my food, carpeting, and other belongings, just in case there's some trace element of something that might maybe cause a side effect. But I do drink "fizzy" water like Perrier and San Pellegrino, which I assume comes in the same sort of BPA bottles, and the evidence of BPA's connections with cancer and other medical dangers—added to my family's particular medical history—is pretty convincing. Therefore, in this case, I'll choose to be paranoid. Unfortunately, fizzy water can't be as easily replaced with tap water and a non-BPA thermos. I'm not really sure what to do about this. The fizzy water began as a more healthful alternative to my first love, diet soda, so I don't want to revert!

As for meat, the bottom line is no antibiotics. This covers the most important health issue for eaters and inherently guarantees that the animals had a close-to-natural diet and some decent living space. Ideally, I'll get "grass-fed" or "free-range" or "family farmed" or whatever term the meat company uses, because that would mean a nicer life for the animals. But I have to admit that my family's welfare comes before a cow's, and how far I go beyond my bottom line will depend on the relative prices.

Ah yes, price. That's a significant hurdle to ethical living for most of us, and not just when it comes to food. Price affects what we buy (two dollars more for recycled paper?) and where we buy it (big-box discounts?). It's not easy to tell people, especially in uncertain economic times, to spend whatever it takes to be ethical.

There are basically three solutions: get a bigger income, shop harder for bargains, or stop worrying about how much things cost. (Note to publisher: If you'd provide a little help with that first solution, I could have a lot more examples for this chapter.)

To solve a slew of problems in one blow, I rejoined the Park Slope Food Coop. Although not all of its offerings are local, organic, organic-kosher, vegetarian, vegan, fair-trade, wholewheat, not tested on animals, packaged in recycled material, or sold unpackaged in bulk, I can feel confident that I won't be buying from manufacturers with the very worst records. In other words, the co-op saves me time, research, and label-reading. It also has ethically satisfying items, like grass-fed beef, that I couldn't find easily elsewhere. And people who have comparison-shopped swear that the prices are usually the lowest in the neighborhood.

On the negative side, the mandatory work shift can be an inconvenience—I start clock-watching about an hour into my nearly three-hour shift—but it does have its pleasures. I enjoy the chance to escape my day job, "play cashier," and chat with the old friends who invariably show up. In sum, after all the agonizing I've been going through over food, the co-op promised to be a little sanctuary where I could relax my vigilance.

Then, barely three weeks after I'd joined, the sanctuary was destroyed. Two co-op members stood up at the monthly meeting and proposed a boycott of all goods from Israel. Two other members followed with letters to the editor of the co-op newsletter.

It was as though I'd been punched in the gut with one of the co-op's own crates of organic canteloupes. But why should I have expected the co-op to be different from other collections of liberals? Like Alan Dershowitz—like almost every American Jewish leftist I know—I have repeatedly found that the liberal hearth turns cold when the topic turns to Israel. Carie Carter, the rabbi at my synagogue, encounters this animosity at meetings of community activists. So does Morris Allen, the Minneapolis rabbi who pioneered the new humane kosher certification.

It is the most painful juggling act many of us are forced to perform. What are we left-wing supporters of Israel to do when we're in a meeting or at a dinner party with our fellow liberals, and the talk turns to denunciation of Israel? Or a petition supporting Palestinian "resistance" is passed around? Should we say what we really think, even if that might provoke a fight? Is that appropriate at a social event? Is it worth alienating friends, or people we cooperate closely with on so many other issues? Yet are we cowards if we keep our mouths shut?

The chief reason for this painful split is the starkly different ways that standard liberals and liberal supporters of Israel view that country. Is it an arrogant military power crushing the poor

Palestinians? Or is it an unfairly criticized, democratic under-dog fighting for survival? I won't repeat here Alan Dershowitz's arguments in defense of Israel, which I largely agree with, or catalog the mainstream liberal criticisms of Israel's treatment of the Palestinians, much of which I also share. But the pain is personal, too. I'm Jewish, and that means I have a primal, three-thousand-year-old attachment to the land of my ancestors and a desperate belief that it must survive as a Jewish state and an ethical beacon.

Sure, Israel has plenty of faults, but is it the worst villain in the world? Why are liberals always so eager to blame Israel? Where's the co-op's boycott of China for trying to wipe out the culture of Tibet and putting dissidents in prison? (I can't begin to count the plastic rulers, potato peelers, oven thermometers, and other China-made gizmos I could buy at the co-op.) Or the boycott of Côte d'Ivoire, which presumably provides half the chocolate the co-op sells, and where most young girls are forced to undergo genital mutilation? Why don't we hear calls to boycott Saudi Arabia for denying women equal rights? How about Russia, for invading Georgia in the summer of 2008? And for that matter, where's the moral indignation at the Palestinians who deliberately shoot rockets into Israeli cities and make martyrs out of teenagers who blow up pizza parlors?

The next few times that I shopped at the co-op, I could hardly look at the cashiers, the shelf-stockers, or my fellow shoppers. Which of them would join a boycott of Israel? Had they written any of the letters? And I had to ask myself: what's more important, cheap organic cucumbers or the land of my religion? The answer was obvious. If the boycott ever passed, I would write a searing letter to the co-op newsletter and then resign my membership.

Of course, the passions at the co-op soon cooled, including mine. I was heartened to see that the next issue of the newsletter had seven letters opposing a boycott, with none in support. Co-op officials explained the bureaucratic process before a boycott proposal could reach a membership vote, and long-timers assured me that the issue would never get that far, because the vast majority of staff and members don't want any kind of controversy. I could put away my juggling balls. This time.

In more mundane ways, as well, the co-op isn't perfect. For all its ten thousand items, it doesn't stock everything my family needs. (I will not give up my diet soda entirely.) And with only 130 member stores in the main national co-op organization, most Americans don't have that choice anyway. So we ethical consumers need to keep searching.

Still, the alternative doesn't have to be Big Bad Boxes. I can patronize regional, unionized chains, one of which, C-Town, claims to consist of "individually owned and operated neighborhood food stores." For the moment, I also am maintaining my membership in Costco. There's something about walking into that warehouse with its shelves of twelve-packs stretching to the ceiling that makes shopping fun, and I want to support a Big Box that supports unions. (Besides, I love snacking on the free samples.) The problem is juggling the co-op and Costco. To save energy and trees, I should purchase recycled toilet paper at the co-op; but isn't there an environmental—and convenience—value if Costco's nonrecycled, jumbo thirty-packs reduce the number of times I have to shop? I can get organic carrots, cage-free eggs, and non-animal-tested shampoo at both places, so are Costco's bulk packages cheaper than the co-op's 21-percent-over-wholesale? Yet, if I keep whittling away like this, there won't be much left to buy at Costco, and it's a hassle to drive there, besides.

I've concocted a weird, temporary green-and-price juggling act that involves purchasing recycled toilet paper and tissues, and green dish detergent and laundry detergent, at the co-op, but taking the environmentally bad versions if Costco is offering special discounts. Clearly, this compromise makes no sense, and I need to do more price comparisons. In the end, sadly, Costco may get dropped.

Where else might I find my nourishment? I'd like to go to the farmers' market more often. It feels good to help local farmers and to know that my food is about as fresh as I can get. However, I can't always make it there for the limited Saturday hours. (Also, even though I'm not a particularly observant Jew, I feel some residual guilt about *assuming* that I'm going to spend money on the Sabbath.) One option that has no appeal is a CSA, or community-supported agriculture program. I prefer to select my own groceries instead of just taking whatever some farmer wants to dump on me each week. And it seems that the CSA would drown my family in vegetables.

No need to change my habits regarding Wal-Mart or Whole Foods, because I never darken those doors anyway. In the case of Whole Foods, a thank-you to CEO John Mackey for creating a broad market for natural products might be acceptable, but we don't need him anymore. With demand for organic products growing 20 percent annually—at least, until the 2008–2009 financial collapse—stores of all sorts are happy to sell me cage-free eggs and antibiotic-free chicken, often at lower prices and without any union-busting baggage. And really, I'd much rather get my organic goods from the food co-op, which tries to obtain those goods from small farms, rather than the industrial-organic behemoths that supply Whole Foods.

As for nonfood shopping, I'm sure I could make more of an effort to patronize little, independent stores. (Doesn't the food co-op count in this "independent" category, when I buy toilet paper or string there?) However, local stores tend to have a more limited selection, shorter hours, and higher prices than the chains, and—well—to be honest, it comes down to convenience. I don't care to spend my time dashing around to six different places looking for a little guy who has what I want at a price competitive with Staples or Barnes & Noble. If I can conveniently shop local, I will, but I'm afraid this is one of the areas where I run out of ethical space.

Two other topics in which my "before" list lags are workers' rights and animal rights.

Shunning Whole Foods and Wal-Mart and shopping at unionized Costco and regional supermarket chains are a start on making up that first shortfall. Additionally, I buy Big Three cars. I'm not saying that unions are a miracle solution to all the problems workers face. They can't prevent the natural job losses of global trade, their work rules can be wastefully rigid, and sometimes their leaders are corrupt, among other negatives. Nevertheless, without a healthy labor movement to keep companies on their toes, things would be a lot worse. It's especially crucial to preserve union strength in groceries and autos, two of the few industries that still do a significant amount of collective bargaining.

Forget about buying U.S.-made or union-label clothes, however. It's simply not practical for me. The only way to reliably locate such items is by trolling through the links on Web sites like Stillmadeinusa, most of which lead to other URLs or to bricks-and-mortar outlets nowhere near me, and I won't buy clothing that I can't try on. To find a union-made, American-made garment in a store in New York—one that also fits, makes me look good, is the right color, is reasonably priced, and doesn't need to be dry-cleaned—sure. Good luck.

As a strong supporter of unions, I feel bad about this decision. A couple of factors ease my guilt a little. First, my research has convinced me that sweatshop jobs, awful as they seem to Americans, truly are better than the alternatives for many women in Honduras, Bangladesh, Vietnam, China, and the other developing countries that manufacture our clothing. Second, I purchase so few clothes that my failure to buy American-union-label probably doesn't make much difference to any workers. (The last time I got a new dress was for my son's bar mitzvah, and he's almost sixteen now.)

And what about animals? Although I may be a carnivorous speciesist, I'm not completely hard-hearted. Switching to shampoo, eye make-up, and suchlike that aren't animal-tested seems a relatively easy move, maybe a way to compensate for eating meat. Who cares what brand of shampoo I use? Yes, the ethical stuff costs more, but price is less of an impediment than with organic food, because I buy these items less frequently. And I can find them everywhere: the co-op, Costco, chain drug stores. So, as I use up my old skin lotion and shampoo, I am slowly replacing them with goods that let my conscience rest easy.

I have to confess that I haven't done much thinking about clothes made of animal fabrics. Then again, considering how rarely I shop (see "bar mitzvah dress," above), I probably don't have to face this issue until—I don't know—my son's college graduation?

In light of how much I already do in my daily life to help the environment, can't I just rest on my (organic) laurels?

Well, I actually have found other things to do—some of them, admittedly, so minor that they seem uncomfortably like the preaching in the books that I hate. For example, I've become so eco-obnoxious that I turn off lights when I leave restaurant bathrooms and hotel fitness centers (if no one else is in the room, of course). Amazingly, I have learned to shut down my computer overnight. Until I researched this book, I didn't realize that aluminum foil was more ecologically friendly than plastic wrap, because it can be recycled and it isn't derived from petroleum; now I'll switch. (Stewart Acuff of the AFL-CIO pointed out the related benefit of buying beer and soda in cans rather than plastic bottles: not only are the cans easier to recycle, but they're also made by unionized steel and aluminum workers.) I also searched a little harder and found recycled printer paper; actually, it wasn't hard. I was probably just too lazy to look before.

More changes: my family is buying carbon offsets again. We had a TerraPass a few years ago, then let it lapse because "everyone said" most of the money goes to administration rather than to carbon-reducing initiatives that wouldn't have been done otherwise. After interviewing officials from both TerraPass and the nonprofit offset provider Carbonfund, I'm persuaded that the offsets are worth buying. Although the companies don't spell out their expenditures in as much detail as I'd like, and my money may do nothing more than plant two trees, it still seems to me that two trees are better than none. Knowing my family's habits, I'm not worried about another common criticism: that we'll end up using more energy than we did before on the assumption that the offsets make up for it.

Then there are the two biggies, home and car. Should I install solar panels or a "green" roof with grass and plants that will absorb sun and provide insulation? Do I live in the right kind of building, in the right location? How much would it cost? I haven't researched all this as much as I should, but I'll try. I regret that we didn't buy a hybrid when our thirteen-year-old minivan died in 2006—the technology seemed too unproven at that point—and if we ever get another car, it definitely will be a hybrid, all-electric, or whatever the mass-market green alternative is by then. However, I'm not about to run out and trade in my fairly gas-efficient (American-union-made!) Pontiac Vibe for a hybrid right now. Since the trade-versus-keep debate is inconclusive, it seems like a waste of raw material, time, and money. One more thing: if my local utility someday institutes a "smart meter" system so that I would pay less for running my washing machine at off-peak hours, sign me up!

In a few cases, I've done some rethinking as a result of my research but decided not to alter my way of living. I refuse to give up my clothes dryer, even though *A Good Life* tells me it's "one of the most energy-hungry domestic appliances." I remember trying to use a clothes line in the past, and not just for the diapers I talked about in chapter 1. For several years, I conscientiously pinned up nearly all of my family's wash during the spring, summer, and early fall on a line stretched across our tiny backyard. But the towels and jeans came out so rough and scratchy that they had to be run through the dryer anyway. I was too embarrassed to hang my underclothes where all the neighbors could gawk. And it always seemed as if, barely ten minutes after I'd finally gotten everything up, I'd have to pull it all down because the sky looked like it was about to rain. An indoor clothes line would be even less feasible for city dwellers like me, who have nowhere to put it except the middle of the living room.

And no, I will not read all the damn lists and look for more things to do!

In the midst of these practical changes, I don't want to forget Alex Steffen's and Thomas Friedman's point that living well isn't enough. If you believe in something, get out there and advocate for it. I do feel the tug of wanting to work for a bigger purpose than just my little patch of the world.

Of course, that leads to the same dilemma we face with everyday ethical decisions: since I don't have time to advocate for every cause I care about, which do I focus on, and via which method of activism?

There are plenty of choices of methodology, including penning letters to newspapers and government officials, starting a blog, launching an online network, circulating petitions (by Web or foot), donating money, doing a fund-raising walk, or—well—writing a book. Being a political junkie, I consider volunteering on an election campaign the height of excitement. This has the added advantage of multiplying my effectiveness, since any candidate I work for is likely to support a number of issues I care about.

Until the last few years, I wouldn't let myself get involved in politics, however. As a reporter and editor, I clamped myself into a straitjacket, telling myself I didn't dare have anything to do with campaigning because you never can know who might see my name on some list, and that would destroy my claim to journalistic objectivity.

Why did I change my mind over the last few years and ease into activism? Mainly, I got frustrated. Besides, I no longer wrote about government or politics, so there was no immediate conflict of interest. I saw other journalists being a lot more open about their political views. And damn it, I care too much about issues like climate change, tax inequality, the ignored budget deficit, teaching true science instead of creationism, women's rights, endangered species, protecting forests and oceans, and Israel's security to sit back and just watch. Ultimately, it was my son who got me moving. In 2004, when he was ten, he asked if he and I could work on a campaign. I found a place to sign up, and suddenly one Saturday we were on a chartered bus full of volunteers and donated doughnuts, headed to the Philadelphia suburbs to knock on doors.

Since then, it's been true love. (Love of the act of volunteering, not the candidates.) I've volunteered for Senate, congressional, presidential, and local races. When my candidate wins, there's an extra thrill, because I feel like I played a tiny role in the victory. But even when the candidate loses, it's no worse than if I didn't volunteer; I'm still depressed. And in any case, the trip there is a lot of fun.

So now I'm back where this book began, overwhelmed by my ethical to-do list, even though I was supposed to have sorted out the juggling, and even though I already have made so many changes. How come life didn't get simpler? I still need to research solar panels and green roofs, compare prices at the food co-op and Costco, find a safe way to drink fizzy water, remember to turn off my computer, volunteer on a political campaign, look for non-RBST milk, read the labels on meat, and work my food co-op shift. Then there are topics I haven't started thinking about, like shifting more investments to socially responsible mutual funds or figuring out how to speak out against Israel-bashers.

How much of this list will I really do? I honestly don't know. I've tried to keep my ambitions within reasonable limits—less than a thousand and one—but I could be overestimating my abilities (or willingness), like those daffodil-promisers at Cornell. Still, I know that whatever I do will help make the world a little better.

All I can promise is to try, and to care.

Acknowledgments

This book began as an intellectual debate with a colleague about whether Whole Foods is a good store (it sells a wide range of natural foods and organic produce at convenient locations) or a bad store (it charges high prices, fights unions, and pushes out little organic markets). Back in the fall of 2007, when I started shaping that debate into a book outline, I didn't foresee how far beyond Whole Foods the book would travel. I certainly didn't foresee how it would change my life.

First, I want to thank my agent, Lauren Abramo of Dystel & Goderich Literary Management, and my editors at Beacon Press, Brian Halley and Allison Trzop, for having faith in this book and helping me figure out how to convey this journey of dilemmas in a way that others could share. In particular, Allison, thanks for your sensitive and sharp editing eye.

(And to Allison, a pledge: may we soon meet at a Mets-Red Sox World Series game.)

Thanks, too, to the friends who so openly discussed their habits and quandaries, including Carie Carter, Louise Heit-Radwell, Alyssa Lappen, Jean Leung, Cathy Monblatt, and Stew Pravda.

For that matter, I probably should thank everyone I know. It seems like any time I'd tell people about this book, they would leap in with examples of their own, statistics, or points of view I hadn't considered.

Almost all of the experts I interviewed were willing to veer off the professional track a little and talk about their private lives, and I appreciate that. In particular, I want to thank those who went into a lot of detail: Bruce Friedrich of PETA, Chip Giller of Grist, Nancy Hwa of the Pension Rights Center, Carroll Muffett of Greenpeace, Kimberly Danek Pinkson of the EcoMom Alliance, Carol Tucker Foreman of the Consumer Federation of America, and Christian Weller of the University of Massachusetts.

Finally, thanks, as always, to my husband, Pete Segal, and my son, Joseph Hawthorne, for putting up with a half-time wife and mom while I worked on this project, for accepting the changes that I have shoved into our lifestyle, and for spurring some challenging discussions in the process.

Notes

Introduction

xi   *Some animal-rights* . . . Duncan Clark and Richie Unterberger, *The Rough Guide to Shopping with a Conscience* (London: Rough Guides Ltd., 2007), 258.

xii *When animal-rights* . . . Miyun Park, "Opening Cages, Opening Eyes," *In Defense of Animals: The Second Wave,* ed. Peter Singer (Malden, MA: Blackwell Publishing Ltd., 2006), 174–80.

Chapter One: Juggling Lessons

8   *These issues of* . . . Robert Reich, *Supercapitalism: The Transformation of Business, Democracy, and Everyday Life* (New York: Alfred A. Knopf, 2007), 99.

10   *But if a building* . . . Andres R. Edwards, *The Sustainability Revolution: Portrait of a Paradigm Shift* (Gabriola Island, Canada: New Society Publishers, 2005), 124.

12   True Green *tells* . . . Kim McKay and Jenny Bonnin, *True Green: 100 Everyday Ways You Can Contribute to a Healthier Planet* (Washington, DC: National Geographic, 2006), 5.

13   *As the book says* . . . Lisa Barnes, "Greening Mealtimes for Children," *Llewellyn's* 2009 *Green Living Guide* (Woodbury, MN: Llewellyn Worldwide, 2008), 55.

13   *"The certification industry* . . ." Elizabeth Laskar, "The Rise of Ethical Fashion," *Llewellyn's 2009 Green Living Guide,* 38.

16   *A 2008 cover* . . . Leslie Crawford, "Green with Worry," *San Francisco,* February 2008.

16   *The* New York Times *soon* . . . Patricia Leigh Brown, "For 'EcoMoms,' Saving Earth Begins at Home," *New York Times,* February 16, 2008.

17   *"Ecology and economy* . . . " Edwards, *The Sustainability Revolution,* 17.

18   *"Once colonialism, racism* . . . " Richard D. Ryder, "Speciesism in the Laboratory," in Singer, *In Defense of Animals,* 87–103.

Chapter Two: Morals at the Mall

22   *The* New York Times *in 2007*…Eric Wilson, "A World Consumed by Guilt," *New York Times,* December 13, 2007.

22   *That's a recipe*…http://www.consumerreports.org/cro/home-garden/news/december-2006/homemade-cleaning-products-12-06/overview/0612_homemade-cleaning-products.ov.htm. Accessed March 2009.

23   *The Rough Guide*…Clark and Unterberger, *The Rough Guide to Shopping with a Conscience,* 34.

27   *Two economics professors*…Emek Basker and Michael Noel, "The Evolving Food Chain: Competitive Effects of Wal-Mart's Entry into the Supermarket Industry," working paper 0712 (Dept. of Economics, University of Missouri, July 2007).

28   *"Recognizing the power…"* Stacy Mitchell, *Big-Box Swindle: The True Cost of Mega-Retailers and the Fight for America's Independent Businesses* (Boston: Beacon Press, 2006), 134.

29   *"They found that the opening…"* Mitchell, *Big-Box Swindle,* 37.

29   *"And the consulting firm…"* "Local Works! Examining the Impact of Local Businesses on the West Michigan Economy," *Civic Economics,* September 2008.

32   *If, as Mitchell's…* Mitchell, *Big Box Swindle,* 9.

32   *Price Club was founded…* Mitchell, *Big Box Swindle,* 60.

33   *Another good quality*…Michael Moss and Andrew Martin, "Food Safety Problems Elude Private Inspectors," *New York Times,* March 6, 2009.

33   *Press reports have*…Jena McGregor, "Costco's Artful Discounts," *BusinessWeek,* October 9, 2008.

33   *In her book, Mitchell*…Mitchell, *Big-Box Swindle,* 135.

35   *"It's incredible to…"* John Mackey, Karen Dawn, and Lauren Ornelas, "The CEO as Animal Activist: John Mackey and Whole Foods," in Singer, *In Defense of Animals,* 206–13.

35   *Organic goods, plentiful*…Andrew Martin, "A Fresh Image in Lean Times," *New York Times,* August 2, 2008.

37   *The* New York Times *in 2007*…Marian Burros, "Is Whole Foods Straying from Its Roots?" *New York Times,* February 28, 2007.

40   *Thomas Friedman, in*…Thomas L. Friedman, *Hot, Flat, and Crowded: Why We Need a Green Revolution—and How It Can Renew America* (New York: Farrar, Straus and Giroux, 2008), 209.

41   *"I am very thankful…"* Barney Gimbel, "Russia's King of Crude," *Fortune,* February 2, 2009, 88.

41 *Lukoil "has always…"* Isabel Gorst, "Lukoil: Russia's Largest Oil Company" (paper presented at the James A. Baker III Institute for Public Policy at Rice University, March 2007), 1.

43 *That dual…*Aviva Chomsky, *"They Take Our Jobs!" and* 20 *Other Myths about Immigration* (Boston: Beacon Press, 2007), 34–35.

43 *"The answer to the low-wage…"* Ibid., 27.

43 *Charney has been sued…*These lawsuits have been covered extensively in the press, including Claire Hoffman, "Barely Legal," *Conde Nast Portfolio,* November 2008, 114; and Jaime Wolf, "And You Thought Abercrombie & Fitch Was Pushing It?" *New York Times Magazine,* April 23, 2006.

45 *Leslie Crawford, the author…*Crawford, "Green with Worry."

45 *More significantly, Texas State…*James E. McWilliams, "Our Home-Grown Melamine Problem," *New York Times,* November 17, 2008.

46 *The California attorney general's…*J. Liaw, "USDA to Define 'Natural' Personal Care Products," *Sacramento Bee,* July 7, 2008.

47 *Similarly,* A Good Life…Leo Hickman, ed., *A Good Life: The Guide to Ethical Living* (London: Transworld Publishers, 2005), 165.

50 *Even some Goodwill…*Rob Walker, "Goodwill Hunting," *New York Times Magazine,* November 2, 2008.

51 *A whole industry…*Alejandra Laviada, "Recyclable House," *New York Times Magazine,* September 28, 2008.

52 *Just in time for…*Alex Williams, "Jolly and Green, with an Agenda," *New York Times,* November 25, 2007.

53 *When Barney's New York…*Wilson, "A World Consumed by Guilt."

Chapter Three: Can an Ethical Liberal Eat Meat?

59 *One Cambridge University…*Bruce Friedrich, "Effective Advocacy," in Singer, *In Defense of Animals,* 187–95.

60 *it takes about…*Clark and Unterberger, *The Rough Guide to Shopping with a Conscience,* 104.

62 *"We need to…"* Peter Singer, introduction, in Singer, *In Defense of Animals,* 1–10.

63 *"Most adult mammals …"* Gaverick Matheny, "Utilitarianism and Animals," in Singer, *In Defense of Animals,* 13–25.

64 *He asserts in…*David DeGrazia, "On the Question of Personhood beyond *Homo sapiens,*" in Singer, *In Defense of Animals,* 40–53.

65 *Ecuador's 2008 constitution…*"The Year in Ideas," *New York Times Magazine,* December 14, 2008.

67   *"What's wrong with…"* Michael Pollan, *The Omnivore's Dilemma: A Natural History of Four Meals* (New York: Penguin Books, 2007), 328.

69   *In his book, Pollan…* Ibid., 171.

75   *"While occupying just…"* Fred Pearce, *Confessions of an Eco-Sinner: Tracking Down the Sources of My Stuff* (Boston: Beacon Press, 2008), 90.

75   *The* Wall Street Journal, *in analyzing…* Jeffrey Ball, "Six Products, Six Carbon Footprints," *Wall Street Journal*, October 6, 2008.

78   *And* The Rough Guide… Clark and Unterberger, *The Rough Guide to Shopping with a Conscience,* 94.

82   *Home Depot faced…* Claudia H. Deutsch, "For Suppliers, the Pressure Is On," *New York Times*, November 7, 2007.

82   *A pair of New Zealand…* Caroline Saunders and Andrew Barber, "Comparative Energy and Greenhouse Gas Emissions of New Zealand's and the UK's Dairy Industry," AERU Research Report No. 297 (Lincoln, New Zealand: Lincoln University, July 2007).

83   *"When a team…"* Sarah Murray, *Moveable Feasts: From Ancient Rome to the 21st Century, the Incredible Journeys of the Food We Eat* (New York: St. Martin's Press, 2007), 131.

83   *Just as cows…* Ball, "Six Products."

83   *For PepsiCo's…* Andrew Martin, "How Green Is My Orange?" *New York Times,* January 22, 2009.

83   *Murray cites a…* Murray, *Moveable Feasts*, 132.

85   *Foodies say that…* Pollan, *The Omnivore's Dilemma,* 257.

87   *From just $178 million…* The statistics come from Keith Naughton, "Natural Response," *Newsweek,* May 12, 2008; Carol Marie Cropper, "Does It Pay To Buy Organic?" *BusinessWeek,* September 6, 2004, 102; and Mark Bittman, "Eating Food That's Better for You, Organic or Not," *New York Times*, March 20, 2009.

Chapter Four: Enough Green, Already!

92   *Transportation is responsible…* Friedman, *Hot, Flat, and Crowded,* 290.

94   *Not only that, but many…* Elizabeth Rosenthal, "In German Suburb, Life Goes on without Cars," *New York Times*, May 12, 2009.

96   *Altogether, some automobile…* Keith Naughton, "Is There a Hybrid Auto in Your Future?" www.newsweek.com, June 28, 2008.

98   *Although they may…* Simon Romero, "In Bolivia, Untapped Bounty Meets Nationalism," *New York Times*, February 3, 2009.

100   *The* Los Angeles Times *reported…* Dawn C. Chmielewski and Ken

Bensinger, "Stars Test the Waters for Hydrogen Cars," *Los Angeles Times*, June 15, 2008.

100 *One of them*...Greg Melville, "Greased Lightning," *New York Times*, June 9, 2008.

103 *A 2004 report*..."Report to the California Legislature: Accelerated Light-Duty Vehicle Retirement Program" (Sacramento, CA: Air Resources Board, May 2004), iii.

103 *For the Mercedes*...Salon, April 21, 2008, www.salon.com/mwt/feature/2008/04/21/ask_pablo_cars/index.html.

115 *According to an article*...Elizabeth Kolbert, "The Island in the Wind," *New Yorker*, July 7–14, 2008, 67.

117 *The book* A Good Life...Hickman, *A Good Life,* 89.

Chapter Five: Beyond Apartheid and Tobacco

131 *The Securities and Exchange*...Ron Lieber, "Socially Responsible, with Egg on Its Face," *New York Times*, August 23, 2008.

134 *"A declaration of corporate..."* Reich, *Supercapitalism,* 170.

134 *"McDonald's employs more..."* Ibid., 171.

135 *In an August*...Alicia H. Munnell, "Should Public Plans Engage in Social Investing?" (Chestnut Hill, MA: Center for Retirement Research at Boston College, August 2007), 7.

136 *Two professors at*...Karen Fisher-Vanden and Karin S. Thorburn, "Voluntary Corporate Environmental Initiatives and Shareholder Wealth" (Hanover, NH: Dartmouth College Centre for Economic Policy Research, February 2008).

136 *"The meta-analytic..."* Marc Orlitzky, Frank L. Schmidt, and Sara L. Rynes, "Corporate Social and Financial Performance: A Meta-analysis," *Organization Studies* 24, no. 3 (2003), 403.

136 *Another meta-study*..."Corporate Environmental Governance," white paper (Innovest Strategic Value Advisors, September 2004), 109.

137 *"Given the large..."* Munnell, "Should Public Plans Engage in Social Investing?"

Chapter Six: The People Who Make Our Stuff

142 *"Half of all workers..."* The book for which I interviewed Francis Vitagliano was *Pension Dumping: The Reasons, the Wreckage, the Stakes*

for Wall Street (New York: Bloomberg Press, 2008); however, this quote is not from that book.

145 *The* New York Times *in September*...Alex Williams, "Love It? Check the Label," *New York Times*, September 6, 2007.

146 *"Back home, there..."* Pearce, *Confessions of an Eco-Sinner,* 105.

147 *The Cambodian women*...Nicholas D. Kristof, "Where Sweatshops Are a Dream," *New York Times*, January 15, 2009.

147 *Wal-Mart, which*...Stephanie Strom, "A Sweetheart Becomes Suspect: Looking Behind Those Kathie Lee Labels," *New York Times*, June 27, 1996.

147 *"cotton farmers in West Africa..."* Edward Gresser, "All Fall Down," Yale Global Online, July 27, 2006.

148 *"the alternative for..."* Clark and Unterberger, *The Rough Guide to Shopping with a Conscience,* 49.

149 *By buying this fruit*...Ibid., 136.

149 *We should also*...James MacGregor and Bill Vorley, "Fair Miles? The Concept of 'Food Miles' through a Sustainable Development Lens" (London: International Institute for Environment and Development, 2006).

149 *"The moment consumers look..."* Heather Green and Kerry Capell, "Carbon Confusion," *BusinessWeek*, March 6, 2008.

151 *"Take the Fender..."* Patricia Marx, "Made in U.S.A.," *New Yorker*, March 16, 2009, 64.

154 *"If shunning third-world..."* Clark and Unterberger, *The Rough Guide to Shopping with a Conscience,* 52.

Chapter Seven: The Price of Purity

162 *In addition, writes*...Ibid., 82.

162 *"We should stop..."* Hickman, *A Good Life,* 28.

164 *What about that soy*...Wilson, "A World Consumed by Guilt."

166 BusinessWeek *in 2004*...Cropper, "Does It Pay to Buy Organic?" 102.

167 *Looked at another*...Jim Dwyer, "(Solar) Power to the People Is Not So Easily Achieved," *New York Times*, January 23, 2008; and Mireya Navarro, "With Green Intentions, Entering the Realm of Co-Op Board Politics," *New York Times*, March 23, 2009.

167 *A few states*...Leslie Kaufman, "Harnessing the Sun, with Help from Cities," *New York Times*, March 15, 2009.

168 *And in a handful*...Rob Walker, "Panel Discussion," *New York Times Magazine*, April 5, 2009.

169 *However, it's had an unintended result...* Jenn Abelson, "Lead Law Puts Thrift Stores in Lurch," Boston.com, February 27, 2009.

171 *Anti-hunger advocate...* Mark Winne, *Closing the Food Gap: Resetting the Table in the Land of Plenty* (Boston: Beacon Press, 2008), 111, 123.

171 *"Prices at the independent..."* "Cost of Being Poor: Retail Price and Consumer Price Search Differences across Inner-City and Suburban Neighborhoods," *Journal of Consumer Research* (cited in the *Atlantic,* November 2008, 21).

172 *"Millions of us..."* Reich, *Supercapitalism,* 90.

Chapter Eight: How the Experts Set Their Priorities

184 *When the membership voted...* Jim Dwyer, "Bottled Water Is a Paradox: Both Banned and Required," *New York Times*, May 14, 2008.

187 *Oxford economics professor...* Paul Collier, *Wars, Guns, and Votes: Democracy in Dangerous Places* (New York: HarperCollins, 2009), 111.

187 *There were "sick..."* Fabrice Weissman, ed., *In the Shadow of 'Just Wars': Violence, Politics, and Humanitarian Action* (Ithaca, NY: Cornell University Press, 2004), 99.

194 *Another Bon Appétit...* Kenneth R. Weiss, "With Low-Carbon Diets, Consumers Step up to the Plate," *Los Angeles Times*, April 22, 2008.

Chapter Nine: My Choices

197 *"At age five, a child..."* T. Berry Brazelton and Joshua D. Sparrow, *Touchpoints 3 to 6: Your Child's Emotional and Behavioral Development* (New York: Da Capo Press, 2002), 214.

197 *Before that point...* Steven P. Shelov, ed., The *American Academy of Pediatrics Complete and Authoritative Guide to Caring for Your Baby and Young Child, Birth to Age Five* (New York: Bantam Books, 2005), 365.

197 *"Small children of..."* Benjamin Spock and Michael B. Rothenberg, *Dr. Spock's Baby and Child Care* (New York: Pocket Books, 1992), 537.

198 *The writer Caleb...* Caleb Crain, "Children of the Left, Unite!" *New York Times Book Review*, January 9, 2009.

199 *In a famous study...* Benedict Carey, "Stumbling Blocks on the Path of Righteousness," *New York Times,* May 5, 2009.

212 *I refuse to give...* Hickman, *A Good Life,* 72.

DATE D'